Drawing the Line

PATRICIA RUGGLES

Drawing the Line

Alternative Poverty Measures and Their Implications for Public Policy

THE URBAN INSTITUTE PRESS
Washington, D.C.

Library of Congress Cataloging in Publication Data

Drawing the Line: Alternative Poverty Measures and Their Implications for Public Policy/Patricia Ruggles

1. Poor—United States—Statistical methods. 2. United States—Economic Conditions-1945-   —Statistical methods. I. Title.

HC110.PR83   1990   362.5'8'0973—DC 20   90-30367
                                                                                      CIP

ISBN 0-87766-447-1 (alk. paper)
ISBN 0-87766-446-3 (alk. paper; casebound)

Urban Institute books are printed on acid-free paper whenever possible.

Printed in the United States of America.

9   8   7   6   5   4   3   2   1

Distributed by:
            University Press of America
4720 Boston Way   3 Henrietta Street
Lanham, MD 20706   London   WC2E 8LU   ENGLAND

THE URBAN INSTITUTE is a nonprofit policy research and educational organization established in Washington, D.C., in 1968. Its staff investigates the social and economic problems confronting the nation and government policies and programs designed to alleviate such problems. The Institute disseminates significant findings of its research through the publications program of its Press. The Institute has two goals for work in each of its research areas: to help shape thinking about societal problems and efforts to solve them, and to improve government decisions and performance by providing better information and analytic tools.

Through work that ranges from broad conceptual studies to administrative and technical assistance, Institute researchers contribute to the stock of knowledge available to public officials and private individuals and groups concerned with formulating and implementing more efficient and effective government policy.

Conclusions or opinions expressed in Institute publications are those of the authors and do not necessarily reflect the views of other staff members, officers or trustees of the Institute, advisory groups, or any organizations that provide financial support to the Institute.

CONTENTS

Tables

Figures

FOREWORD

Measuring poverty is a problematic endeavor. Viewed one way, it is an arbitrary and subjective process; viewed another, it is a careful process based upon a consensus of experts who apply a variety of analytical methods in reaching their judgments. The thesis of this book is that we need to reassess where the consensus stands.

Official poverty standards were adopted more than two decades ago and were based on data from the mid-1950s. Patricia Ruggles calls for an update of our poverty definition to take into account both technical factors that affect the poverty standard and, more importantly, fundamental issues such as changes in consumption patterns and changing concepts of what constitutes a minimally adequate standard of living. Owning a telephone may not have been part of Americans' expectations of what was included in a minimally adequate standard of living fifty years ago, but probably is today. Poverty is a normative measure that must be adjusted to changing social norms and expectations. This makes the task of devising a balanced means of measuring poverty all the more difficult and, at the same time, all the more important.

However contentious, drawing a poverty line is essential. It is a way of letting us know how much progress we are making in reducing the numbers of economically underprivileged in America and, in very practical terms, it is a standard used by federal and state governments to implement programs that aid the poor. Contributing to this dialogue on how to measure poverty and how to make our current measure of it more useful is part of a process of enormous value; it is part of a process to which The Urban Institute attaches great importance. Because so much of the research conducted by the Institute relates to social and economic problems that arise from poverty, such as homelessness, crime, and unemployment, the topic of this study is of fundamental concern to the Institute.

The evidence presented here suggests that if a poverty threshold were to be computed today, in order for it to be comparab!e in normative terms to the original threshold established in the 1960s, it would need to be about 50 percent higher than the current official poverty line. This suggestion underscores the author's recommendation that we conduct a complete update of our consumption patterns roughly every decade to help our poverty measurements keep pace with changing social and economic norms.

While the judgments about how to improve the poverty measure are the author's alone, The Urban Institute stands behind the quality of thinking reflected in this study and its contribution to the important subject of poverty measurement.

William Gorham
President

Poverty is ultimately a normative concept, not a statistical one. Although this book focuses on a set of detailed statistical issues in the measurement of poverty, in the final analysis setting the poverty level requires a judgment about social norms, and such a judgment cannot be made on statistical grounds alone. As Adam Smith put it more than 200 years ago, poverty is a lack of those necessities that "the custom of the country renders it indecent for creditable people, even of the lowest order, to be without." Such necessities cannot be identified in some neutral, scientifically correct way—they do indeed depend on the "custom of the country," and some judgment as to what that custom requires must enter into their selection.

It has been more than 25 years since our current poverty line was established, and the necessities defined by the "custom of the country" have undeniably changed during that time. Even if we accept, as this book does, the view that our current standards represented a reasonable social minimum in 1963, normative standards change over time, and norms such as the poverty line must consequently be reassessed periodically. This book does not attempt to establish some entirely new norm for poverty, but instead argues that to be comparable *in normative terms* to its 1963 level our current poverty standard would have to be substantially higher.

The poverty line is important today not only as a tool for general policy assessment, but also because eligibility for many specific assistance programs is tied directly to this standard. A major increase in our poverty line would result in automatic eligibility increases in these programs, resulting, at least in some cases, in increased program costs (although of course Congress could always choose to revise eligibility rules to maintain current spending levels). Thus today the poverty line is being used not only for statistical purposes but also to make very basic choices about who will receive help and who will not. Under these circumstances it is particularly important that our standard should in fact allow consumption of those goods that the custom of the country renders it indecent to be without.

The research for this book was supported in part by the National Science Foundation, under grant number SES-87-13643. This supported research was carried out at the U.S. Bureau of the Census, under the American Statistical Association/National Science Foundation Fellowship Program, which is sponsored by NSF and the Bureau of the Census. Additional support for the book was provided by the Urban Institute under a grant from the Ford Foundation and by the Rockefeller Foundation.

I am particularly grateful to my husband, Paul Cullinan, who demonstrated great tolerance in reading and discussing multiple drafts of each chapter, and who provided generous support and encouragement throughout the project. Roberton Williams also read more than one draft of almost every chapter, and in addition was an important participant in much of the original research reported here. This research could not have been done without the extensive programming help of Taube Wilson, and the work on the Current Population Survey done by Al Shelly. I also would like to thank Richard C. Michel for his continuing advice and encouragement, and Harold Watts, Sheldon Danziger, Rebecca Blank, and Marilyn Moon for their helpful comments on earlier drafts of the manuscript.

In addition, Constance Citro, Joseph Minarik, Jim Klumpner, Lars Osberg, Lee Price, Isabel Sawhill, Kathleen Scholl, Chad Stone, and Michael White, as well as several other colleagues at the Urban Institute, the Joint Economic Committee, and the Census Bureau, made valuable suggestions on the topics discussed in specific chapters. I also would like to thank Gordon Fisher for correcting several factual errors and for providing background information on the development of the official poverty measure; Joseph Richardson and Carla Pedone for information on specific assistance programs; and Daniel Kasprzyk and David McMillen for their support in working with the Survey of Income and Program Participation. Finally, Brenda Brown cheerfully and competently prepared several versions of the manuscript.

I am, of course, solely responsible for any remaining errors. Opinions expressed in this book are mine only, and should not be attributed to The Urban Institute or its funders, the National Science Foundation, the Bureau of the Census, or the Joint Economic Committee.

Chapter One

INTRODUCTION: WHY MEASURE POVERTY?

What is poverty, and why should we measure it? Many writers have considered the definition of poverty, and much of this book is devoted to exploring the implications of alternative poverty concepts. Before trying to define—or redefine—poverty, however, it is useful to think about why we need a poverty measure at all. Indeed, a central argument of this book is that the "right" measure may vary, depending on the specific purpose for which it is to be employed.

One fundamental reason for having a poverty measure is to allow comparisons of economic well-being—across families, across population groups, across regions, and perhaps most of all, across time. These comparisons in turn may help us to judge the effects of economic growth and of public policies and to evaluate the need for public intervention of one type or another. Poverty measures are only one possible indicator of economic well-being, of course, and others, such as median income, per capita income, and various other adjusted income and consumption measures, can be used to compare economic well-being across groups and across time. The choice of a specific poverty measure rather than one of these broader measures has the effect of focusing attention not just on general economic well-being but on the well-being of the least-well-off members of society.

From a public policy perspective, however, a second application of poverty measures is equally important. For those who help to design policies and programs, as well as for those who must implement and evaluate them, the major purpose of a poverty measure is to allow us to assess the effects of our policies and programs and to identify people and groups whose most basic economic needs remain unmet.

This book is written primarily for policymakers and those interested in assessing policies and programs, and therefore it focuses on poverty measures designed with these purposes in mind. In other words, this book is neither about poverty as a generalized measure of economic well-being nor about inequality or the distribution of income. Although these are all interesting issues, they are not of direct concern to policymakers charged with designing and assessing specific antipoverty policies and programs. Instead, therefore, the poverty measures examined here focus quite narrowly on poverty as a lack of access to minimally adequate economic resources.

Defining and measuring "minimally adequate economic resources" is still a large job, of course. Limiting the topic in this way, however, explicitly excludes a number of approaches. Specifically, it excludes issues concerning the behavior of the poor—whether they form a deviant "underclass," for example, or whether there is a "culture of poverty." The book also does not consider the welfare of the poor in some broader sense—that is, it does not try to measure how happy the poor are, or how satisfied they are with the conditions of their lives. Instead, the concern of this study is with more fundamental economic questions—for example, whether or not people have enough money to pay the rent and to buy food.

Judged by this very basic standard, official poverty measures in the United States are deficient. These measures probably identified people with truly inadequate access to consumption reasonably well when the measures were introduced in the mid-1960s. Now, however, the consumption data underlying these measures are very outdated, and the resulting poverty standards have not been updated adequately to reflect changes in consumption patterns and needs over the past 25 years. As a result, the official "poverty line" is no longer realistic as a standard for minimally adequate consumption.

A complete updating of our consumption standards is needed every decade or so. This updating should be based on detailed expert judgments about minimally adequate budgets. Even the much less detailed examination of consumption patterns and needs offered here implies that the poverty line should probably be substantially higher than it is currently—close to $15,000 for a family of three in 1988, for example, rather than at its official level of about $9500.

Other aspects of the official measures are also questionable. The specific adjustments used to compute relative needs for families of different sizes are again based on data that are very outdated and that probably were inappropriate even when more current. As a result, these adjustments contain some strange quirks, and they need to be reexamined in light of more detailed and up-to-date estimates of actual family needs. In addition, the official poverty measure uses separate thresholds for several groups—for the elderly and for detailed family composition groups within each family size category, for example—

that simply cannot be justified on the basis of current data. Other distinctions that might be more appropriate, however—notably, adjustments for differences in price levels in different parts of the country, which clearly do affect the amount of money a family needs to spend on necessities like rent or food—are not included.

The specific poverty measures that we use have played an important role in shaping our perceptions both of the extent of real economic need and of the characteristics of those who are most deserving of our help. Ultimately, different measures may well lead to different priorities in setting antipoverty policies. If we believe that the poverty rate is already fairly low and is declining, for example, we are less likely to consider additional spending for antipoverty programs a vital national priority. Similarly, if we believe that circumstances are improving more (or more rapidly) for some population subgroups than for others, we may choose to reallocate spending to provide more to those whose need appears to be greater. For these reasons, basic flaws in our current measures that result in misleading conclusions about the incidence of real economic need should be of concern to policy analysts and policymakers.

Although this book criticizes many aspects of the official measures, it argues that from the policy analyst's perspective a measure that is in some ways deficient is still preferable to no measure at all. Thus, the suggestions put forth here should be read as attempts to make our current measures more accurate and useful rather than as fundamental objections to the entire business of poverty measurement. Before turning to a more detailed discussion of those suggestions, however, current measurement practices must be outlined briefly.

OFFICIAL POVERTY MEASURES IN THE UNITED STATES

The United States has an "official" poverty measure that the federal government uses both in publishing statistics on income and in setting eligibility standards for certain public programs.[1] This measure is produced by comparing the current money incomes of families with a set of predefined poverty "thresholds." It provides a basis for comparing the adequacy of family incomes across types of families, across regions, and across time. The United States has not always had such a measure, however—the official measure is less than 30 years old, and it became the "official" standard of the federal government through a haphazard process of use rather than through any systematic approach.

It is no coincidence that the adoption of a national poverty standard in the United States occurred in the late 1960s, during the War on Poverty, when concern about the living standards of the poor reached a peak. As James Tobin (1969) put it, "Adoption of a specific quantitative measure, however arbitrary and debatable, will have durable and far-reaching political consequences. Administrations will be judged by their success or failure in reducing the officially measured prevalence of poverty. So long as any family is found below the official poverty line, no politician will be able to claim victory in the war on poverty or ignore the repeated solemn acknowledgements of society's obligation to its poorer members."[2]

Unfortunately, Tobin's prediction has not been entirely borne out. Concern about poverty is no longer as high on the national agenda as it was in 1969, and at least one politician has claimed "victory" in the War on Poverty, despite continuing high poverty rates. Nevertheless, the existence of a national poverty standard and the production of annual estimates of the population in poverty have served as reminders that even in times of sustained economic growth some Americans continue to live in need.

The current official poverty standard grew out of a series of studies undertaken by Mollie Orshansky for the Social Security Administration in the mid-1960s (see, for example, Orshansky 1963, 1965). Orshansky started with a set of minimally adequate food budgets for families of various sizes and types that had been calculated by the Department of Agriculture. She simply multiplied these by a factor of three, on the assumption (borne out by some survey evidence) that food typically represented about one-third of total expenditures. Because the original food budgets that were their basis varied by family size and by factors such as the age and sex composition of the household, Orshansky's poverty thresholds also varied by these factors.[3]

Although Orshansky's thresholds bore only a very approximate relationship to a "scientifically" determined minimum level of subsistence, the fact that they did incorporate at least some adjustment for family size and composition made them an advance over much previous work. The adjustments for a differences in need across families of different sizes and types found in Orshansky's thresholds were based entirely on the Department of Agriculture's estimates of differences in their necessary food consumption, with no adjustment for differences in their other consumption needs. Nevertheless, even these crude adjustments were better than none, and these scales, with only minor differences, are still built into today's official poverty thresholds.

Once Orshansky's poverty scale had been published, it was widely adopted by other government researchers. Finally, in 1969 a slightly modified version of the Orshansky scale was mandated by the Bureau of the Budget as the standard poverty measure for the government statistical establishment as a whole. Since 1969 the Orshansky poverty scale has been subject to considerable criticism, but, with relatively minor changes, it still forms the basis for our official poverty measures.

Official statistics produced using Orshansky's methodology show major declines in the incidence of poverty since the early 1960s, as figure 1.1 illustrates. But the degree of improvement has not been constant across all demographic groups. Although the elderly, for example, now appear much less likely to be poor than they were 20 years ago, children's poverty rates actually were higher in 1987 than they were in 1967. Poverty rates for people in female-headed families have fallen somewhat from their levels of the 1960s, but they still remain very high. Perceptions of poverty based on these statistics continue to shape our antipoverty policies.

Figure 1.1 OFFICIAL POVERTY RATES BY DEMOGRAPHIC GROUP, 1960–1987

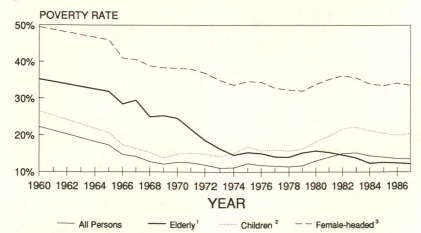

Source: Committee on Ways and Means, 1989, Table 2, p.944.
Notes:
1. Aged 65 and over. 1960 figure based on 1959 data.
2. Related children under 18 in families and unrelated subfamilies.
3. Persons in female-headed families.

Two major types of criticism have been leveled at the methodology used to prepare these official statistics. First, many researchers, especially academics, have criticized the conceptual basis of the measure. These critics have focused on the definition of poverty and on the extent to which the official measure does or does not conform to particular concepts of what it means to be poor. These criticisms are outlined in much more detail in chapter 2, which considers alternative poverty concepts and their implications for measurement. Because these broad-scale proposals for rethinking our poverty measures would have potentially large and unpredictable empirical results, however, few have been seriously considered for adoption by federal statistical agencies.

A second type of criticism has involved a host of proposals for specific small-scale revisions in the poverty measure. These proposals often arise in response to the particular economic or political circumstances of the moment. For example, the very high rates of inflation of the late 1970s sparked a widespread concern about the indexing procedures used to adjust poverty thresholds from year to year, whereas the dramatic growth in noncash benefits over the past two decades has inspired much research on the effects of including or excluding these benefits in calculating income. Although the researchers who have proposed and analyzed these incremental changes in poverty measures typically have been familiar with the broader context of conceptual and policy issues involved in measuring economic well-being, the press and even the policy community at large have tended to treat each new issue as if it were the only problem with an otherwise perfect measure.

This book takes a middle path between these two approaches. Its major aim is not to recommend some entirely new conceptual approach to measuring poverty, although some specific reassessments of the existing measures are proposed. Instead, its major purpose is to explore the empirical implications of some concrete and particular choices in poverty measurement while providing enough background to allow those who are not familiar with the theoretical debate in this area to appreciate the conceptual arguments for and against specific measurement options.

The book does not propose some specific new standard as the one "right" way to measure poverty, but it does conclude, after assessing the evidence, that the current official measures could be improved in several areas. In each of these areas the book suggests guidelines for developing improved measures and presents some possible alternatives that would come closer to meeting those guidelines.

PLAN OF THIS BOOK

The major focus of this book is on methods of measuring poverty and their implications for estimates of the size and characteristics of the poverty population. Although "poverty" is potentially a very broad concept, this book follows current official measurement practices in focusing primarily on lack of economic resources rather than on more general forms of deprivation. In other words, this book considers people poor if they lack access to minimally adequate levels of income or consumption. Although other problems such as homelessness, drug use, teenage pregnancy, and unemployment all may be related to poverty, they are not the focus of this investigation.

The chapters that follow explore the effects of variations in several specific dimensions of poverty measurement and discuss the implications of each for public policy analysis. The next chapter examines the definition of poverty in detail, identifying three major conceptual approaches and discussing the pros and cons of each from the perspective of public policy analysis. The chapter argues that for assessing programs and policies, poverty measures that focus on comparing individuals' utility levels—in some sense, their overall level of satisfaction or welfare—are less helpful than measures that focus more narrowly on economic well-being. Differences in satisfaction arise from many different causes, not all of them in the realm of public policy, but differences in the availability of minimally adequate economic resources are much more likely to be a matter of policy concern.

Chapter 3 considers the level of the U.S. poverty thresholds, focusing particularly on methods of adjusting thresholds for changes in income and consumption patterns over time. The chapter demonstrates that it is possible to construct poverty thresholds that are either higher or lower than the official ones but argues that long-term price-indexing of the thresholds—the current method of adjusting them for changes over time—eventually leads to very unrealistic poverty lines. The chapter considers other methods of constructing a set of thresholds, demonstrating that even the method originally used by Orshansky, if applied today using current consumption data, would result in much higher poverty thresholds than the official ones.

The chapter concludes that the basket of consumption goods implicitly underlying the U.S. poverty concept should be updated every decade or so to reflect both changing consumption patterns and changing concepts of minimal adequacy. Although a complete re-evaluation of consumption needs is beyond the scope of this study, estimates based on approximate food and housing need standards imply that if such updates had been done, today's thresholds would be at least 50 percent higher than the official ones. These thresholds in turn would imply overall poverty rates of more than 20 percent, compared to the official poverty rate of about 13 percent. This recommended update, therefore, is both the most pressing and the most controversial change proposed in this book.

Chapter 4 discusses the wide variety of methods that could be used to adjust poverty thresholds for differences in family needs. It demonstrates that the choice of a specific set of adjustments can be important in determining poverty rates for families of different sizes and types. The set of adjustments for family size implicit in the official U.S. poverty thresholds is shown to be very irregular, with relatively large adjustments for additional family members in large families but small adjustments in small families. Because economies of scale are normally expected to rise rather than fall as family size rises, this set of adjustments is counterintuitive and unrealistic.

As averaged across the scale as a whole, however, the family size adjustment implicit in the official thresholds is fairly typical of adjustments found in the scales used by other countries for purposes such as program evaluation and the assessment of needs. Although a general reevaluation of needs by family size would be desirable, a more limited approach that simply smoothed out the irregularities in the existing scale would be defensible, given the evidence that most other expert-designed family size adjustments fall into the same overall range. Chapter 4 gives an example of a set of adjustments that would meet this need while preserving the general magnitude of our current adjustments.

Even if no general program of reevaluation and reform of the adjustments for differences in family size and type is instituted, the chapter proposes that the Census Bureau should consider some smaller scale changes in the details of the current adjustments. There is no justification for the continued use of the specific detailed family type adjustments that the Census Bureau now employs, which are based on extremely outdated data. Also, there is little evidence that the elderly as a whole need less than others, and therefore it advocates eliminating separate thresholds for the elderly. On the other hand, there is sufficient evidence for differences in price levels across regions to warrant introducing regional differentials into the poverty thresholds. As chapter 4 demonstrates, most of these changes could be implemented with little change in estimated poverty rates overall.

Chapter 5 discusses the issue of time in measuring resources and looks specifically at short- versus long-term poverty. The size of the poverty population is shown to vary in a systematic way with the amount of time over which resources are measured, but the long-term poor are shown to be much more likely to be nonwhite, old, disabled, and/or in female-headed families than are the short-term poor. On the other hand, the median poverty spell is shown to last for less than one year.

The chapter concludes that poverty measures are very sensitive to the specification of the accounting period and that for many purposes the "spell" is a much more natural way to measure poverty than is an arbitrarily defined period such as a year. The Census Bureau therefore is urged to produce spell-oriented measures of income and poverty levels as well as the more familiar estimates based on annual cross-sectional income data.

Chapter 6 discusses the unit of analysis in measuring poverty. Should analysts consider the resources of persons, families, households? Because some types of people typically live in smaller families than do others, the composition of the poverty population will look quite different if the proportion of families with a particular characteristic—for example, an elderly head—rather than the proportion of people in such families is considered. The chapter considers the effects of alternative analytic units both in a cross-sectional context and in considering changes in individual and family circumstances over a period of time. In the latter case in particular, a person-related standard is seen to give more consistent and more easily interpreted results.

Chapter 7 is devoted to problems in the measurement of economic resources, a key component of most types of poverty measures. This chapter first discusses the definition of income, including topics such as noncash income and the treatment of taxes. It is shown that although dramatically different poverty rates are obtained with alternative income measures, trends in poverty over time are not extremely sensitive to the income concept used. The chapter also argues that health care and other benefits that are not very fungible cannot be included in a meaningful way in a poverty measure that uses a simple set of monetary values as thresholds. Instead, alternative thresholds for certain nonfungible necessities such as health care are proposed.

In addition to income, chapter 7 also considers assets and other resources that contribute to economic well-being but that are not easily incorporated into a simple income measure. The distribution of asset holdings in the low-income population is discussed, and it is shown that few of the poor have any significant liquid assets. In fact, most of those who have assets of any type are elderly, and even in this group those who would not be poor if their assets were counted are in the minority. Various methods of incorporating an asset measure into a poverty standard are discussed. The chapter also considers various sources of nonmarket income, ranging from home production to crime, and their potential effects on our poverty statistics.

The final chapter, chapter 8, summarizes the effects of the various measurement alternatives examined and discusses their implications for an understanding of the low-income population in more detail. The measurement alternatives considered in the previous chapters are reconsidered in light of what they say about the needs of specific population groups, such as families with children and the elderly. The relative empirical importance of particular variations in poverty measurement is assessed. Finally, the chapter summarizes the areas of new research and the specific measurement changes recommended to enhance our ability to track the changing needs and characteristics of the low-income population.

Notes

1. In fact, the United States has two sets of official cutoffs relating to the measurement of poverty. The first, established for each year by the Census Bureau, is used primarily for statistical purposes. Poverty thresholds under this standard are determined retrospectively. Because the analysis of income data takes place after the income year in question is over, the Census Bureau already knows what price increases actually occurred over that year, and it simply can adjust the previous year's poverty thresholds accordingly. It is this measure that is discussed in detail in this book.

The second set of poverty cutoffs is calculated and issued each year by the Department of Health and Human Services (HHS), although it is known, confusingly, as the "OMB guidelines." These guidelines are calculated prospectively, to apply to the upcoming income year, and are used to determine eligibility in about two dozen federal programs, including the Food Stamp Program, Headstart, and some parts of Medicaid. To compute these guidelines for 1990, for example, HHS took the Census Bureau's thresholds for 1988—the most recent then available—and updated them for price changes between 1988 and 1989. (There are also minor differences in the HHS and Census Bureau methods of computing family size adjustments.) As a result, the poverty guidelines actually used for most program purposes lag about a year behind the Census Bureau thresholds in level—the guidelines issued in February 1990 and used for 1990 program eligibility determination, for example, will be comparable roughly to the Census Bureau poverty thresholds for 1989. For details on how to compute the poverty guidelines from the Census Bureau thresholds see Fisher (1984).

2. Tobin's comment reflected a widely held view—both Michael Harrington (1969) and Robert Lampman (1971) expressed similar ideas, for example. See also further discussion in Danziger and Gottschalk (1983), which also cites Tobin's comment.

3. Orshansky set higher thresholds for one- and two-person families to take account of the higher fixed costs such as housing expenses that such families face. More recently, separate thresholds for male- and female-headed families and for farm and nonfarm residents also were dropped, although lower thresholds for the elderly in one- and two-person families still are maintained. For a detailed discussion of the origins and early revisions of the official thresholds, see U.S. Dept. of Health, Education and Welfare (1976). Orshansky's methodology also is discussed in more detail in chapter 3.

Chapter Two

CHOICES IN POVERTY MEASUREMENT

Any measure of poverty involves a large number of choices. Indeed, perhaps one reason the definition developed by Orshansky in the 1960s has been so durable in the United States is that any redefinition would involve so many possible areas of change that it is difficult to know where to start. For the policy analyst or data user whose primary interest is in outcomes rather than in measurement issues, many of the questions debated by economists seem confusing and obscure. This chapter, then, outlines in nontechnical terms the major categories of choices facing the researcher and discusses the implications of each for poverty measurement.

Because the major purpose of this book is to provide practical guidance to those seeking to use poverty measures in public policy analysis, choices that are very far from current practices or that could not be implemented under any likely data collection plan receive less attention than do choices that are more immediately available. The first two sections of the chapter outline some broad issues in defining and identifying poverty. The last two sections focus on specific components of the poverty measure and on alternative indexes for measuring poverty.

EMPIRICAL DEFINITIONS OF POVERTY: A BRIEF SURVEY

Before the 1960s relatively few studies requiring a precise empirical definition of poverty were carried out. Perhaps the earliest such study, and the source for many later concepts of poverty, was Rowntree's study of poverty in York, England, around the turn of century (Rowntree 1901). This study defined primary poverty as income below that needed to obtain the minimum necessities for the maintenance of physical efficiency.

The Roundtree definition, with its focus on income and on poverty thresholds based on some estimate of the amount needed for subsistence, is very similar in concept to the Orshansky standard as implemented in the United States, and it also served as the underpinning for many subsequent studies of poverty in Britain and in other English-speaking countries. Most notable, perhaps, was the use of this approach in the Beveridge Report (United Kingdom, Parliament 1942), which established a subsistence standard that became the basis for the provision of income support for the poor in the United Kingdom.[1]

Most of these empirical studies of poverty concentrated primarily on counting the number of poor rather than on measuring the depth of their poverty, and this approach was continued in the early work in the United States by Orshansky (1963, 1965) and others. In commenting on this work, however, Harold Watts (1968) pointed out that a simple head count of this type is in many ways unsatisfactory. A person with an income one dollar below the poverty line is not dramatically different in economic well-being from one with an income one dollar above the line. Watts suggested various other poverty measures that would take into account the depth of poverty as well as its incidence, and the recent literature on poverty measurement has expanded on this theme. Much of this literature follows on an influential article by A. K. Sen (1976a), which divided the measurement of poverty into two stages: first identifying the poor, and second aggregating their poverty "gaps"—the amounts by which they fell short of some specific poverty threshold—into some sort of comprehensive poverty index.

This book focuses primarily on the first problem—identifying the poor—and considers only very briefly issues relating to the construction of poverty indexes. The major reason for this approach is that although the statistical properties of various indexes have been examined intensively, from a policy analyst's viewpoint the crucial differences between measures most often arise not from the details of the indexes and their construction but rather from the underlying concept of poverty on which they are based. As a result, the major outcome variable considered here is the simple poverty count—the number or percentage of the population that would be counted as poor under various definitions.

Clearly, the depth of poverty also matters for public policy purposes. Programs that raise the incomes of many poor people should not be judged valueless even if no single individual is actually removed from poverty altogether. This book argues, however, that in practice poverty gap measures are likely to be more sensitive to the original definition of poverty than to alternative aggregation procedures within a given poverty definition. In addition, as Atkinson (1987) suggests, within a given definition it is relatively simple to produce a variety of aggregate measures and to see if the choice of a measure affects in any way the comparisons (across time, across groups, and so on) that one wishes to make.[2] As a result, the emphasis here is on deriving and comparing alternative poverty definitions.

IDENTIFYING THE POOR: ALTERNATIVE CONCEPTS OF POVERTY

The construction of an official poverty measure carries with it an implied judgment about social welfare. It says that it is not just the total welfare of all individuals in society that matters but also specifically the well-being of those who are least well-off. Although the problem of poverty is often seen by economists as a special subset of the problem of inequality—after all, if there were no inequality presumably there would also be no poverty—from the viewpoint of the policymaker a concern about poverty does not necessarily imply any interest at all in broader issues of distribution. Many policymakers start instead with the notion that underlay the War on Poverty—that there is some minimum "decent" standard of living, and a just society must attempt to ensure that all its members have access to at least this level of economic well-being.

Although the concept of a minimum decent standard of living can be made operational in a number of different ways, as discussed below, all of the poverty standards that might do so have two important features in common. First, they focus on economic well-being, not on welfare or utility in some broader sense. In other words, such measures determine people's poverty status by considering their command over goods and services, not their patterns of behavior, beliefs, or general levels of satisfaction or happiness.

This does not imply that these other factors are not important. It means only that policies that are explicitly designed to improve economic circumstances are best evaluated using a scale that considers economic resources. Whether U.S. policies ought to focus on economic status rather than on some other outcome is another issue. As Watts (1968: 318–19) has persuasively argued, however, "The task of evaluating and ranking programs for their effect on poverty is not responsibly discharged by usurping the Presidential-level problem of balancing the claims of all social objectives."

The second feature common to all poverty standards considered here is their focus on members of society whose command over goods and services is most limited. It is this feature, of course, that distinguishes these measures from broader measures of inequality. Again, if providing some minimum access to consumption for all members of society is a policy goal, then a standard that focuses on defining a minimal acceptable level of such access is appropriate in assessing policies designed to meet this goal. For this purpose, poverty measures must be designed primarily to assess the adequacy of resources available to the least-well-off, rather than the shares of resources going to people of different types.

Poverty measures can be, and often are, used more broadly as social indicators to compare the relative well-being of different groups. It is important not to overgeneralize in using measures in this way, however. Comparisons of relative poverty rates can lead to valid statements about the proportion of those in various groups with unacceptably low incomes or consumption levels, or about the size and distribution of the resulting income or consumption gaps. But because poverty measures focus on the low end of the distribution, they do not provide a valid means of comparing the total economic well-being of two population groups that each contain both poor and nonpoor members. If the poverty rates of the two groups are very different, one may perhaps infer that one of the groups is likely to be better off in general. Any comprehensive assessment of the relative well-being of the two groups as a whole would require a more detailed examination of the comparative resources of all their members, however, not just those who are poor. Measures of total resources and of the inequality of distribution of resources would be more relevant to such a comparison than would a poverty measure.

A poverty standard, then, must be defined in economic terms and must focus on those whose resources are most limited. Three major approaches to defining poverty can be taken within these broad guidelines. Hagenaars and De Vos (1988: 212) have neatly summarized the three types of poverty definitions that result from these approaches: (1) Poverty is having less than an objectively defined, absolute minimum. (2) Poverty is having less than others in society. (3) Poverty is feeling that you do not have enough to get along.

Each of these definitions, in turn, has different implications for the construction of a poverty measure, although, as will be seen, widely varying measures can be constructed within the same general class of definitions. The remainder of this section briefly outlines the rationale for and use of each type of poverty definition.

"Absolute" Poverty

Poverty measures that define poverty as either income or consumption below some absolute level that represents an "objective" minimum constitute the earliest and broadest class of poverty measures. Rowntree's original measure was of this type, as is the official U.S. poverty standard. This type of measure seems "scientific," since the minimums used are usually established through some sort of appeal to expert opinion. More important, an absolute standard provides a fixed benchmark that can be used to measure progress over time. Lampman (1971), for example, argued for an absolute scale on these grounds.

Politicians who are concerned about providing a "minimum decent standard of living" often conceive of such a standard in absolute terms. Indeed, as anyone who has heard an elderly relative's account of what things were like "in my day" is likely to recognize, individuals may not change their own concepts of an acceptable minimum standard even when the standards of society as a whole change quite dramatically. Thus, the political consensus in favor of an absolute, fixed measure can be quite strong, and those designing official poverty standards are likely to choose this type of definition.

The disadvantage of this type of measure is that in fact it is very difficult to establish an "objective" minimum that really is applicable over a long period (or even across very divergent population groups). Over time, for example, the goods people consume are likely to change dramatically, and the definition of the minimum needed for subsistence is likely to change as well. "Experts" constructing a market basket of normal consumption goods 50 years ago, for example, would not have included a telephone, a television, or air conditioning, but all might be included in 1990 (especially, in the last case, if those constructing the market basket were spending the summer in Washington). An absolute poverty standard that adjusts only for changes in prices and not for changes in consumption patterns will miss these consumption shifts, and thus is likely to overstate any improvements in the lot of the poor. Indeed, for just these reasons Orshansky (1988; personal communication 1987) has expressed considerable dismay at the codification of her original standard into a rigid, absolute scale—instead, she feels that attempts should have been made to adjust her thresholds to reflect changing patterns of consumption over time.

In addition to absolute poverty scales defined in terms of minimum thresholds, an "appropriate maximum" proportion of income or consumption may be assigned to certain subsistence goods. Thus Watts (1967), for example, proposed that families spending more than one-third of their income on food might be considered poor. Similarly, the Canadian "Low Income Cut-offs" (LICOs), an unofficial poverty line used for statistical purposes by the Canadian government, are computed by estimating the income level at which families of different sizes typically spend a percentage of income on basic needs that is at least 20 points higher than the average (Statistics Canada 1987).

A variant of the "appropriate maximum" measure that (according to Hagenaars and De Vos 1988) has been used in social policy debates in the Netherlands focuses on total fixed costs as a proportion of income. The principal components are housing, heat, and food. The theory behind such "maximum" measures is that as family income rises, smaller and smaller proportions are likely to be spent on such basics, and more is available for discretionary purchases. Thus, households that spend a smaller share of income on basic commodities are in effect better off than those with little or nothing left over for "luxuries."

The appropriate maximum approach can be used to adjust for differences in consumption needs across families of different sizes and types. Indeed, Van der Gaag and Smolensky (1982) have proposed a method of adjusting for such differences based on such comparisons of consumption patterns, as is discussed in chapter 4. Yet this approach has the problem that at least some spending differences may arise from differences in tastes rather than differences in resources. Further, it is still true that as both relative prices and tastes change over time the appropriate share of the budget to be allocated to specific basic consumption needs may change as well. For example, if food costs go down but the cost of housing rises, an index based on food costs alone would then overstate increases in the economic well-being of the poor.

Relative Poverty

The second largest class of poverty definitions are those that define poverty in relative terms. Such measures range from the fairly simplistic—for example, definitions that arbitrarily label the bottom 10

or 20 percent of the income distribution as "poor"—to the complex—
for example, the measure proposed in Townsend (1979), which examines each individual's consumption of a long list of commodities
and social services and then calculates a "deprivation index" based
on the number of areas in which the individual's consumption falls
below social norms.

The most common approach to a relative poverty standard, however, is to choose some income or consumption cutoff that can be
expressed as a proportion of the median for society as a whole. Fuchs
(1967) and Rainwater (1974), to note only two of the many who have
advanced such proposals, both have argued for a standard equal to
one-half the median income, for example.

Interestingly, this was approximately the level of the Orshansky measure for a family of four when it was introduced in the early 1960s.
Because official poverty thresholds have been adjusted only for changes
in prices and not for general growth in income over time, however,
they are now equal to about one-third of the median income at this
family size. This relative decline in the official poverty standard illustrates the key practical difference between an absolute and a relative
measure. The specific set of poverty thresholds constructed using the
two approaches may not be significantly different at a given point in
time, since "expert" opinions on the minimum needed for subsistence
are quite likely to correspond at least roughly to popular ideas based
on relative income or consumption levels. Over time, however, an
absolute standard that is adjusted only for price changes will decline
in relative terms if there is any growth at all in family incomes.

Opponents of the relative income or consumption approach to poverty measurement argue that it presents too much of a "moving target"
for policy assessment and that it is in some sense not fair to judge our
antipoverty efforts against such a standard. Indeed, this type of standard
will rise most rapidly in periods of rapid economic growth, when most
people, including most of the poor, are likely to experience growth in
their real incomes and consumption opportunities. Even though low-
income families may consider themselves better off under such circumstances, they would not be judged less poor under a relative poverty
measure unless their income or consumption levels actually rose relative to the median level for society as a whole. To put it another way,
poverty cannot decline under a relative poverty measure without some
change in the shape of the income distribution as a whole.[3] It is much
more difficult to design (let alone enact) policies to carry out such a
major redistribution than it is to design programs to improve the consumption opportunities of the poor.

A poverty standard that does not take changing relative income and consumption levels into account at all, however, runs the risk of becoming increasingly unrealistic over time. As the line becomes further from social norms, those whose incomes and consumption levels fall under it are increasingly likely to be out of the economic mainstream in other ways as well. For example, in the last decade alone the proportion of poor adult, nonelderly household heads who work full-time has fallen from about 43 percent to less than 36 percent.[4] As real wages rise and the poverty line remains fixed in real terms, it is increasingly unlikely that someone who works a significant number of hours will remain "poor," at least under the official definition. As a result, the poverty population comes to exclude most low-wage workers.

Nevertheless, many such workers (and others among the near-poor, such as retirees) still may experience real economic hardships, in the sense of being unable to consume commodities that "the custom of the country renders it indecent for creditable people, even of the lowest order, to be without," to quote Adam Smith (1776, vol. 1, p. 691). Moreover, those who are still poor under the absolute scale even as it declines in relative terms are in some sense a much more "hard core" poverty population than were those who were judged poor under this scale in 1965. That is, because the line is so much farther from the norm for our society, people who fall under it are more likely to be those with particularly severe problems, or perhaps even multiple problems—the disabled; young single mothers; and those with little education, low job skills, or both. It is indeed a challenge to design programs that will help people with such major problems to become more self-sufficient. Further, if the measurement-related aspects of this shift are not well understood, some analysts may misinterpret the evidence of increases in these problems among the poverty population as a sign that our existing antipoverty programs are backfiring and actually creating a more severely handicapped poverty population over time.

"Subjective" Poverty

Subjective definitions of poverty are a relatively new entry into the field of poverty research. These definitions are based on surveys that use households' own assessments of the minimum or "just sufficient" amounts of income or consumption needed by people like them. Most of this work follows on an article by Goedhart et al. (1977) and is associated with Bernard Van Praag and others at the University of

Leyden. Important applications of this method appear in Van Praag et al. (1980), Van Praag et al. (1982), and in Aldi Hagenaar's (1986) book, *The Perception of Poverty*. The only studies that have applied this method to U.S. data are Colasanto et al. (1984), which used Wisconsin data; Danziger et al. (1984), which used data from a special supplement to the 1979 Income Survey Development Program (ISDP) Research Panel; and, most recently, De Vos and Garner (1989), which compares results from the 1982 Consumer Expenditure Survey (CES) in the United States with results obtained from Dutch survey data.

The basic idea underlying subjective poverty measures is that one way to discover the minimum amount of income or consumption that people need to maintain what they consider to be a "decent" or minimally adequate level of living is to ask them directly. The ISDP data analyzed by Danziger et al., for example, are dollar amounts given in response to the question: "Living where you do now and meeting the expenses you consider necessary, what would be the very smallest income you and your family would need to make ends meet?"(1984:501). Similarly, in the survey done by Goedhart et al. (1977) people were asked what income they considered to be "just sufficient" for their household, and the CES questionnaire analyzed by De Vos and Garner (1989) asked the same question as the ISDP.[5]

As might be expected, people's answers to such questions tend to vary systematically with income and family size. For example, Goedhart et al. (1977) estimated the income elasticity of their poverty line estimate as 0.60 (that is, for each dollar of additional income, people raise their estimate of a "just sufficient" income by 60 cents, on average), and Danziger et al. (1984) found an income elasticity of about 0.38. Both sets of authors attributed the relationship between current income and estimated needs to the effects of habit on people's perceptions. Following the method introduced by Goedhart et al. (1977), subjective poverty lines have been calculated from such survey responses by finding the income level at which a "just sufficient" income is the same as reported income—in other words, the point at which the distributions of actual and "minimally necessary" incomes intersect.[6]

Subjective poverty definitions have a certain appeal as a solution to the problem of setting a poverty threshold. After all, "poverty" is a socially determined state, and in the end official thresholds come down to what some collection of politicians and program administrators consider an adequate level of resources to support life in a particular community. It seems in many ways more appropriate to ask the members of that community directly what they consider a minimally adequate income level. And, because the answers to such questions tend to rise as income rises, but not as fast, this approach could represent a compromise between absolute and relative measures as a means of adjusting thresholds for economic change over time. In answering these questions, people may be effectively separating out the component of their increased resources that has become "necessary" from the component that still represents purely discretionary spending.

This approach also has some drawbacks, however. As Hagenaars and De Vos (1988:213) note, the use of a subjective poverty definition to set poverty thresholds in the first place requires the assumption that terms such as "sufficient income" or "enough to make ends meet" are associated with the same level of real welfare by all respondents. As the art of political polling has taught us, questions that require the respondent to express an opinion often receive dramatically different answers with apparently small changes in wording. In the case of the question used in both the ISDP and CES surveys and cited above, for example, it seems likely that by including the phrases "living where you do now" and "meeting the expenses you consider necessary" the surveys will elicit answers that pertain to individuals' current specific living situations—the house they currently live in, the car they currently drive. In other words, the answers may reflect the level of spending needed in the very short run, if no real changes in standards of living are to ensue.

But these answers may by no means represent the consumption levels these individuals actually consider minimally necessary. For example, some families may have high mortgages that they must pay in the short run—but in the slightly longer run they could sell their houses and buy something smaller without reducing their welfare below the level they consider minimally acceptable. Other families may consider their current housing totally inadequate—but because the survey specifies "living where you do now" they may not include the amount that it would cost to obtain better housing in their estimate of needs. If respondents take this question very literally, in fact, they may be providing much more information about their current family budgets than about their minimum needs.

Although the version of this question used in the U.S. surveys seems to be phrased in a particularly ambiguous way, any survey that asks respondents to say how much they in particular would need to meet expenses is likely to obtain a set of answers that is heavily influenced by the respondents' current circumstances. To the extent that economic circumstances vary in systematic ways across subgroups within the population, comparisons across these groups based on subjective measures may tell us more about these underlying differences in expectations and current circumstances than they do about relative needs. One of the major findings of the Danziger et al. (1984) study, for example, was that subjectively derived poverty rates for elderly women were substantially below those found using the official measure, whereas rates for nonelderly men were higher than the official rates. Because the objective circumstances of elderly women are indeed substantially worse than those of prime-age men, it seems plausible that this result largely may reflect the fact that the latter group is currently better off and so has both higher current expenses and more expensive tastes.

More generally, people who currently are getting along without certain amenities—a home of their own, a car, a diet high in meats and other expensive foods—are not as likely as those who have these things to consider them "necessary." Even if the "just sufficient" standard is successful in eliciting responses that correspond to the same level of welfare—that is, the same level of satisfaction or utility—for these disparate individuals, it still is questionable whether it is consistent with our notions of justice to base public policy on this type of measure. First, as we already know, people's estimate of the "just sufficient" amount will rise as we increase their incomes. Thus, even if today's poor do not think they need cars, for example, if they become less poor they may change their minds.

Second, and more fundamentally, this type of measure, by comparing welfare rather than economic circumstances across individuals, violates the basic axiom that policies whose aims are primarily economic should be evaluated with measures that focus on economic well-being. One could argue that policies ought to focus on true welfare rather than simply on economic needs, but it is difficult enough to design programs that function well even with the fairly limited goal of enhancing economic well-being. Further, although there is some social consensus that issues of economic need are within the domain of public intervention, there is no such consensus, at least in the United States, with regard to most of the other variables that shape individuals' welfare in some broader sense.

COMPONENTS OF THE POVERTY DEFINITION

All of the poverty definitions discussed in the last section have their advantages and disadvantages. By now, however, it should be clear

that in whatever way poverty is defined, the method of identifying
the poor that results generally will involve two major components:
a poverty threshold (or set of thresholds) and a measure of resources.
This section summarizes the analytic choices involved for each of
these in turn.

Setting the Poverty Threshold

Watts has characterized our existing poverty measures as "simply a
collection of more or less arbitrary and eminently vulnerable
rules"(1986:18). Although, as demonstrated above, some justification
can be marshaled in support of a variety of different poverty concepts, each of which would lead to its own set of poverty lines, the
choice of a level for that line ultimately will be fairly arbitrary (although possibly less so than our current set of standards). If an
absolute poverty measure tied to some market basket of "necessary"
goods is chosen, for example, the selection of the appropriate goods
and the appropriate levels of consumption for each good still will
be open to debate—there simply is no one "correct" basket that
includes all necessities (but no luxuries) for every possible type of
household. Similarly, although a relative poverty line at one-half the
median income is often proposed, there is no inherent reason why
one-half is the "right" level, and, say, 45 percent is not.

One of the appeals of the subjective poverty measure is that it
seems less arbitrary—after all, the poverty thresholds come from the
respondents themselves, not from the researchers who design the
study. As discussed above, however, even these thresholds may be
subject to considerable swings, depending on the exact wording of
the questionnaire and the preexisting economic circumstances of the
respondents. Further, the responses still must be aggregated by the
researcher into a single set of poverty lines, and the groups over
which this is done and the specific methods used still will be open
to some essentially arbitrary choices.

The essential arbitrariness of the poverty threshold in itself should
not be a cause for despair, however. Instead, it should lead to two
important realizations. First, there is no "right" way to set poverty
thresholds. Rather, a variety of useful thresholds can be estimated,
and the specific threshold should be chosen for its applicability to
the problem at hand. Second, even fairly crude poverty measures
can be useful for many policy purposes, as long as their limitations
are borne in mind.

For many public policy applications the variable of interest is not the poverty rate itself but rather differences in the poverty rate (or "poverty gap") across groups, across regions, and most of all, across time. Within broad limits, comparisons of this type typically are more sensitive to methods of adjusting the threshold for changing circumstances or for differences in needs than to the original level chosen. The exception to this rule arises when the distribution of income over certain groups within society—for example, the elderly—is very uneven, with the bulk of households bunching at certain levels. In such cases, across-group comparisons can look very different depending on whether the poverty line is set just above or just below such a level. This problem emphasizes the importance of considering the relationship between the specification of the poverty line being used and the particular analysis being done.

Most sources of bias in making poverty comparisons, however, arise not from the original level of the threshold but from methods of making adjustments in the threshold to account for differences across groups and across time. There are two major types of adjustment, in particular, that are often sources of controversy and that may cause some biases in intergroup comparisons. First, there is the problem of adjusting the thresholds for differences in family size and composition. Because this is usually done by calculating some scale that purports to give "equivalent" incomes or consumption needs for families of different sizes and types, this problem generally is referred to as the *equivalence scale* problem. Second, there is the equally serious problem of adjusting for changes in prices and living standards over time, which can affect not only the composition of the population seen as poor but also its size. These problems are examined in detail in the next two chapters of this book, which also offer some empirical comparisons of the implications of alternative poverty thresholds.

Measuring Economic Resources

The second component of a typical poverty definition is the measure of economic resources. Although the poverty threshold may give us some idea of economic needs, it is only by comparing those needs with actual resources that we can determine whether, under this definition, a given individual is poor. Chapters 5, 6, and 7 cover a host of specific issues that arise in attempting to measure economic resources in a way that is useful for understanding poverty.

The first and most enduringly controversial issue concerning the measurement of resources is whether the measure should focus primarily on people's incomes or on their level of consumption. Consumption-based measures are attractive for a number of reasons. First, most people think of poverty as inadequate access to consumption, and it seems most natural to measure that access by examining consumption directly rather than by examining income and then estimating its relationship to consumption possibilities. Indeed, some people with low incomes are able to maintain consumption levels above their income levels, either by borrowing or by drawing on assets, and it can be difficult to adjust income-based measures for these additional resources. Second, many analysts would exclude those whose poverty is merely transitory and who can expect much higher incomes in the longer run—for example, students—from the "real" poverty population. The argument here would be that "permanent" or lifetime income is a better measure of a person's true welfare than is his or her current income status and that consumption is a better proxy for permanent income than is current income (see, for example, Sen 1976b, for more on this view). Although this study has argued that for the policy analyst it is specifically *economic* welfare rather than some broader "true" welfare measure that is of interest in measuring poverty, nonetheless some consideration of longer-range prospects may be appropriate in assessing need or at least in designing policies to alleviate need.[7]

Despite the arguments in favor of a consumption-based poverty measure, however, most empirical studies of poverty in fact use a measure based on income. There are two reasons for this, one practical and one conceptual. The practical reason is that it is simply much easier to obtain reasonably reliable, regularly produced estimates of personal incomes than it is to obtain such data on consumption. Several large-scale surveys that collect data on income in conjunction with many other variables are regularly undertaken by the U.S. government. The CES, our only regular consumption survey, has a smaller sample size than our major income surveys, and because it must collect very detailed data on the consumption of individual goods, it has less room for additional detailed information on other characteristics of people and families.

Consumption data also may be more difficult than income data to collect reliably. Most people have only a few sources of income, and these tend to be fairly stable over time. Further, because income is important in determining tax liabilities, people tend to have reasonably good records of any income changes. Consumption, on the other hand, can involve a vast array of possible goods and services, and getting people to keep reliable records of the amounts and types of goods they consume can be very difficult.

It is this set of practical concerns that has caused most analysts to choose income as the primary source of information about material resources in measuring poverty. A second reason for choosing an income-based measure, however, is that at least in some respects it may be a better indicator of an individual's command over goods and services than is his or her actual consumption. If individuals have the resources to consume adequate levels of goods and services but for reasons of taste choose not to, it is arguable that they are not in fact poor. This argument is particularly relevant to consumption-based measures that take into account only a few key consumption items, such as food.

Conversely, if people find some way to consume more than can be accounted for through measured income, this may simply mean that we have defined income too narrowly—for example, we may wish to include loan proceeds and gifts in our total income measure. And finally, if some individuals can maintain minimally adequate levels of consumption only by pursuing sources of income that are socially unacceptable—for example, by begging or stealing—it is perhaps realistic to count them among the poor.

This book follows the lead of most empirical studies of poverty in using income as the primary basis for estimating economic resources. This decision still leaves a broad array of possible choices in defining and measuring those resources. The chapters that follow consider several of these choices. First, whose income should be considered—the individual's, the family's, or the household's? Second, over what period should this income be measured—a month, a year, a decade, or even a lifetime? Third, there is the issue of the income definition itself—how should factors such as taxes be treated, and should income received in kind instead of in cash be included? And finally, should other resources such as assets or nonmarket incomes be adjusted for, and if so, how?

In each case the primary goal of this book is not to present some definitive answer to these questions but rather to consider the pros and cons of various alternatives, and, perhaps more importantly, to estimate the impact of alternative choices on the size and characteristics of the population identified as poor. The goal of this analysis is to consider how these apparently technical measurement issues affect our views about who the poor are, which, in turn, helps determine the allocation of public resources across the low-income population.

INDEXES FOR POVERTY MEASUREMENT

Before considering the definitional choices in detail, however, a brief review of alternative methods of aggregating poverty data is in order, if only because some basis for aggregation—even if only a head count—is also a necessary component of any poverty measure that applies to more than one case. Although, as discussed above, most of the analysis in this book is presented in terms of effects on very simple poverty measures—principally, counts of the number of people in poverty—it still may be helpful to consider briefly the principles for designing aggregate measures of poverty that have been advanced in the literature. Much of the poverty measurement literature of the past two decades has concentrated on this problem, and specifically, on developing indexes that have certain desirable statistical properties. For example, most analysts agree that a poverty index should be affected only by changes in the resources (or consumption) of the poor, not by changes affecting only the nonpoor. Indexes that violate this axiom may relate to inequality but cannot really be said to measure poverty.

A second widely accepted axiom holds that if a poor person becomes more poor, the index should increase. This axiom is satisfied by a simple summing of poverty gaps across those in poverty, but not, for example, by a head count. A more difficult to satisfy but often-included axiom is that transfers between poor persons also should affect the index, causing it to rise, for example, if a person who is deeper in poverty makes a payment to someone whose poverty is less severe. Satisfaction of this axiom requires some weighting of poverty gaps in relation to individuals' poverty status. In addition, some care is required in dealing with cases in which such transfers actually remove someone from the poverty population altogether. Finally, Hagenaars (1986), among others, argues for a "decomposition axiom." That is, if poverty indexes are computed separately for each of several mutually exclusive groups—say, for example, age categories—then changes in poverty within each category should aggregate systematically into a change in the poverty index for the population as a whole.[8]

Within these broad parameters, it is possible to develop a wide variety of indexes that relate to different concepts of poverty and inequality, and ultimately to different underlying social welfare functions (see Foster 1984 for a review of this literature). Although these statistical properties undoubtedly enhance our ability to make unambiguous comparisons across groups and across time, these advantages must be balanced against certain potential drawbacks in choosing indexes for public policy analysis, and especially in designing measures to be used in producing official poverty statistics. First, most of the resulting indexes have no clear intuitive interpretation that can be easily understood by busy policymakers with little or no grounding in statistics. Indeed, as the indexes become more and more complex it can be difficult even for analysts who are familiar with them to pinpoint the sources of change from period to period or to predict how alternative indexes will react to specific changes in the distribution of income or consumption. For a measure to be useful in evaluating policy, the sources of changes in that measure should be easily understood. Even with a fairly simple poverty index, it can be difficult to relate specific policy options to resulting changes in the measure, and this problem only grows worse as the measure itself becomes more complex.[9]

Second, as Atkinson (1987) demonstrates, even when a class of specific poverty measures does not give unambiguous rankings of poverty under all conditions, it may do so under a broad enough range of conditions to be satisfactory for many analytic purposes. Here the trick is to be fairly clear in advance as to exactly what one's analytic purpose is. Measures that are perfectly satisfactory in relation to some concepts of poverty potentially could be misleading with regard to others. As Atkinson notes, however, "there is likely to be a diversity of judgments affecting all aspects of measuring poverty and . . . we should recognize this explicitly in the procedures we adopt. This will lead to less all-embracing answers. We may only be able to make comparisons and not to measure differences; and our comparisons may lead only to a partial and not a complete ordering. But such partial answers are better than no answers." This last sentence, in particular, represents a fundamental article of faith for the policy analyst.

Notes

1. See also Fiegehen et al. (1977) or Townsend (1979) for a discussion of poverty measures for Britain; Poduluk (1968) or Wolfson (1986) for Canada.

2. The United States Bureau of the Census currently publishes its survey data on income in the form of computer-readable microdata files as well as in tabular form,

allowing individual analysts with relatively sophisticated programming abilities (and large computer budgets) to construct their own aggregation procedures under the official thresholds (or any simple permutation of the official thresholds). In addition, the Census Bureau publishes annual reports containing tables showing a distribution of income deficits by family characteristics. Although these estimates are not as widely publicized as the poverty rate figures, they can be used to construct a variety of aggregate "poverty gap" measures. (It would be very helpful if the Bureau would provide these estimates by family size as well as by other characteristics, however.) In addition, estimates of a simple poverty gap measure (and of the effectiveness of various antipoverty programs in filling this gap) are available for recent years in Weinberg 1986 and U.S. Congress, House of Representatives, Committee on Ways and Means (1989: 962–71).

3. Clearly, poverty cannot decline at all, in percentage terms, if the standard is defined simply as the bottom x percent of the income definition. This limits the usefulness of such poverty definitions in policy analysis.

4. Calculated from U.S. Bureau of the Census (1980, Table 27) and U.S. Bureau of the Census (1989a, Table 21), which show hours and weeks worked for household heads aged 22 to 64 in 1978 and 1987, respectively.

5. The CES version of the question adds the parenthetical phrase "before any deductions" after the phrase "the smallest income."

6. These functions are normally specified in log form, so that the poverty line becomes the income level where

$$\log(Y\_min) = a_0 + a_1 \log(Y),$$

where Y_min is the dollar amount given in response to the "minimum income" question and Y is reported current household income. By adding other variables to the regression equation specific poverty thresholds for various population subgroups can be calculated. This use of subjective poverty measures is discussed further in chapter 4.

7. This issue is discussed in much more detail in chapter 7, which considers assets, including human capital, in relation to the resource measure.

8. This brief list by no means exhausts the many alternative axioms advanced in the literature—see, for example, Sen (1976a), Sen (1979), Thon (1979), Clark et al. (1981), and Foster et al. (1984) for other suggestions.

9. Against this, Kapteyn (1977) argues that as a given measurement—for example, IQ—is used over time, it gains acceptance and understanding regardless of its complexity, and so one's focus should be on the development of the "best" measure rather than the simplest one.

Chapter Three

SETTING THE POVERTY THRESHOLD

Given a basic concept of poverty, the first step in actually identifying the poor is to choose a poverty threshold—some level of resources that represents a minimum acceptable standard of economic well-being. As the last chapter discussed, a number of different concepts can serve as the basis for this choice, but within a given definition of poverty many aspects of the choice will be essentially arbitrary, at least within broad bounds. In choosing among specific alternatives, therefore, it is helpful to understand not only their conceptual differences but also the empirical implications of a specific choice. Choices that are conceptually very different in fact may lead to very similar conclusions, at least at a point in time. On the other hand, distinctions that seem very minor in theory can result in very major differences, both in the estimated thresholds themselves and in comparative poverty rates for people in different population groups.

This chapter, therefore, reviews some of the major conceptual issues that must be addressed in setting a poverty threshold, once one has made some basic choices among alternative poverty definitions. The chapter focuses particularly on the problem of adjusting thresholds for differences across time. Even thresholds that start out very close together can differ substantially after a period of 10 or more years, depending on the methods used to adjust for changes in prices and consumption patterns. These differences in turn can lead to very different measures of poverty, as the chapter demonstrates by estimating some specific alternative thresholds and exploring their implications for comparative poverty rates. The next section starts this exploration by reviewing the alternatives considered when the current official thresholds were established in the mid-1960s.

SETTING THE POVERTY THRESHOLD AT A POINT IN TIME: ORIGINS OF THE OFFICIAL THRESHOLD

As discussed in detail in the first chapter, current official poverty thresholds are pegged to a standard that was based originally on estimated minimum consumption needs. That standard has been adjusted to reflect changes in prices over time, but little has been done to adjust for any other source of changes in needs. Further, the original standard considered primarily food needs and adjusted only roughly for other differences in consumption across families of different types. Despite these shortcomings, the original thresholds developed by Orshansky (1963, 1965) were a significant improvement over several of the other threshold estimates in use in the early 1960s. As noted below, however, there were at least a few estimates available at that time that would have made plausible alternatives to the Orshansky approach.

Poverty Measures Before the Adoption of the Official Thresholds

Although empirical data were not widely available before 1960, Orshansky's studies were not the only source of detailed poverty estimates available in the late 1950s and early 1960s. A comprehensive and well-reasoned study of the size and characteristics of the low-income population that predated Orshansky's work was Robert J. Lampman's study undertaken for the Joint Economic Committee (Lampman 1959). This admirable study not only examined the composition of the low-income population in detail but also considered alternative thresholds and issues such as the income definition, as well as broader questions such as sources of change in the low-income population and the effects of economic growth on low-income families of various types. Lampman's work anticipated most of the issues still debated among poverty researchers today.

Although Lampman considered a number of different sets of thresholds, his preferred set was derived from an even earlier study produced in 1949 by the staff of the Subcommittee on Low Income Families (U.S. Congress Joint Committee, 1949). This study used a cutoff of $2,000 in 1948 dollars as the poverty threshold for a family, which Lampman adjusted for price changes to get a 1957 threshold of about $2,500 for a family of four. He then drew on a 1947 study by the Bureau of Labor Statistics (BLS), which estimated minimum budgets for families of different sizes, to adjust this threshold for families of other sizes. His resulting set of thresholds differed from

Orshansky's in two major ways. First, the overall level of the thresholds, even if further indexed for price change up to 1963, would have been a bit lower—Lampman's value for a family of four in 1963 dollars, for example, would have been about $2,750, compared to Orshansky's threshold of about $3,100. Second, the relative value of the threshold would have increased slightly more—and in a somewhat more regular pattern—for each additional family member under Lampman's threshold than under Orshansky's.[1]

The Orshansky Thresholds

Unlike Lampman, who took an essentially arbitrary cutoff established a decade earlier and simply updated it, Orshansky started over with a new estimate of basic needs designed to have some "scientific" justification. Her use of the Department of Agriculture's minimum food consumption standards, along with data from a USDA study of food as a share of family budgets, gave her thresholds the appearance of a basis in fact. (Construction of the Orshansky thresholds is discussed in more detail in chapter 1, and in more detail below.)

An additional feature in favor of Orshansky's thresholds was that they came close, in terms of the total poverty population identified, to estimates already produced by the Council of Economic Advisors (CEA) using a much less sophisticated set of thresholds that did not even vary by family size. Because these cruder estimates were already accepted in the policy community as defining the broad scope of the poverty problem, these new and similar estimates were much more likely to gain broad policy acceptance.

Table 3.1, which is reprinted from Orshansky's 1965 article on poverty, illustrates the importance of using some adjustment for family size and type by comparing the composition of the poverty population in 1963 under her definition and several others, including the CEA measure. Orshansky's measure (shown in column D of the table) resulted in an estimate of the total size of the poverty population that was very similar to those found using a variety of other approaches, but unlike those approaches it used a systematic adjustment for family size and for other family characteristics, such as farm/nonfarm residence. The other measures that had been in use included at best relatively crude adjustments for family size (and no adjustment for other family characteristics).[2]

For example, the measure shown in column A of the table was taken from the 1964 CEA report mentioned above and used a simple

Table 3.1 PERSONS IN POVERTY STATUS IN 1963, BY ALTERNATIVE
DEFINITIONS (in millions)

Type of Unit	A[a]	B[b]	C[c]	D[d]	Total U.S. population
Total number of persons	33.4	34.0	34.5	34.6	187.2
Farm	4.9	6.4	5.1	3.2	12.6
Nonfarm	28.5	27.6	29.3	31.4	174.6
Unrelated individuals	4.9	4.5[e]	4.9	4.9	11.2
Farm	.2	1.4	.2	.1	.4
Nonfarm	4.7	2.6	4.7	4.8	10.8
Members of family units	28.5	30.0	29.6	29.7	176.0
Farm	4.7	5.0	4.9	3.1	12.2
Nonfarm	23.8	25.0	24.6	26.6	163.8
Children under age 18	10.8	15.7	14.1	15.0	68.8
Farm	1.8	2.4	2.1	1.5	4.8
Nonfarm	9.0	13.3	12.0	13.5	64.0

Source: Orshansky (1965).
Notes:
a. Under $3,000 for family; under $1,500 for unrelated individuals (interim measure used by Council of Economic Advisers).
b. Level below which no income tax is required, beginning in 1965.
c. $1,500 for first person plus $500 for each additional person, up to $4,500. See testimony by Walter Heller on the Economic Opportunity Act, *Hearings Before the Subcommittee on the War on Poverty Program of the Committee on Education and Labor, House of Representatives, Eighty-eighth Congress, Second Session*, Part 1, page 30.
d. Economy level of the poverty index developed by the Social Security Administration, by family size and farm-nonfarm residence, centering around $3,100 for 4 persons (Orshansky thresholds).
e. Estimated; income-tax cutoff is $900; Census 1963 income data available only for total less than $1,000; this figure has been broken into less than $500 and $500-999 on basis of 1962 proportions.

$3,000 cutoff for families (and $1,500 for single individuals). The measure shown in column C, which came from congressional testimony given in early 1964 by Walter Heller of the CEA, was somewhat more sophisticated. It allowed $1,500 for a single individual and an additional $500 for each additional family member (up to a total of seven). A fixed family size adjustment of this type probably overstates the economies of scale available to couples and small families, however, and understates those for large families. The final measure (shown in column B) was estimated by applying the income tax thresholds in effect in 1965 to incomes in 1963. Again, these thresholds did vary by family size and marital status, but they were not chosen to correspond to any systematic estimate of family needs.

Although the conceptual bases for these different measures were quite different, they had some important similarities. For example, all four resulted in thresholds for a four-person family that were in the neighborhood of $3,000. Other levels were discussed by various analysts at about this time. Lampman (1959), for example, considered both a $2,000 minimum and a $4,000 level, the latter derived from a market-basket study undertaken by the Bureau of Labor Statistics. But most estimates prevalent in the early 1960s seem to have centered around the $3,000 range.[3]

Similarly, all four sets of thresholds examined by Orshansky resulted in estimates of the total population in poverty that were fairly close. They ranged from 33.4 million under the simple $3000 cutoff to 34.6 million under the Orshansky measure. These gave estimated poverty rates—the percentage of the population in poverty—that ranged from 17.8 percent to 18.5 percent. (All of the measures except the $3,000 cutoff gave rates over 18 percent.)

Even though these totals were quite similar, however, the composition of the poverty population implied by these alternative approaches was quite different. For example, the measure based on tax thresholds would have found a poverty rate of more than 50 percent for the farm population, whereas Orshansky's measure for this population came in at about 25 percent. Similarly, the simple $3,000 threshold would have given a poverty rate of less than 16 percent for children, whereas Orshansky's measure found a rate of nearly 22 percent (and the tax-based measure would have resulted in a poverty rate of almost 23 percent).

Thus, the alternative poverty thresholds considered by Orshansky illustrate two important points. First, and most obviously, it is possible to get essentially the same overall poverty rate at a given point in time using very different methods of selecting a set of thresholds. In practice, most people probably have some existing set of beliefs about how much a typical family needs in order to get by, and this in turn implies some rough ideas about the appropriate poverty rate. "Expert" scales that are far out of line with these beliefs are likely to meet resistance. Second, however, within these broad guidelines very different relative poverty rates for different groups can be calculated, depending on the specific scales used.

Early Criticism of the Orshansky Approach

The adoption of Orshansky's thresholds by a variety of researchers, and ultimately by the federal statistical establishment as a whole, gives some indication that they represented an estimate of minimum needs that many found reasonably acceptable. The Orshansky thresholds were not without their critics, however. These critics fell into three main groups—those who thought Orshansky's thresholds were too high, those who thought them too low, and those who argued that an income-based definition of poverty was in itself inherently unacceptable.

The major critic who argued that the Orshansky thresholds were too high was Rose Friedman of the American Enterprise Institute. As discussed in chapter 1, Orshansky's thresholds were based on minimum food consumption standards for families of different types. Using data from a 1955 food consumption survey, Orshansky estimated that the typical family spent one-third of its budget on food. She reasoned that if families becoming poor could cut back food consumption to the level of the economy food budget, they could cut back the consumption of other goods and services proportionately. She therefore multiplied her minimum food budgets by a factor of three to get an estimate of total consumption needs.

Friedman (1965) argued that Orshansky's use of three as her multiplier was unrealistic, in light of the actual spending patterns of the poor. Because the poor typically spent about 60 percent of their incomes on food rather than the 33 percent estimate for the general population used by Orshansky, Friedman believed that the "correct" multiplier for the poor should have been proportionately lower.[4] Using this approach, she reestimated the 1963 threshold for a family of four at $2,200. This threshold level produced an estimate of the total poverty rate of about 10 percent—only about half the level found by Orshansky.

Other writers also criticized Orshansky's multiplier, but from the perspective that it was too low rather than too high. The consumption data Orshansky used to construct her multiplier came from a 1955 food consumption survey done by the USDA. Between 1955 and 1963, however, there was some growth in family incomes, which probably was accompanied by some decline in the share of family budgets typically spent on food. Indeed, the 1960-61 Consumer Expenditure Survey (CES) indicated that the typical family now spent about one-fourth rather than one-third of its income on food.

Orshansky argued that this survey understated food consumption, but Alan Haber (1966), for example, pointed out that there was no evidence that food expenditures were understated relative to those for other goods and that in any case even comparison of the CES data from the early 1950s with the 1960-61 data clearly indicated the declining share of food in family budgets. Using a higher multiplier derived from the CES data, Haber estimated the threshold for a family of four at almost $3,500.[5]

Other writers agreed that both Lampman's and Orshansky's thresholds were unrealistically low. Michael Harrington (1962), for example, discussed Lampman's (1959) study in the appendix to *The Other America*, arguing that the $4,000 threshold for an urban family of four derived from the BLS market basket study cited by Lampman was a much more reasonable estimate of minimum adequacy. Harrington also pointed out that other studies, including both an AFL-CIO study and a more recent BLS (1960) study, came up with even higher estimates. In the introduction to the 1969 edition of the book Harrington also criticized the official poverty thresholds, arguing that the economy food plan that was their basis was designed for emergency use only, not as a guide to long-term consumption needs, and that the thresholds in any case should be adjusted for changing consumption standards over time, and not just for price changes.

Finally, a number of writers of the 1960s were critical of the entire idea of an income-based poverty measure. Indeed, the fundamental argument of Harrington's book was that poverty has ramifications far beyond simple lack of income—that people who are poor eventually become "internal exiles" in America, who "develop attitudes of defeat and pessimism and who are therefore excluded from taking advantage of new opportunities" (Harrington 1969:179). This thought is echoed in Oscar Lewis's (1966) concept of a "culture of poverty," as well as in much of the more recent literature on the "underclass" today.[6]

In more technical terms, Martin Rein (1969) argued that any subsistence-level definition was "arbitrary, circular, and relative," because it relied on consumption data that were themselves influenced by lack of income, and that in any case were simply averages over broad groups, which might be very far from the needs of any particular family. Rein's preferred strategy would have been a comprehensive assessment of inequalities in the distribution of specific material needs, as was later undertaken by Townsend (1979), for example, in the United Kingdom.

There is much that can be said for a concept of poverty that considers deprivation from some broader perspective rather than relying on some arbitrary income cutoff as the sole indicator of need. Indeed, the deprivation suffered by those who are poor over a very long period is almost certainly greater than that experienced by those undergoing relatively short spells of poverty—an issue considered in more detail in chapter 5. Many analysts have advocated approaches to poverty measurement that would try to measure this deprivation more directly—either by measuring material hardship directly as suggested by both Townsend (1979) and Christopher Jencks (Jencks and Torrey 1988; Meyer and Jencks 1989), for example, or by considering other types of deprivation, such as lack of access to educational opportunities, lack of appropriate health care, or lack of political participation or power.

As research topics leading to a better understanding of the origins and meaning of economic and social deprivation in America these various approaches undoubtedly have merit. As an approach to assessing the successes and failures of income support programs, however, they are less than ideal. As Harold Watts (1968) has argued, programs whose primary aim is to improve the economic status of their beneficiaries must be assessed, at least in the first instance, using a measure whose primary focus is on that economic status. Although it is certainly possible to argue for the development of other measures as well, as long as our major antipoverty policies focus on providing minimally adequate levels of income we also will need a poverty measure that defines what "minimal adequacy" means in income terms. Like Lampman's and Orshansky's studies, therefore, this book focuses primarily on measures of income poverty and not on inequality or even deprivation in some broader sense.[7]

Although, as the above discussion has shown, it is certainly possible to argue with Orshansky's methodology, this book largely accepts the benchmark of about $3,000 for a family of four in 1963 as a reasonable starting place in measuring poverty. This acceptance is based partly on the perception that however it was generated, Orshansky's measure received widespread acceptance that can be seen as some sort of validation, at least as a subjective measure if not as a perfectly objective or "scientific" standard. This study considers a variety of other means of setting the threshold, but none of them, if taken back to 1963, would imply a very different starting place from that used by Orshansky. The fact that it is possible to derive such a large range of measures starting from essentially the same base, however, points up a problem that is perhaps even more difficult than setting the threshold in the first instance—adjusting poverty thresholds for changes in prices, consumption, and needs over time.

ADJUSTING THRESHOLDS FOR CHANGE OVER TIME

A major policy application of poverty statistics is to allow comparisons of the numbers of people who are poor at two different points in time. The poverty rate (or some variant, such as a poverty gap measure) serves as a benchmark against which to judge the success of our policies in reducing the most severe forms of want. To make these comparisons, however, it is necessary to have some way to adjust poverty thresholds to make them comparable across a period of several years.

Poverty thresholds can be set in any number of ways in the first instance. It is argued above that if they achieve widespread acceptance they probably fall into some broad range that represents a social consensus about the needs of the "typical" family, but clearly within that broad range a number of variations are possible. Nevertheless, such poverty thresholds may allow useful and valid comparisons across time that may depend very little on the detailed specification of the original thresholds. Indeed, once a set of poverty thresholds has been chosen, changes in family size adjustments, for example, will have only relatively small effects on the total poverty rate or poverty gap for the population as a whole, although the impacts for specific groups may be much larger. Alternative methods of adjusting for change over time, however, can have dramatically different effects on the level of the thresholds as a whole, especially after a number of years have elapsed. These differences in turn can result in very different poverty rates and poverty gaps.

Why Adjust for Change Over Time?

Why do we need to adjust poverty thresholds for change over time at all? The most obvious answer is because prices change. An amount of money that was adequate for a family in 1967 would have been able to buy far less 10 years later. Even if one thinks of poverty as resources below some "absolute" level of consumption that is not expected to change in real terms over time, it is still necessary to adjust for these price changes—in other words, to make the real purchasing power of the standard the same over time.

Prices, however, are not the only things that change over time. People's incomes and family structures also change, and so do the goods and services that are available for consumption. Major changes in consumption patterns have occurred since 1955, when the consumption data underlying the official thresholds were collected. Some goods commonly consumed today did not even exist in 1955, and others were relatively rare. For example, many of the poor, especially in rural areas, had no plumbing—a rarity today. Moreover, most families with children could count on the services of a full-time homemaker in 1955, and many fewer children lived with only one parent. These changes, and others like them, contribute to changes in minimum family needs over time.

Over time, any fixed "market basket" of necessary goods will become outdated, as changes occur in both consumption patterns and the structure of family needs. Further, as long as there is some continued real growth in the economy as a whole, incomes generally will rise relative to prices (although during recessions price gains may temporarily exceed wage increases). As a result, if poverty thresholds are adjusted only for prices, they will fall further and further behind average standards of living. Finally, as discussed in the last chapter, even subjective thresholds—those based on surveys asking how much families need—also move with changes in income, although changes in such thresholds would probably occur more slowly than would changes in, for example, median income levels.

All of these factors lead to the conclusion that indexing poverty thresholds for price changes alone over very long periods does not offer a very realistic measure of changes in minimum needs. This chapter therefore considers two other methods of updating poverty thresholds as well—linking them to changes in incomes rather than in prices and reestimating them directly to account for changes in consumption patterns and in the relative prices of goods consumed.[8]

Once one has decided among the absolute, relative income-linked and "adjusted market basket" approaches, however, one still has a number of possible choices within each system of adjustment. This chapter considers six specific sets of poverty thresholds adjusted for change over time—two adjusted for price changes only, two based on changes in relative incomes, and two that adjust roughly for changes in consumption patterns. Both sets of price-indexed thresholds and the first set of "relative" thresholds are derived directly from the first "official" thresholds of 1967. The other three sets of thresholds have been calculated independently at each date considered, based on income and consumption data relevant to that date. All these approaches, however, are consistent with the Orshansky methodology, in that all would have given thresholds near Orshansky's if applied in 1963 using the data then available.[9] To allow consistent comparisons across these approaches, the family size and family type adjustments used in the official thresholds also have been used in each case examined here, although, as the next chapter argues, they too are potentially vulnerable to criticism.

Adjusting for Changes in Prices

The existing official poverty thresholds are based on an "absolute" measure of poverty that has been indexed for changes in prices over time. This means that each year's poverty thresholds are multiplied by the percentage change over the past year in the Consumer Price Index (CPI) to arrive at the next year's set of thresholds.[10]

The CPI, in turn, is constructed through a complicated process that involves "shopping" for a fixed market basket of goods in a subset of U.S. cities. The prices collected are weighted by population and other factors across the cities and are adjusted for factors such as seasonal variation. Further, although an effort is made to maintain comparability in the goods included in the index, realistically the goods available in the marketplace change over time—new products appear and old ones stop being consumed or change so much that they are not really comparable across time. The index is adjusted on an ongoing basis for technological change in existing products, but until recently has been reweighted for changes in consumption patterns only at very long (and irregular) intervals. Thus, even though consumption patterns are likely to change as relative prices change, for example, the methodology used to compile the CPI explicitly prohibits the substitution of one good for another as prices change.[11]

Finally, the consumption weights used to construct the CPI are supposed to be representative of urban consumers as a whole.[12] To the extent that the poor have different patterns of consumption from this population—for example, spending more on food and housing, and less on consumer durables such as refrigerators or home computers—that fact is not reflected in the price index. Therefore, if prices for food and housing rise at a different rate than for other goods, the index may misrepresent the actual spending power of those with very low incomes.[13]

Thus, even if one were convinced that an exactly correct "absolute" poverty standard had been set in 1967, indexing this standard by the CPI would still represent only an approximate measure of its buying power for the poor today. Further, the details of the specific index used to adjust for price changes are likely to matter most in periods of high inflation, when prices are changing rapidly. Small methodological differences in price indexes that would have no practical effect in a period of relatively stable prices can mean big differences in thresholds when prices are rising at 10 percent or more per year.

Not suprisingly, therefore, the use of the CPI to measure price changes became most controversial in the late 1970s. Between 1978 and 1979, for example, the CPI rose 11.3 percent, and it rose another 13.5 percent between 1979 and 1980. Although rapid increases in prices occurred to some extent during this period for almost all goods and services, the CPI's treatment of housing in particular was a contributing factor to its unusually fast rise. Although the weight for housing in the index represented its budget share for urban consumers as a whole, the index calculated changes in housing prices based on each year's new purchases of housing.[14]

This methodology is inappropriate, however, if the majority of consumers, who do not buy new housing in a given year, experience a smaller change in their housing costs than the minority who do. In a period when housing price increases are outstripping general price rises, as in the late 1970s, this methodology can overstate substantially the price increases that consumers actually face.

Many analysts, therefore, urged a change to a modified version of the CPI. Known as the CPI-X1, this modified index used a different measure of housing price changes, the change in housing rental prices, which was thought to be more representative of average housing price increases. This method of adjusting housing prices also was adopted for the official CPI in 1983. The official poverty thresholds, however, are currently higher than they would have been if they had been indexed by the CPI-X1 all along, because the high price rises of the 1978–81 period have been incorporated into the base used for subsequent years' indexes.[15]

Table 3.2 illustrates poverty thresholds in 1987 under a variety of measures, including both the official measure and a CPI-X1-based measure.[16] In both cases it is assumed that indexing has been in effect since 1967. As the table shows, by 1987 poverty thresholds would have been only 92 percent of their current levels if the CPI-X1 had been used for indexing all along.[17]

Although price-indexing of the poverty thresholds does adjust them for changes in prices over time, it does not take into account other changes that also may affect the amount of income needed to provide a minimally adequate standard of consumption. Over the long run, incomes tend to rise faster than prices, so that eventually the "custom of the country" changes, and new goods come to be seen as necessary. Shifts in consumption patterns also may be caused by other factors, including changes in the goods available in the marketplace, changes

Table 3.2 POVERTY THRESHOLDS IN 1987 UNDER ALTERNATIVE METHODS OF ADJUSTING THE THRESHOLD OVER TIME

Family size	Official threshold	Threshold indexed by CPI-X_1	Threshold indexed by growth in median income	Relative threshold— 4 person standard[a]	Housing consumption standard[b]	Updated multiplier standard[c]
1 person	5,778	5,314	6,582	7,717	8,918	9,695
nonelderly	5,909	5,434	6,732	7,891	9,120	9,915
elderly	5,447	5,010	6,205	7,174	8,407	9,139
2 persons	7,397	6,802	8,427	9,879	11,416	12,411
nonelderly head	7,641	7,027	8,705	10,205	11,793	12,821
elderly head	6,872	6,320	7,829	9,178	10,606	11,530
3 persons	9,056	8,328	10,317	12,094	13,977	15,195
4 persons	11,611	10,677	13,227	15,506	17,920	19,482
5 persons	13,737	12,633	15,649	18,346	21,201	23,049
6 persons	15,509	14,262	17,668	20,712	23,936	26,022
7 persons	17,649	16,231	20,106	23,570	27,239	29,613
8 persons	19,515	17,947	22,231	26,062	30,119	32,744
9 or more	23,105	21,248	26,321	30,857	35,659	38,768
Ratio to official threshold	1.0	0.92	1.14	1.34	1.54	1.68

Source: Calculated by the author from price and income data presented in Williams 1988 (Tables B1–B4) (with corrections supplied by Williams). Indexing assumed to start in 1967. Official thresholds shown are weighted average thresholds by family size, and are from U.S. Bureau of the Census 1989a (Appendix A-2).

Notes:

a. Poverty threshold for four-person families set at 50 percent of the median income, and all other thresholds adjusted accordingly, using equivalence scales implicit in official thresholds.

b. Based on Fair Market Rents and housing affordability guidelines used in the Section 8 subsidized housing program. See text for general discussion and appendix A for details on the method of calculation.

c. Calculated using the same general methods as the original Orshansky standard, but with a "multiplier" updated to reflect the changing share of food in family budgets. See text for general discussion and appendix A for details on the method of calculation.

in relative prices, and changes in family characteristics, needs, and incomes.

Survey data provide some support for the view that today's poverty thresholds no longer represent a consensus about a socially adequate minimum. Both the ISDP question and the 1982. CES question on the minimum amount that a family would need to "make ends meet" cited in the last chapter consistently received answers that were well above the official poverty thresholds. For example, Danziger et al. (1984, Table 1) reported that the income level associated with "making ends meet" for a family of four was over $15,000 in 1979, or more than twice the official poverty threshold of $7,355 for a family of four in that year. Similarly, De Vos and Garner (1989, Table 2) reported an estimated threshold of $20,700 for a family of four in 1982 based on the CES data—again, slightly more than twice the official threshold. Although these estimates may be biased upward for the reasons discussed in the last chapter, a similar Gallup Poll question, which asked, "What is the smallest amount of money a family of four needs to get along in your community?" received a median response of $11,600 in 1979—or about 158 percent of the official 1979 threshold (Danziger et al. 1984:10).

One way to adjust for changing consumption standards over time— at least, for changes caused by rising real incomes—is to tie adjustments in poverty thresholds to changes in incomes rather than to changes in prices. Under this approach, as incomes rise in general, poverty thresholds would be adjusted upward by a similar percentage. As the next section demonstrates, however, there are at least as many options for this type of adjustment as for adjustments based only on prices.

Adjusting for Changes in Relative Incomes

The most commonly proposed relative poverty measure is a threshold set at some specific percentage of median family income—most often, 50 percent. Such a standard could be implemented in several different ways. In theory, for example, one could simply set the standard equal to half the median income for each family size. In practice, however, this approach would be undesirable, because the median income actually peaks for four-person families and starts to decline with family size thereafter. The major purpose of a poverty standard is to represent some minimally adequate level of consumption, and it seems very unlikely that the addition of more family members actually would reduce the level of resources needed. More generally, even though the equivalence scales in the official poverty standard may leave a great deal to be desired, there is no reason to believe that the income ratios implicit in the actual distribution of income are in any way preferable as a measure of relative needs.

Many analysts who have proposed the 50 percent of median income standard, therefore, in practice have set the standard for four persons at one-half of the median for all families and have calculated all other thresholds from this basis.[18] Historically, the earliest thresholds calculated by Orshansky, which were for 1959, had a four-person standard equivalent to about 49 percent of the median income for that year. Because growth in incomes substantially outstripped growth in prices between 1959 and 1967, however, by 1967 the four-person standard had declined to about 43 percent of the median income for families as a whole. By 1987 this standard had declined further to about 37 percent of the median income. As a result, as table 3.2 indicates, if the nation had returned to a four-person standard at about 50 percent of the median income (adjusting all other thresholds accordingly), 1987 poverty thresholds would have been about 1.34 times the official thresholds.

Not only has median income changed since 1967, however, but so has the average family size. In 1967 the average family size was approximately 3.6 persons, making the choice of a four-person family as "typical" appear fairly reasonable. By 1987 the average family size had declined to about 3.1 persons. Interestingly, this occurred not because of any change in the proportions of three- and four-person families. These remained quite stable, at about 17 percent and 15 percent of all families, respectively. Rather, there has been a dramatic decline in larger families—those with five or more members—and a simultaneous increase in the number of people who live either alone or with one other person.

This decline in family sizes might suggest setting the threshold for three persons rather than four at 50 percent of the median, because the average family size is now so much closer to three. To maintain a level that was roughly consistent with Orshansky's original estimates, the present analysis focuses on a four-person standard at 50 percent of the median, but it is worth noting that if a three-person standard had been used instead the 1987 poverty threshold would have been even higher—about 1.71 times the official threshold.

Other variations on this theme could be invented, of course. For example, one could index for changes in median per capita income, or median "equivalent" income, where some specific adjustment for family size differences has been made. Such approaches would take

changes in family size and income levels into account simulta-
neously and therefore would give threshold adjustments that fell
between those for the three-person and four-person standards. Any
such standard that is tied to 50 percent of the median income will
result in higher thresholds than the official ones even at the beginning of the indexing period, however, because the official thresholds
in 1967 were below 50 percent of the median income for all but the
largest families.

Thus, to compare thresholds indexed by income growth with those
indexed only by prices more directly, table 3.2 also shows a set of
thresholds calculated by inflating the official 1967 thresholds by the
growth in median income over the 1967–87 period. These thresholds, shown in the third column of the table, are about 14 percent
higher than the official thresholds, indicating that median income
grew about 14 percent more than prices (at least as measured by the
CPI) over the period as a whole. If the 1967 thresholds did represent
a rough social consensus on minimum income adequacy, this indexing method would give 1987 thresholds that represented the same
relative level of income (except for the impacts of family size changes).

As discussed in chapter 2, opponents of a relative approach to
poverty measurement argue that relative standards present too much
of a moving target and are not closely linked to real changes in
economic well-being. Under such a standard, for example, general
increases in real income would increase poverty rates if the incomes
of the poor increased less than those of other families. Similarly, in
recessions, poverty thresholds—and potentially, poverty rates—would
fall in real terms under a relative standard. In this sense, relative
measures may be more closely tied to changes in income distribution
or inequality than to changes in minimum needs.

It is argued elsewhere in this book that the major policy purpose
of a poverty line is to set a standard of "minimum adequacy" to be
used in program and policy assessment. For this purpose, a standard
that, for example, falls in real terms during recessions is less than
ideal, because presumably the real needs of the poor do not fall
similarly.[19] More broadly, an income-based measure, although in-
volving fewer apparently arbitrary judgments of "needs" than an
absolute standard, is correspondingly less closely linked to the basic
concept of "minimum adequacy." A more direct approach to adjusting for changes in consumption patterns, therefore, is to reesti-
mate the market basket of "minimum needs" at regular intervals—
for example, every decade.

Adjusting for Changes in the Consumption of "Necessary" Goods

Over short periods—even as much as a decade—indexing thresholds for income or even price changes may be a perfectly reasonable way to adjust them for changing needs as well. Any approach that relies on indexing alone will fail to take into account changes in consumption patterns, however. Such changes also may affect the amount of income needed to provide a minimally adequate standard of consumption.

The most obvious problem in adjusting an absolute standard only for price changes is that over the very long run the goods available for consumption will change almost beyond recognition, and these changes in turn will affect perceptions of needs. A century ago, for example, few households had indoor plumbing or electricity. A set of minimum consumption needs established in 1890 and indexed for changing prices alone would today exclude such goods, therefore, even though they are now considered basic needs. Even our current standards, based on 1955 consumption data, implicitly exclude many goods that have become common among lower-income households only within the last 35 years, such as the telephone.

Over a period of several decades the social and economic conditions that define "need" also will undergo changes as family characteristics change. Even 25 years ago relatively few mothers worked outside the home, and few families paid for child care. Today, however, child care costs consume a large share of the budgets of many low-income families who no longer have a parent at home during the day. Similarly, because more families have two earners, work expenses such as commuting costs and taxes take a bigger share of total earnings.

Over a long period the relative share of family budgets devoted to different goods and services also will change. To the extent that such changes reflect changing tastes, they are not necessarily of concern. To the extent that they are induced by changes in prices, however—and particularly, by changes in the prices of basic necessities such as food and housing—such shifts should be taken into account in defining the market basket of basic goods that in some sense underlies any absolute definition of minimum needs. Changing consumption weights in the Consumer Price Index (CPI) may not capture these changes adequately, because the CPI focuses on changes in all prices rather than on shifts affecting a "minimally adequate" market basket.

Although absolute poverty standards have real advantages in making comparisons over the short run, over the long run poverty is indeed a relative concept. While an explicitly relative standard—one tied directly to income changes—may have some important drawbacks, if an absolute standard is to maintain any meaning over several decades it must be updated periodically.

This book argues that the appropriate way to update a set of absolute poverty thresholds for changes in needs and consumption standards over time is to call on some set of "experts" to set normative standards of consumption for a market basket of specific goods, and then to have additional experts revise those standards for changes in consumption at a set interval such as a decade. Both Watts (1980) and Rein (1969), among others, have argued that "expert" opinion about family needs is really just as arbitrary and subjective as any other opinion—that there is no "scientific" way to determine just how much of what goods any particular type of family really "needs." In some abstract sense, this is true. As the Department of Agriculture demonstrated in 1983 when it revised the Thrifty Food Plan, for example, it is possible to meet even scientifically devised nutritional standards with very low-cost food budgets, although those food budgets may represent a distribution of food expenditures that very few families would or could actually choose.

In a broader sense, however, the same factors that constrained Orshansky's original thresholds presumably would constrain their revision. Extremely unrealistic estimates would meet with substantial criticism and would be difficult to adopt.[20] Family budgets that detailed projected spending on a variety of different goods would be criticized by advocacy groups interested in specific goods if they were truly unrealistic. Indeed, constructing a realistic poverty market budget should not be much harder, in theory, than constructing a market basket for the CPI, which is done now. To facilitate this process, however, certain safeguards would be appropriate—proposed revisions by expenditure category should be published in advance, for example, with provision for public comment, and analyses of actual spending patterns at various income levels could be required for comparison.

Rein (1969) correctly commented that a subsistence standard based on the actual consumption patterns of the poor is inherently circular, in that presumably those consumption patterns already have been constrained by a lack of resources and therefore may be inadequate in important respects. A normative market basket should not mirror exactly the consumption of middle-income families either, however, because such families may spend more on "luxuries" than would be consistent with minimum adequacy. Presumably, most categories of consumption should fall somewhere between these two sets of consumption standards. A standard that in fact implies even higher proportions of the budget going to "inferior" goods than is typical of the consumption of existing poor families—as is the case, for example, with the Department of Agriculture's current version of the basic low-cost food plan, the Thrifty Food Plan—is not realistic and deserves public criticism.[21]

In other words, even though there is no one "right" bundle of consumption needs for the poor that all experts would agree on, we do know enough to eliminate a very large number of clearly wrong answers. In this sense, an expert-determined market basket need not be seen as essentially arbitrary, even conceding that an exact "scientific" determination of needs is not really possible. Although experts who work for the government may be under political pressure to come up with poverty lines that are as low as possible, any consumption-based standard is still likely to exceed a standard that has been adjusted only for price changes over a very long period.

Until 1981 the Bureau of Labor Statistics (BLS) actually published three sets of family budgets—for lower, intermediate, and higher living levels—that were based on such a set of normative market baskets. Because the consumption studies underlying the market baskets were based on Consumer Expenditure Survey (CES) data from 1960-61, however, BLS recognized that by 1981 they were seriously in need of revision. Given the cutbacks in domestic federal spending that occurred in the early 1980s, BLS felt that it could not fund the needed program of research and instead chose to stop producing the data series. Although the "lower living level" budget was designed to estimate a set of consumption needs somewhat above the subsistence level, when BLS stopped producing it, its level was substantially higher than the corresponding poverty thresholds.[22]

Setting normative consumption standards for a wide range of basic goods is indeed a job for experts, and it is clearly beyond the scope of this study. As a substitute, however, this study considers two much more limited consumption-based measures—one, like Orshansky's original thresholds, that is tied to food consumption, and one that is based on housing needs. These two standards are shown in the final two columns of table 3.2. Both imply that a consumption-based approach would result in substantially higher thresholds than those found under the official measure.

The "housing consumption" standard shown in table 3.2 has been derived using data and consumption standards established under the Section 8 Subsidized Housing Program. That program, which provides rental subsidies to low-income families, uses data on the rents paid by recent movers to establish a "Fair Market Rent" (FMR) for rental units of various sizes.[23] The program also establishes a maximum proportion of income that tenants can be required to pay for housing costs—in 1987, for example, this share was 30 percent.[24]

Because the maximum number of people that can live in a two-bedroom unit without violating the Department of Housing and Urban Development's (HUD) standards on overcrowding is four, the FMR for a two-bedroom unit was chosen as an estimate of minimum housing needs for a four-person family.[25] Treating this amount as the "housing share" under HUD's Section 8 guidelines, one can derive an implied minimum standard for total consumption for a four-person family—in 1987, for example, by dividing the annualized FMR by 0.30. This standard has been adjusted for other family sizes using the same needs ratios inherent in the official poverty thresholds. Poverty thresholds under this approach would be about 1.54 times the official thresholds in 1987. More details on the HUD guidelines and on the computation of this standard are given in appendix A.

The other consumption-based standard shown in table 3.2—the "updated multiplier" standard—is computed using an even simpler methodology. In this case, Orshansky's original approach of multiplying a basic food need standard by the inverse of the share of food in the average family budget has been duplicated exactly—but with updated data on budget shares. As is shown in detail in appendix A, the share of food has fallen considerably over the years, with average families today spending less than one-fifth of their budgets on food. As a result, today's multiplier would be about five rather than the estimate of about three that Orshansky used. Much of this decline in food spending can be explained by increases in the costs of other goods—for example, food, housing, and medical care together accounted for 66 percent of the average budget in both the 1960–61 Consumer Expenditure Survey (CES) and in the 1982–84 CES. Again, the "updated multiplier" approach produces thresholds well above the official ones. In 1987, for example, they would have been 1.68 times the official level.

It is worth reiterating that both the "housing consumption" and "updated multiplier" thresholds are only rough proxies for a standard based on a more complete market basket of necessary goods. It is possible that a set of thresholds based on a broader survey of minimum consumption needs would not be as high relative to the official thresholds as are the two alternatives considered here. If, for example, increases in housing costs since the 1960s were offset by major declines in the costs of other goods consumed by the poor, total needs may not have risen as much as would be implied by a standard based on housing costs alone.

Estimates of Fair Market Rents were not produced in the 1960s, and so detailed comparison of the housing-based standard with the original Orshansky standard is not possible. As shown in appendix A the share of family budgets going to housing has certainly increased over this period, however, implying that market rents in the 1960s were indeed lower in relative terms than they are now. Because housing costs make up a very large share of the budgets of most poor families, increases in housing costs relative to other goods particularly affect the income needs of the poor. As a result, the use of HUD's relatively conservative estimates of the appropriate budget share for housing actually may understate the impacts of housing cost increases on the needs of poor families.

In addition, as detailed in appendix A, this study has followed HUD's changes in housing cost guidelines, allowing housing costs to account for a larger share of family budgets over time. This in turn reduces the growth in poverty thresholds observed as housing costs increase, and offsets any decline that might have occurred in the costs of other necessary goods. And finally, this study has implicitly assumed that three-person families, who would also need a two-bedroom apartment to avoid overcrowding, would be able to find one at about 78 percent of the Fair Market Rent, since the standard threshold for three persons is only about 78 percent of the four-person threshold.

As discussed above, however, a detailed examination of changes in the costs of a complete market basket of necessary goods would be a better approach to constructing a good estimate of changes in the needs of the poor since the mid-1960s. Such a market basket would almost certainly cost substantially more than allowed for under our current official thresholds. Food and housing costs as measured by the Thrifty Food Plan and the FMR together account for about 76 percent of the official four-person threshold. A comprehensive market basket of minimum needs would presumably include many other goods as well as food and rent—for example heat, electricity, a telephone, transportation, medical care, clothing, child care, and perhaps various other things that are commonly needed to run a household, such as cleaning supplies and money for the laundromat.

Even if as little as possible were spent on each of these goods, their total would surely come to more than the approximately $230 per month that a four-person family with an income at the official poverty line would have left after paying for food and housing. For a three-person family at the poverty line the problem would be even worse—only about $180 per month would be available to meet all expenses other than food and housing, even if housing expenditures could be held to 78 percent of the FMR for a two-bedroom apartment. These budgets are clearly unrealistic, in other words, even if poor families spend nothing on common "luxuries" like televisions and Christmas presents for the children.

Although a more comprehensive approach would be preferable, in the absence of a detailed market-basket study the housing consumption standard developed here, which has been designed to be relatively conservative, should provide a reasonable (albeit possibly somewhat low) estimate of the current minimum consumption needs of poor families. The "updated multiplier" threshold, which produces a somewhat higher estimate, has been constructed using exactly the same methodology as the original Orshansky thresholds, and therefore shares many of their virtues and flaws. Although neither of these estimates is ideal, in other words, together they strongly imply that a realistic consumption-based standard would be considerably higher than our current official thresholds.

Comparing Poverty Thresholds Across Time

So far this chapter has focused on the thresholds for 1987 under various methods of adjusting for change over time. The relationships seen in table 3.2 are not constant over time, however. As discussed above, in periods of recession incomes grow relatively slowly and may even decline relative to prices, whereas in high-growth periods an income-based index will rise much more rapidly than one adjusted for price changes alone. Similarly, consumption needs may change at different rates in different periods.

Table 3.3, which shows alternative thresholds for a three-person family at several points in time, demonstrates the differential growth rates of alternative indexes. For example, the threshold indexed by the growth in median income (shown in column 3), which was defined to start at the same level as the official threshold in 1967, had

Table 3.3 ALTERNATIVE POVERTY THRESHOLDS FOR A THREE-PERSON
FAMILY AT FIVE-YEAR INTERVALS, 1967–87

Year	Official threshold	Threshold indexed by CPI-X₁	Threshold indexed by growth in median income	Relative threshold— 4 person standard[a]	Housing consumption standard[b]	Updated multiplier standard[c]
Dollar Value in:						
1967	2,661	2,661	2,661	3,098	N/A	3,379
1972	3,339	3,254	3,729	4,341	N/A	4,241
1977	4,833	4,631	5,370	6,252	2,008	6,380
1982	7,693	6,998	7,860	9,152	11,386	11,540
1987	9,056	8,328	10,317	12,094	13,977	15,195
Ratio to Official Standard:						
1967	1.0	1.0	1.0	1.16	N/A	1.27
1972	1.0	0.97	1.12	1.30	N/A	1.27
1977	1.0	0.96	1.11	1.29	1.45	1.32
1982	1.0	0.91	1.02	1.19	1.48	1.50
1987	1.0	0.92	1.14	1.34	1.54	1.68

Source: Calculated from price and income data presented in Williams 1988 (Tables
B1–B4). Indexing assumed to start in 1967. 1987 estimates based on unrevised data.
Notes:
a. Poverty threshold for four-person families set at 50 percent of the median income,
   and all other thresholds adjusted accordingly, using equivalence scales implicit
   in official thresholds.
b. Based on Fair Market Rents and housing affordability guidelines used in the Section
   8 subsidized housing program. See text for general discussion and appendix A for
   details on the method of calculation. Data on Fair Market Rents not available before
   1975, when the Section 8 program was established.
c. Calculated using the same general methods as the original Orshansky standard,
   but with a "multiplier" updated to reflect the changing share of food in family
   budgets. See text for general discussion and appendix A for details on the method
   of calculation.

risen to be about 12 percent higher than the official threshold by
1972. Over the next five-year period, however, it remained almost
constant, and between 1977 and 1982 it fell in relative terms, because
of the recession of the early 1980s. As a result, in 1982 this threshold
was only 2 percent higher than the official threshold. Strong growth
over the 1982–87 period caused this threshold to rise sharply in
relative terms, however, to a peak at 14 percent above the official
threshold.

The other poverty standard tied to relative incomes—the 50 percent standard in column 4—shows the same pattern of growth in the early 1970s, followed by relative stability and then decline in the early 1980s, with a strong comeback over the past five years. The threshold indexed by the CPI-X1 (column 2), on the other hand, remained close to the official threshold through the mid-1970s but declined fairly rapidly in relative terms between 1977 and 1982. Since 1983, when the official measure switched its method of counting housing costs to the one used by the CPI-X1, the two sets of thresholds have moved in tandem. Unless further changes are made in one of the indexes, the CPI-X1 thresholds will remain at 92 percent of the official thresholds.

Finally, the two consumption-based standards rise over time relative to the official thresholds, although the rate of increase varies somewhat over time.[26] The increase in the food-based standard has been greater than the increase in the housing standard since 1977, partly because the Section 8 norms for both rents and housing budgets were tightened in the early 1980s. Both standards imply thresholds in the same general range over the 1977–87 period, however.

EFFECTS OF ALTERNATIVE THRESHOLDS ON MEASURED POVERTY RATES

Alternative poverty thresholds clearly have different implications for measured poverty rates. In general, the higher the threshold the more people will be counted as poor. Because income is not evenly distributed, however, a given percentage increase in the poverty threshold does not necessarily translate into a proportional increase in poverty rates. In fact, because so many families have incomes in the neighborhood of the poverty line, changes in poverty thresholds almost always have a more-than-proportional effect on measured poverty rates, as the next section shows.

Poverty Rates under Alternative Thresholds

Table 3.4 shows the measured poverty rate in several years under each of the six sets of thresholds discussed above, as calculated using data from the Current Population Survey. This table demonstrates that even fairly small changes in thresholds can have relatively large effects on measured poverty rates. For example, a switch to the CPI-

Table 3.4 POVERTY RATES FOR ALL PERSONS UNDER ALTERNATIVE
THRESHOLDS, SELECTED YEARS, 1972–1987

Year	Official threshold	Threshold indexed by CPI-X$_1$	Threshold indexed by growth in median income	Relative threshold— 4 person standard[a]	Housing consumption standard[b]	Updated multiplier standard[c]
1972	11.9	11.3	14.3	17.9	N/A	17.3
1977	11.6	10.7	13.8	17.4	20.7	18.0
1982	15.0	13.2	15.3	18.9	25.1	25.5
1987	13.5	12.0	16.1	19.7	23.4	25.9

Source: Calculated from the Current Population Survey for years shown. 1987 data
based on unrevised data.
Notes:
a. Poverty threshold for four-person families set at 50 percent of the median income,
and all other thresholds adjusted accordingly, using equivalence scales implicit
in official thresholds.
b. Based on Fair Market Rents and Housing Affordability guidelines used in the
Section 8 subsidized housing program. See text for general discussion and appendix A for details on the method of calculation.
c. Calculated using the same general methods as the original Orshansky standard,
but with a "multiplier" updated to reflect the changing share of food in family
budgets. See text for general discussion and appendix A for details on the method
of calculation.

X1 as the basis for indexing would have resulted in an overall poverty
rate that was about one and a half percentage points lower in 1987,
and almost two points lower in 1982.

The relationship between the two income-linked thresholds and
the state of the economy is illustrated even more clearly in table 3.4.
In 1987, when the economy was fairly strong, both of these indexes
would have produced poverty rates that were substantially above
the official poverty rate. In 1982, however, near the trough of the
recession, poverty rates under the relative measures would have been
much closer to those under the official measure.

As a result, the trend in poverty over the past decade looks even
more ominous under the relative measures than under the official
measure. Under the price-indexed measures the recovery appears to
have reduced poverty rates substantially. Because inequality in the
distribution of income has increased over this period, however, with
increases in the median income significantly exceeding increases in
the incomes of low-income families, poverty rates actually have risen
over the last five years under both of the relative income-linked
standards.

Poverty rates are the highest under the two consumption-based standards. Under the housing consumption standard, for example, the 1987 poverty rate was more than 23 percent, and the 1982 rate was about 25 percent. Under the updated multiplier standard the poverty rate was between 25 and 26 percent in both those years. In other words, under a consumption-based measure, about one American in four was poor during the 1980s. The percentage decline in the poverty population since 1982 is also smaller under the consumption-based measures than under the official measure. Indeed, the updated multiplier approach, like the relative income approaches, finds an absolute increase in the poverty rate over this period.[27]

Poverty Rates for Demographic Subgroups within the Population

Just as striking as the differences in total poverty rates under alternative thresholds are the effects of these alternatives on the composition of the poverty population, shown for 1987 in table 3.5. Because the distribution of income varies across population groups, relative poverty rates also will vary depending on the level of the poverty threshold. This can be seen most clearly by comparing the poverty rates for the elderly with those for all persons under the various thresholds. Under the price-indexed thresholds, the poverty rate for the elderly is well below that for all persons—12.2 percent for the elderly compared with 13.5 percent for all persons under the official threshold, for example. Under the threshold indexed by the growth in median income, however, the two rates are closer, and the rate for the elderly in fact slightly exceeds that for the population as a whole—16.9 percent for the elderly, compared with 16.1 percent for the population as a whole. As poverty thresholds rise, the proportion of the elderly shown as poor rises even more relative to the proportion for the population as a whole. Under the updated multiplier approach, for example—the highest standard examined here—about 32 percent of the elderly would be counted as poor, compared with about 26 percent of the population as a whole.

This shift in relative poverty rates has important implications for public policy. One of the great antipoverty success stories of the past two decades has been the decline in poverty rates for the elderly population. Almost 30 percent of the elderly were poor in 1967 under the official thresholds, but by 1987 only 12.2 percent were. In contrast, the official 1987 poverty rate for the population as a whole is much closer to the 1967 level—13.5 percent in the later year, compared with 14.2 percent in the earlier one. The official poverty rate

Table 3.5 POVERTY RATES FOR SELECTED POPULATION GROUPS UNDER ALTERNATIVE THRESHOLDS, 1987

Group	Official threshold	Threshold indexed by CPI-X₁	Threshold indexed by growth in median income	Relative threshold— 4 person standard[a]	Housing consumption standard[b]	Updated multiplier standard[c]
Poverty rate for:						
All persons	13.5	12.0	16.1	19.7	23.4	25.9
Persons under 18	20.5	18.8	23.5	27.7	31.7	34.7
Persons 65 or over	12.2	9.6	16.9	22.9	28.5	32.3
Persons in female-headed families	33.6	30.7	38.2	44.1	49.0	52.2
Whites	10.5	9.2	12.9	16.4	19.9	22.2
Nonwhites	29.9	27.5	33.8	38.1	42.6	46.3
Ratio of threshold to official threshold	1.0	0.91	1.14	1.34	1.54	1.68

Source: Calculated from the Current Population Survey for 1987 (unrevised).

Notes:

a. Poverty threshold for four-person families set at 50 percent of the median income, and all other thresholds adjusted accordingly, using equivalence scales implicit in official thresholds.

b. Based on Fair Market Rents and Housing Affordability guidelines used in the Section 8 subsidized housing program. See text for general discussion and appendix A for details on the method of calculation.

c. Calculated using the same general methods as the original Orshansky standard, but with a "multiplier" updated to reflect the changing share of food in family budgets. See text for general discussion and appendix A for details on the method of calculation.

for the elderly fell below that for the general population for the first time in 1982 and has remained below the overall poverty rate since then.

Some analysts have argued that as the relative position of the elderly has improved—even as federal budget constraints have become tighter—a smaller proportion of national resources should be directed into programs serving the elderly. The data shown in table 3.5 make it clear that the degree of improvement in the relative status of the elderly seen is quite sensitive to the specific set of thresholds used, however. Under any set of thresholds there is no question but that the economic status of the elderly has improved more than that of children, for example, who, even under the official poverty definition, are significantly more likely to be poor now than they were 20 years ago. Much of this improvement for the elderly results from the Social Security program, which has provided an income floor for most of the poorer elderly. The incomes available to the bulk of the elderly population have not increased nearly as much, however, especially relative to those of the rest of the population. Further, without the relatively costly transfer programs that now serve the elderly, their poverty rates would be much higher.

Although changes in the relative poverty status of the elderly under alternative thresholds are the most dramatic examples of the effects of the level of the threshold on the composition of the poverty population, the relative poverty status of other population subgroups also can be affected. Poverty rates for children, for those in female-headed families, and for nonwhites, for example, are always well above those for the population as a whole, but the gap does narrow slightly, at least in percentage terms, as thresholds rise.[28] In general, as poverty thresholds rise, the population seen as "poor" comes to resemble more closely a cross-section of the population as a whole—although obviously under any of these definitions children, those in female-headed families, and nonwhites are still far more likely to be poor than is an average white adult.

Conversely, a threshold that is fixed in absolute terms, and that thus tends to fall relative to median income, will come to identify a narrower subset of the population as poor over time. This will occur even if there is no change in the overall distribution of income across demographic subgroups within the population as a whole. Of course, being identified as "poor" or "not poor" does not make the individuals involved any better (or worse) off, but such a shift may have political consequences. As the characteristics of the poverty population diverge farther from those of the "typical" family—even if this divergence is an artifact of the measurement process—the poor are more likely to become more isolated politically and to be seen as an underclass whose problems are caused by their own "aberrant" behavior. This perception may in turn undermine support for programs designed to combat poverty.

Notes

1. In addition to Lampman's 1959 study, an important empirical survey of the distribution of income and well-being was carried out by Morgan et al. (1962). This study did discuss the measurement and prevalence of poverty, but its major focus was a broader survey of family incomes. Early poverty research in the United States is comprehensively reviewed in Haveman (1987) and Danziger et al. (1986).

2. Lampman's estimates were a partial exception, in that their family size adjustment was based on BLS data that in fact reflected a somewhat better estimate of total family needs by family size than were Orshansky's adjustments. They did not adjust for differences other than size-related ones, however. Because Orshansky's measure was based on a set of food budgets, and the need to purchase food was in fact likely to be substantially less for those on farms, her thresholds for the farm population were only about 60 percent of those for nonfarm families (raised to 70 percent in later studies). These levels almost certainly overstated any differences in needs. The separate farm thresholds were revised upward to 85 percent of the nonfarm standard in 1969 and were eliminated altogether in 1981. Orshansky also used separate thresholds for families depending on the gender and age of head and on the number of children in the family. The first of these distinctions also was eliminated in 1981.

3. Lampman's preferred threshold for a four-person family was about $2,500 in 1957, which would have been equivalent to about $2,750 by 1963. Various writers reacting to Orshansky's work in the mid- to late 1960s also came out in favor of either higher or lower thresholds, as discussed in the section of this chapter on criticism of the Orshansky approach.

4. Friedman (1965) did not attempt to determine whether poor families spending this high a proportion of their incomes on food had an "adequate" amount of income remaining to cover other needs.

5. Haber (1986) also adjusted for the fact that both consumption studies were based on consumption as a share of income after taxes, whereas Orshansky's income data were based on gross income estimates. Further, Haber argued that using the economy food plan understated real food needs and that the "low-cost food plan," a more generous index, would have been more appropriate. Using this plan as the basis for his estimates, Haber came up with a poverty threshold of $4,263 for a family of four.

6. See Sawhill (1988) for a review of more recent work on the "underclass" in the United States.

7. One could argue, as do Mayer and Jencks (1989), that our real social policy concern is with standards of consumption rather than with income, and that income is merely a poor proxy for total consumption. The relative merits of income-based and consumption-based approaches to the measurement of total resources are discussed in more detail in chapters 2 and 7. A more detailed assessment of Mayer and Jencks's

approach as it applies to estimating needs across families of different types appears in chapter 4.

8. Because data on subjective assessments of poverty have not been collected in a systematic fashion in the United States, constructing meaningful comparisons of subjective measures across time would not be possible at this time using U.S. data. Consequently, subjective means of adjusting poverty thresholds for change over time are not formally considered here.

9. Unfortunately, it is not possible to extend the standard based on housing consumption back to the 1960s because of a lack of consistent national data on rents. Because the budget share going to housing has risen substantially since the 1960s, however, a standard based on typical housing costs would have been closer to the "official" estimates in the 1960s than it is now. See appendix A for more discussion.

10. Before 1969, the CPI for food only was used. Since then, the CPI for all items has been used.

11. See Manser and McDonald (1988) and Kokoski (1989) for discussion of substitution biases in the CPI resulting from changes in relative prices. See U.S. Bureau of Labor Statistics (1989) for details on the construction of the CPI.

12. Before 1978, the index was based on the consumption patterns of urban wage earners rather than all urban consumers. The "urban consumers" group includes about 80 percent of the U.S. population, excluding primarily residents of nonmetropolitan areas.

13. Studies of relative price changes for the poor and the nonpoor indicate that at least over some periods prices for goods consumed by the poor may have risen somewhat faster than those for consumption goods in general, although there is substantial within-group variation in consumption patterns that makes these results difficult to generalize to the poverty population as a whole. See for example Hagemann (1982), Michael (1979), Muellbauer (1974a), and Hollister and Palmer (1972) for more discussion of these issues.

14. This is the same methodology that is used to adjust prices for all other goods and services as well. In most cases, however, goods only enter into the budgets of those who have actually purchased them in the year in question, so that the average budget share for the good is approximately proportional to its share of the market for all goods and services bought in that year. To the extent that purchases of other goods are made over time, however— for example, automobiles—use of budget share weights with purchase prices for the current year only also may distort price change measures.

15. An alternative approach to a CPI-based adjustment would be to turn to one of the implicit price deflators derived from the national income and product accounts, such as the deflator for personal consumption expenditures (PCE). Although this index is less volatile than the CPI, it is affected by changes in the mix of goods consumed as well as by changes in prices, and it includes some institutional as well as household consumption. Thus, it may not be a good choice for indexing poverty thresholds, because the poor may have relatively little flexibility in their consumption choices, and those choices may differ more substantially from those for the entire nongovernment, nonbusiness sector of the economy than they do from the choices of all urban consumers. In practical terms, indexing by the PCE over the 1967–87 period would have almost the same outcome as indexing by the CPI-X1. By 1987, the PCE-based threshold would be about 93 percent of the official threshold, compared with about 92 percent for the threshold based on the CPI-X1. For a more extensive comparison of alternative price indexing options see Levy and Michel (1988, appendix A).

16. The thresholds shown represent weighted averages for each family size and type. Actual thresholds vary depending on the number of family members who are children. For more information see discussion of equivalence scales in chapter 4 of this book and U.S. Bureau of the Census (1989a, appendix A).

17. In response to criticisms of the CPI, the Census Bureau has just produced a set of alternative poverty estimates based on the CPI-X1 as part of its income and poverty report for 1989. See U.S. Bureau of the Census (1989b).

18. See, for example, U.S. Congress, House, Committee on Ways and Means (1985, Appendix J). An alternative approach, used for example by Plotnick and Skidmore (1975) and Rainwater (1981), is first to adjust for family size differences first by using some equivalence scale, and then to calculate median income on an equivalent-income basis. The poverty threshold at one-half the median will then also be expressed in equivalent income terms. Because the actual median family size is now about three persons, this approach results in higher thresholds than if a four-person standard is set at 50 percent of the median, but the exact line is sensitive to the equivalence scale chosen.

19. To deal with this problem, Harold Watts (1980) suggested a "ratchet," allowing family budgets to rise with increases in median income or expenditure levels, but not to fall in real terms during periods of declining real incomes.

20. Some administrations, of course, are more impervious to public outcry than are others—widespread comment on the lack of realism inherent in the revised Thrifty Food Plan did not prevent its adoption by the Reagan adminstration in 1983, for example. On the other hand, proposed changes in the method of calculating Fair Market Rents in the Section 8 Subsidized Housing Program were revised, although not eliminated, in response to negative public reaction.

21. Inferior goods are goods whose proportionate share of the budget rises as income falls. Food in general is typically considered such a good, because a family of a given size can only consume so much, and therefore as family income rises the proportion of income spent on food tends to fall. Within a food budget, however, some items are relatively likely to be bought by the poor, whereas others are consumed in greater proportion by higher income families. For example, poor families as a whole spend more on potatoes and other starches and less on meat than do richer families. The Thrifty Food Plan, however, calls for families to spend an even higher share of their food budgets on potatoes, cereal, flour, pasta, and beans than poor families already do, and it provides for only about two-thirds as much meat, eggs, and sugar as the poor now typically consume. The TFP for a nonaged adult, for example, calls for the consumption of about four pounds of potatoes, cereals, and grain products (other than bread) per week, but for only about a pound and three-quarters of meat. (Men also are allowed another two pounds of bread; women get slightly less than one pound.) See Peterkin et al. (1983) for more details.

22. The lower living level for a family of four in 1981 called for a budget of $15,323, whereas the 1981 poverty threshold for a four-person family was $9,287, or just over 60 percent of the lower living level budget. See U.S. Bureau of Labor Statistics (1982).

23. Details on this and other aspects of the calculation of this standard are given in appendix A.

24. This budget share is actually based on "countable income," which equals gross income minus various deductions. The share of gross income that tenants are required to pay would be even less, therefore. Although gross income is much closer to the income concept used by the Census Bureau in measuring poverty, variation in deductions across households complicated any attempt to compute the share of gross income that tenants typically would be required to pay. Although the 30 percent estimate therefore is somewhat too high, it represents an upper bound on a "reasonable" share of income for housing, and as such it should generate a relatively conservative set of thresholds.

25. Fair Market Rents do not represent the very lowest level at which a unit of a given size may be rented, and in that sense they may overstate "minimum" housing costs. On the other hand, this study has assumed that a four-person family would

occupy a two-bedroom apartment, and that a three-person family, which would also need a two-bedroom apartment to avoid violating overcrowding standards, would be able to find one at about 78 percent of the FMR (the level that would be consistent with the family size adjustments built into the official poverty scale). Similarly, the decreases in allowances for smaller family sizes built into the official thresholds exceed the declines in FMRs for units of smaller sizes. In that sense, therefore, the assumptions used here are quite conservative.

More broadly, one could argue for the use of the FMR, which represents a level slightly below the median for recent rentals, rather than some lower estimate of housing costs on the grounds that, even if lower cost units exist, it may be difficult for poor families in need of housing to rent them. For example, many low-cost units may be in rent-controlled buildings with low turnover and long waiting lists. In lieu of better information on true "minimum" housing needs, therefore, the FMR seems a reasonable proxy. For more details on the FMR see appendix A.

26. Unfortunately, no data on FMRs are available before 1975, when the Section 8 housing program was established, and so the housing consumption standard has been computed back only to the mid-1970s.

27. Changes in the HUD methodology for computing FMRs and for setting budget shares to be spent on rent cause the 1987 thresholds under the housing consumption standard to be relatively understated compared with the earlier thresholds. Without these methodological changes the 1987 poverty rates under this standard also would have risen compared with 1982, and in fact would have been slightly higher than the rates seen under the updated multiplier approach. See appendix A for more discussion.

28. For example, under the official threshold poverty rates for those in female-headed families are about two and a half times as high as those for all persons, whereas under the highest relative threshold they are only about twice as high. Similarly, poverty rates for children are a little more than 50 percent higher than general poverty rates under the official threshold, compared with about one-third higher under the updated multiplier approach.

Chapter Four

ADJUSTING FOR DIFFERENCES IN FAMILY NEEDS

Methods of adjusting poverty thresholds for change over time are crucial in determining the level of the thresholds as a whole, and, as demonstrated in chapter 3, they also may influence the perceived composition of the poverty population. The adjustments for family size and type that are implicit in the existing system of thresholds play a much more direct role in determining the composition of the poverty population, however. If a higher threshold for single people relative to couples had been chosen, for example, one would automatically see more single people in poverty. Similarly, the amount allowed for each additional child has a direct bearing on the number of children who are counted as poor. Indeed, to the extent that family size varies with other characteristics, such as race or female headship, such adjustments may even have an indirect influence on relative poverty rates across such demographic groupings.

There is a large and complex literature on the construction of "equivalence scales," or adjustment factors used in equating needs across different types of families. Indeed, some analysts have argued that at least for the purpose of comparing welfare or utility levels, family income should not be adjusted at all—or, at the opposite extreme, that it simply should be divided by the number of people in the household.[1]

As discussed in chapter 2, however, comparisons of household or family utility levels are less relevant for most policy analyses than are more basic comparisons of income adequacy. Defining an "adequate" income across families of different sizes still is no simple matter, but most analysts probably would agree that larger families typically need more income to survive than do smaller ones. If one also believes that, as seems likely, family members in larger households are able to share some goods such as living space, some method of adjusting our poverty thresholds to take account of such economies of scale will be desirable.

Many different systems of adjusting for differences in family size and characteristics have been devised by economists, and some plausible sets of alternative equivalence scales and their implications are considered later in this chapter.[2] Realistically viewed, however, the equivalence scales that are embodied in the official poverty thresholds were not constructed using a sophisticated assessment of relative family needs. Instead, they are modified versions of the relative food consumption standards that happened to be available to Mollie Orshansky 25 years ago. These equivalence scales are implicit not only in all our official poverty estimates but also in all the estimates presented in this book (except, of course, those based on alternative scales that appear in this chapter). It could be argued, however, that these equivalence scales have some important flaws. Before turning to a broader but more abstract discussion of the impacts of alternative scales, therefore, it may be helpful to examine the scales currently in use a bit more closely.

EQUIVALENCE SCALES IN THE OFFICIAL POVERTY THRESHOLD

The poverty thresholds Mollie Orshansky used to construct her original poverty rate estimates for 1963 (reprinted in table 3.1) varied not only over family size but also over a number of other family characteristics. Because the original thresholds were based on a set of food budgets, the specific characteristics chosen for examination tended to be those that might be expected to affect food consumption in particular. The most striking example was farm/nonfarm residence. Farmers might be expected to need less market income for food if they could consume their own crops. Because the thresholds were derived by multiplying basic cash food budgets by three, however, the original set tended to overstate the differences in needs experienced by farm and nonfarm residents. Just because farmers needed to spend only 70 percent as much as nonfarmers on food, their allowances for other needs should not have been reduced by the same percentage as well. Indeed, thresholds for farm residents were raised to 85 percent of nonfarm thresholds in 1969 and were eliminated as a separate category in 1981.

In addition to the farm/nonfarm distinction, the original thresholds also were calculated separately for families with male and female heads, for one- and two-person families with elderly and nonelderly heads, and for those containing differing numbers of children. Again, the distinctions were based largely on estimated differences in food requirements for men and women, elderly and nonelderly, and children versus adults—and again, these differences were implicitly assumed to carry over to all other needs. In 1981 the distinctions based on the gender of the head were dropped, but all of the others still remain in the official thresholds.[3]

Variations in Need Adjusted for in the Official Thresholds

Although fewer distinctions remain in the official thresholds than were used in Orshansky's original studies, a large number of different family type categories are still considered. The thresholds shown in table 3.2 actually represent weighted averages for each family size. In fact, the Census Bureau uses much more detailed tables to compute the official poverty statistics. Under these tables thresholds differ depending on the specific numbers of children and adults in the family as well as by family size. For example, the threshold for a three-person family consisting of one adult and two children is slightly higher than the threshold for a three-person family with two adults and one child. In 1987, this difference was $9. Although threshold levels show a somewhat irregular pattern, they generally rise relative to the weighted average with additional adults and with the first child, and then decline with each additional child thereafter. In families of up to five members there is also a small increment for single parenthood, but not in larger families.[4]

The thresholds for each family size that are the result of this process thus contain some implicit equivalence scales (shown for the weighted average thresholds in table 4.1). Because they were based on rather outdated consumption data that considered only food requirements, and because they were developed for demographic groupings that probably were not as appropriate for an examination of poverty as for determining food requirements, these equivalence scales contain certain quirks. The second column of table 4.1, which shows the percentage increase in the scale for each additional family member, illustrates the somewhat irregular pattern of allowances for family size increases. For example, the threshold rises by 23 percent when family size goes from two to three, but by 28 percent when it goes from three to four. Because consumption studies indicate that economies of scale are likely to exist as families get larger, one would expect the rate of increase to decline, not rise, as family size grows. The final column of the table, which shows the elasticity of the need standard at each family size—essentially, a measure of the change

Table 4.1 EQUIVALENCE SCALES IMPLICIT IN OFFICIAL POVERTY
          THRESHOLDS

Family size (Persons)	Equivalence value (One person = 1)	Percentage increase from next smaller family size	Implied elasticity of need with respect to family size[a]
1 Average	1.00	—	—
Nonelderly	1.02	—	—
Elderly	0.94	—	—
2 Average	1.28	0.28	0.36
Nonelderly head	1.32		
Elderly head	1.19		
3	1.57	0.23	0.51
4	2.01	0.28	0.85
5	2.38	0.18	0.75
6	2.69	0.13	0.69
7	3.05	0.13	0.80
8	3.38	0.11	0.80
9 or more	4.04	0.20	

Source: Calculated from official thresholds shown in table 3.2
Note: Elderly persons defined as those aged 65 or over.
[a]This elasticity is calculated as the power to which a change in family size must be raised to generate the change in equivalent income for that family size implicit in the official thresholds. See footnote 5 for details.

in estimated needs as family size increases—shows that the official measure does indeed assume that needs increase more with each new family member in families of four or more than in families of two or three.[5] This feature of the official measure seems quite counterintuitive.

To some extent, these irregularities arise because of differences in family composition within family size categories. However, additional irregularities exist even within the detailed set of thresholds for specific cells within the matrix of family sizes by family composition. For example, the marginal effect of an additional child as opposed to an additional adult varies substantially across the different family sizes.

These irregularities apparently result, at least in part, from differences in the age distribution of the children appearing in these cells in Orshansky's original calculations. The food budgets she used to calculate the original thresholds were partially disaggregated by age of child, and so the higher marginal value of a child at some family sizes may reflect the fact that the marginal child was likely to have been slightly older—and therefore, to have had higher food needs—in those family size categories. By now, of course, the distribution of ages of children within a given family size category may be very different from what it was in the early 1960s—but detailed family size and composition adjustments based on Orshansky's original calculations continue to be used.[6]

Need for Revision of the Official Scales

Because these family size equivalences are so irregular, and because they were constructed in a rather ad hoc manner and are in any case by now extremely outdated, their embodiment in our official poverty thresholds for the indefinite future is extremely questionable, even if the thresholds themselves are not otherwise revised. Data producers tend to argue that changes in data series should be avoided because they interfere with comparisons across time. This is indeed a serious concern. Over a long period, however, approximations that were acceptable when put into place may come to diverge further and further from actual conditions and may become quite misleading. Further, as new data and new technologies become available it is sometimes possible to construct new measures that are a significant enough improvement to warrant minor discontinuities in data series. Where discontinuities are large, reestimates of historic data series may be called for.

Indeed, the changes made in 1981, when the farm/nonfarm and gender-of-head distinctions were eliminated, have almost certainly resulted in a more realistic basis for poverty rate comparisons across demographic groups. It is time now for a similar rethinking of our family size adjustments. There is no justification for the continued use of the existing detailed family size by family composition cells, because the basis for the distinctions they embody appears extremely tenuous. More broadly, we should consider estimating a more systematic set of equivalences based on more recent and more comprehensive consumption data. At a minimum, we could alter our existing family size adjustments so that they reflect somewhat more rational assumptions about the effects of family size on consumption needs.

Exactly how to go about reestimating family size equivalences—and the probable effects of alternative strategies—are questions that are discussed further below. Before turning to them, however, the next section considers another questionable distinction that is embodied in our current thresholds—the use of a separate (and lower) set of thresholds for the elderly.

POVERTY THRESHOLDS FOR THE ELDERLY

As the equivalence scales shown in table 4.1 indicate, the Census Bureau uses separate thresholds not only for families of different sizes but also for one- and two-person families with and without elderly heads. For example, the threshold for an elderly person living alone is about 94 percent of the average one-person threshold, or about 92 percent of the level for a nonelderly person. The threshold for a two-person family with an elderly head is also lower than that for a similar family with a younger head—the threshold for the elderly couple is about 90 percent of the threshold for a nonelderly pair.

Like the other distinctions in thresholds discussed above, this lower poverty standard for the elderly is an artifact of the original food budgets used by Orshansky. Because the elderly need fewer calories to maintain their weight than do younger (and presumably more active) people, the Department of Agriculture food budgets that were the basis of the Orshansky thresholds allowed lower spending levels for those age 65 and over, and Orshansky translated these into lower budgets overall. These lower budgets have been maintained over the years.

Pros and Cons of Special Thresholds for the Elderly

Those who favor lower thresholds for the elderly typically argue that the needs of the elderly are indeed less than those of the nonelderly. For example, the elderly may need to eat less than do the nonelderly, as the Department of Agriculture assumed. Further, the elderly are more likely than others to own their own homes, which many analysts assume will tend to lower their housing costs. And, because the elderly are less likely to work than are the nonelderly, their work-related expenses such as transportation and clothing may be lower.

On the other hand, the elderly also have some needs not typically faced by younger people, most notably, health care expenditures not covered by insurance. These have risen rapidly over the last decade and are a much larger share of spending for the elderly than for other families. Further, even though many elderly do own homes, those homes are likely to be both relatively old and relatively large, leading to high bills for maintenance, utilities, and property taxes. And, although the elderly may need fewer calories than young people, many face health limitations that in turn limit their diets and food preparation abilities, leading to relatively high food expenditures.

Evidence on the Relative Consumption Needs of the Elderly

A number of studies have examined rates of change in the costs faced by the elderly and the nonelderly and have largely concluded that although the consumption patterns of the two groups have differed substantially, price increases in the goods they consume have occurred at similar rates, with costs for the elderly perhaps rising slightly faster overall.[7] Fewer studies, however, have focused explicitly on the relative needs of the elderly and the nonelderly in some normative sense. As is discussed later in this chapter, most studies that have explicitly set equivalent need standards for the elderly have relied on either reported consumption, which does tend to be lower for the elderly than for the nonelderly, or on families' own subjective evaluation of needs.[8]

Both these methods, however, are heavily influenced by the fact that the elderly on average have less income than the nonelderly. As a result, studies that rely either on reported consumption levels for specific goods or on subjective evaluations of one's own needs are likely to find lower levels of need for the elderly. Because families headed by elderly people typically consume less than other families, estimates that rely on reported consumption, for example, are likely to find that the elderly "need" less than other families who are currently better off, and who therefore consume more. And as discussed in chapter 2, subjective poverty measures also tend to be correlated with people's current income status, and thus are not necessarily reliable indicators of relative needs for differing family types whose current incomes differ substantially.

Given the differences in family income and family size between elderly and nonelderly family units, it is difficult to make meaningful comparisons between their needs and consumption patterns. Nevertheless, table 4.2 outlines the share of family income going to various categories of consumption expenditures by the age of the reference person in each family unit. As that table shows, units headed by someone age 65 or over do have lower total expenditure levels than those headed by younger people, and are also smaller on average.

Overall, however, the elderly spend a higher proportion of their

Table 4.2 SHARE OF TOTAL CONSUMPTION EXPENDITURES DEVOTED TO SELECTED GOODS, BY AGE OF REFERENCE PERSON, 1984

	All units	Under 25	Age 25-54	55-59	60-64	65-74	75+
Total consumer units (in thousands)	74,884	7,266	42,688	5,418	5,592	8,312	5,608
Characteristics:							
Average number of persons	2.6	1.8	3.1	2.7	2.3	1.9	1.5
Average age of reference person	46.2	21.5	38.0	56.9	62.0	69.3	80.6
Percent homeowners	60.0	10.0	60.0	79.0	79.0	76.0	67.0
Average annual expenditures	$21,788	$13,178	$25,484	$25,369	$20,705	$15,873	$11,196
Share spent on:							
Food	15.6	15.4	15.0	16.1	16.5	17.8	17.1
Housing	30.4	28.4	30.8	27.8	28.4	30.5	35.5
Apparel, etc.	5.5	6.0	5.7	5.8	4.8	4.5	3.1
Health care	4.1	2.3	3.1	3.9	5.5	8.4	13.3
Transportation	20.1	25.1	20.4	18.8	20.3	19.2	13.0
Pension and insurance contributions	9.2	6.2	10.0	11.9	10.8	4.9	2.0
Entertainment, etc.[a]	10.2	14.9	10.2	10.6	8.8	8.7	7.0
Other[b]	4.8	1.8	4.6	5.3	5.0	5.9	9.0

Source: Calculated from Consumer Expenditure Survey data for 1984, as reported in Harrison (1986, Table 3, p. 17).
[a]Includes entertainment, reading, education, tobacco, alcoholic beverages, and personal care.
[b]Includes cash contributions to persons and organizations outside the household.

budgets on both food and housing than do younger people. To some extent, this may also be a result of their relatively low incomes; these goods are likely to consume a larger share of spending for the poor than for those who are better off, as discussed in the last chapter. On the other hand, units headed by people under age 25—which are comparable to elderly units in both size and income level—spend a lower share of their budgets on each of these goods than do the elderly. As expected, health care costs also consume a much larger share of the budget for older people than for the young. In fact, among the various categories of largely "nondiscretionary" spending, only transportation and clothing form a larger share of the budget for the nonelderly than for the elderly, and even in these categories the difference is not very large until the "age 75 and over" category.

Based on the evidence on consumption patterns, it would be easier to make a case for differential poverty thresholds for units headed by those under age 25 than for units headed by those age 65 or over. Indeed, several studies have found greater variations in spending patterns within the elderly and nonelderly populations than between the two (see for example Michael 1979; Hagemann 1982). Without some convincing evidence for consistently lower needs for the elderly, therefore, it is difficult to justify the continuing use of a lower poverty standard for this population. As Harold Watts (1980:6) has put it, "differentials that are based on conjecture may cause more mischief than no adjustments at all." The current set of thresholds for the elderly are indeed based almost entirely on conjecture, and thus no adjustment at all would be an improvement in this case, as it was in the earlier elimination of distinctions based on gender and on farm/nonfarm residence.

Effects of Separate Thresholds on Measured Poverty Rates for the Elderly

As long as distinctions between the elderly and the nonelderly are still used in setting thresholds, however, it is important for the analyst concerned with issues affecting the elderly to be aware of their effects on the poverty statistics. Table 4.3 illustrates this effect by showing 1986 poverty rates for elderly and nonelderly persons under the official thresholds and under a revised set of thresholds that makes no distinctions based on age of family head. If the same set of thresholds were used for everyone, the poverty rate for the elderly would have been almost three points higher than under the official thresholds. Further, instead of being below the poverty rate for the

Table 4.3 ANNUAL POVERTY RATES IN 1986 UNDER ALTERNATIVE POVERTY
THRESHOLDS FOR THE ELDERLY

Measure	Elderly persons[a]	Nonelderly persons	All persons
Official threshold	12.4	13.7	13.6
Same threshold for elderly as for nonelderly	15.3	13.7	13.9

Source: Calculated from the March 1987 Current Population Survey.
[a]Elderly persons defined as those age 65 or over.

nonelderly, the rate for the elderly would have been a point and a half higher.

This relatively large effect occurs because so many elderly are in families with incomes clustered very near the poverty line, so that even small changes in the threshold result in large changes in the measured poverty rate for the elderly. Because the elderly are a relatively small proportion of the total population, however, overall poverty rates would have been increased only slightly by the use of these higher thresholds, from 13.6 percent to 13.9 percent.

Eliminating the separate poverty thresholds for the elderly would be quite simple in practical (if not political) terms. Reestimating our family size equivalences, however, is more difficult and potentially would have larger effects on estimates of the prevalence and composition of poverty as a whole. The next sections therefore briefly review some conceptual issues in estimating family size equivalences and discuss the effects of alternative adjustment methods on poverty estimates.

ALTERNATIVE METHODS OF ADJUSTING FOR FAMILY SIZE DIFFERENCES

As the first section of this chapter discussed, the family size adjustments embodied in the official poverty thresholds are difficult to defend on the basis of what is known about consumption patterns and needs for families of different sizes. Not only are the adjustments for increasing family size irregular in pattern, but they actually increase as family size rises, implying that families of four or more, for example, are able to take advantage of fewer economies of scale than are families of two or three. Like the thresholds themselves, these adjustments are based on outdated and incomplete consumption data and are seriously in need of revision.

Alternative Approaches to Setting Equivalence Scales

It is easier to identify the problems with the current adjustments than it is to design a new set, however. Many analysts using different methods have addressed the problem of constructing family size adjustments to be used in comparing income and needs. Ten different sets of equivalence scales, based on three approaches to the estimation of relative needs, are shown in table 4.4. These scales summarize much of the recent empirical literature on estimating family size equivalences, at least as it applies to the United States, but they by no means exhaust all of the alternatives that have been proposed by writers in this area.[9]

The scales shown in table 4.4 fall into several groups. The first three scales—which include the scale implicit in the official thresholds, the scale used by BLS in computing its family budgets, and the scale from Lampman's 1959 study for the Joint Economic Committee—come from U.S.-government-sponsored studies that relied on "expert" determinations of need of one sort or another to adjust incomes or needs across families of different sizes. The Lampman scale draws on a consumption study done by the Bureau of Labor Statistics in 1947, and the official scale and the BLS scale ultimately are based on consumption data from the 1950s and the early 1960s.

The next two scales come from international official statistics. Although many countries publish statistics on income and poverty that are adjusted in some way for differences in family needs, the most recent set of equivalence scales from Canadian Low Income Cut-Offs (LICOs) have been chosen as relatively representative, both in their general approach and because they were developed using consumption data from an economy and population fairly similar to those of the United States. The Organization for Economic Cooperation and Development (OECD) scales come from the major international agency producing such statistics for use in comparing poverty and needs within developed countries. (See Jenkins and O'Higgins (1987) for discusion of these scales.)

Both the Van der Gaag and Smolensky (1982) and the Lazear and Michael (1988) scales were developed using data on the consumption patterns of different types of families within the United States. The Van der Gaag and Smolensky scales are based on an attempt to

Table 4.4 EQUIVALENCE VALUES UNDER ALTERNATIVE SCALES (ONE ADULT = 1)

Family size	Official thresholds	BLS measure[a]	Lampman thresholds[b]	Canadian LICOs (1986)[d]	OECD scale[e]	Van der Gaag and Smolensky[f]	Lazear and Michael[g]	Danziger et al.[h]	DeVos and Garner[i]	Constant elasticity = .5
1 (Average)	1.0		1.0	1.0	1.0		1.0			1.0
Elderly	0.94	0.80				0.63		0.65	0.75	
Nonelderly	1.02	1.0				1.0		1.0	1.0	
2 (Average)	1.28		1.42	1.36	1.7		2.0			1.41
Elderly head	1.19	1.46				0.89		0.80	1.22	
Nonelderly head	1.32	1.40				1.28		1.25	1.37	
3	1.57	1.77	1.82	1.73	2.2	1.27	2.4	1.40	1.61	1.73
4	2.01	2.86	2.17	1.99	2.7	1.56	2.8	1.54	1.83	2.00
5	2.38	3.32	2.50	2.17	3.2	1.66	3.2	1.65	1.97	2.24
6	2.69		2.80		3.7		3.6	1.74		2.45
7	3.05		3.24[c]							2.65
8	3.38									2.83
9 or more	4.04									

Source: See notes.

Notes:

[a] Equivalence scales derived from family budgets published by the Bureau of Labor Statistics (1982). Single nonelderly person assumed to be under age 35, nonelderly couple also under age 35. Three-person family consists of a husband and wife under 35 and a child under 6; four-person family has husband and wife aged 35-54 and two children aged 6-15; five-person family has a husband and wife aged 35-54, and three children aged 6-15. Alternative scales can be constructed if different age groups are chosen.

[b] Equivalence scales derived from minimum income levels by family size shown in Lampman (1959, Table 1, p. 6).

[c] Seven or more.

[d] Derived from Statistics Canada's Low Income Cut-Offs (LICOs) for 1986. See Wolfson and Evans (1989, Table 5.1).

[e] Based on the recommendations for the OECD's "material deprivation" indicator. See discussion in Jenkins and O'Higgins (1987).

[f] Derived from Van der Gaag and Smolensky (1982, Table 2, p. 21). Adult equivalent based on a male age 35. Nonelderly couple both assumed to be age 35, three-person family assumed to be a couple age 35 with a child under 6; four-person family a couple age 35-54 with two children age 6-11 and 12-17; and five-person family to be a couple aged 35-54 with children 6-11 and 12-17. Alternative scales can be constructed if different age groups are chosen.

[g] Derived from Lazear and Michael (1988, pp. 191-195).

[h] Adult equivalent based on single male under age 65. Derived from Danziger et al. (1984, Table 2, p. 503).

[i] Derived from U.S. data on subjective poverty lines in DeVos and Garner (1989, Table 2, p. 11).

measure consumers' utility indirectly through the preferences revealed in consumption spending. By equating consumers' utility across family types, relative "needs" for different families can be estimated.

Lazear and Michael (1988) focus primarily on estimating the share of total family consumption going to children. Based on the finding that a child's share of family consumption typically is about 40 percent of an adult's, they propose that each additional child should be treated as implicitly "needing" 40 percent as much as an additional adult. (All adults are implicitly treated as equivalent, with no allowances for economies of scale unrelated to age.)

The subjective approach to measuring needs is represented by the scales developed by Danziger et al. (1984) and by De Vos and Garner (1989). Both of these scales come from surveys that ask people about the minimum needed "to make ends meet," as discussed in chapter 2. By analyzing and comparing the responses of different types of families, it is possible to develop a set of equivalence scales for different family types.[10]

Finally, the last column of table 4.4 shows a simple equivalence scale developed for this study. Its aim is to be roughly comparable with the official scale in terms of general implications for family size adjustments, but to smooth out some of the irregularities across family sizes seen in the official scale. The pros and cons of this and the other approaches are discussed in more detail below.

Implications of Alternative Methods for Family Size Adjustments

The 10 different scales shown in table 4.4 have a fairly wide range of implications for family size adjustments. Two-person families, for example, are found to have needs equal to between 1.25 and 1.3 times those of a single adult under the official scales, as well as under the scales developed by Van der Gaag and Smolensky (1982) and Danziger et al. (1984).[11] The OECD scale and the Lazear and Michael (1988) scale, on the other hand, would produce estimates in the range of 1.7 to 2.0 times the single adult value for a family of two.

Similar differences are found in comparing across scales at other family sizes. The Van der Gaag and Smolensky (1982) and Danziger et al. (1984) scales are consistently lower than most others, and the De Vos and Garner (1989) scale also tends to be lower than the average, although not as low as the other two. All of these scales rely either on reported consumption or on subjective evaluations of consumption needs, which they use to attempt to equate "utility" across family types.

This approach may have some attraction for more theoretical studies, but for policy analysis utility-based measures are not generally appropriate, because income support policies usually aim to provide minimally adequate levels of consumption, not to make people equally "happy." If young single males typically "need" new sports cars or elaborate stereo systems to achieve a given level of happiness, in other words, whereas older women may report themselves to be equally well-off without these goods, few policymakers would consider this differential in "needs" a legitimate policy problem.

Utility-based measures are particularly vulnerable to the biases caused by the fact that those who have more typically think that they "need" more—whereas relatively poor families report similar levels of utility at lower levels of consumption. In any consumption-based analysis, therefore, but particularly in one based on the estimation of equivalent utilities rather than equivalent "needs" more broadly defined, care must be taken to avoid simply institutionalizing the status quo.[12]

The OECD scale and the Lazear and Michal scale, on the other hand, both use relatively large fixed adjustments for additional family members, which result in higher than average adjustments as family size rises. In effect, these two scales assume very few economies of scale for additional family members.

The remaining scales are all based on "expert" judgments about consumption needs at different family sizes and typically fall into some broad middle range between the other two approaches. The official thresholds look more like the subjective or consumption-based thresholds than like the other expert scales for family sizes of three or less, but for larger family sizes they come closer to the other expert scales.

The BLS scale, in contrast, is relatively close to other expert scales for smaller families, but looks more like the fixed-adjustment-based scales for larger families. The very large jump in needs between three- and four-person families shown in the BLS scale is accounted for by the fact that larger families were assumed to have older children, on average, and needs were adjusted by age of child as well as by number of children. Because BLS used a considerably higher adjustment factor for older children, the index of needs rose by more than one equivalent adult between these two family sizes.

In their important recent article on equivalence scales, the staff of the Luxembourg Income Study (LIS) generalized the type of findings reported here by examining 32 different equivalence scales that have been used by various researchers or that are implicit in the official poverty or assistance program thresholds of various countries, including the United States (see Buhmann et al. 1988). They pointed out that virtually all of these scales can be approximated reasonably closely with a simple formula that depends on a single parameter: the elasticity of need with respect to family size. Using this parameter (denoted e below), equivalent income (W) can be calculated from the family's disposable income (D) and size (S) in the following way: $W = D/S^e$.

The family size elasticity, e, already introduced in this chapter in the discussion of table 4.1, is an index that varies between 0 and 1, with larger elasticities implying smaller economies of scale. Clearly this formula, which results in a smooth curve relating income and family size, does not perfectly capture all the quirks in an irregular system of thresholds such as that of the United States.

To smooth out these quirks, therefore, the final set of adjustments shown in table 4.4 sets e, the elasticity of need with respect to family size, equal to 0.5. This level is near the overall elasticity for the official scale as a whole and preserves the threshold for a four-person family at its official level of about twice the threshold for a single adult. This level is also close to that found on average under most of the other "expert" scales. Under this scale, however, one need not believe that the addition of a family member increases needs substantially more in larger families than in small ones. Use of this scale, holding constant the four-person threshold at its current level, would have relatively little impact on the poverty rate overall but would increase the poverty rate for families with two or three members and decrease it for families of five or more.

Optimally, the statistical agencies of the United States should undertake a longer term program to update and correct their implicit assessment of consumption needs by family size, estimating actual family budgets for specific family sizes and perhaps types. Overall, however, the general elasticity of needs with respect to family size seen in the official scale seems reasonable, in that it accords well with elasticities found in a large number of other "expert" evaluations of need. There is no a priori reason to believe that it would change dramatically as the result of new research, although presumably the irregularities across family sizes would be reduced.

In the absence of such a program of research and evaluation, an alternative approach would be to adopt a scale with a similar overall elasticity but without the irregular allowances across family sizes. Although there is no assurance that such a scale would be in some real sense more "correct" than the current scale, the relationships across family sizes that it assumes at least would be more neutral. The final scale shown in table 4.4, for example, would meet this need.

EFFECTS OF ALTERNATIVE FAMILY SIZE ADJUSTMENTS ON MEASURED POVERTY RATES

How much effect do alternative equivalence scales have on measured poverty rates in general? Fortunately, the LIS group used its research on alternative scales to attempt to answer this question by examining the impacts of these alternatives on measured poverty rates in 10 different countries (the results with regard to the United States are summarized in table 4.5). Before turning to those results, however, it may be helpful to review the different types of equivalence scales found in the LIS survey and included in its study of equivalence scale impacts.

Family Size Elasticities by Type of Scale

The LIS survey, like the more limited survey of alternative equivalence scales reported here, found that most of the differences between alternative scales arise not from their irregularities and minor differences across family type categories but rather from the differing amounts of weight given to each increment in family size. The LIS researchers found examples of scales with elasticities covering almost the entire range between 0 and 1, but for the most part the elasticities fell into the same major groups found in this survey.

The largest elasticities—implying the largest allowances for additional family members—were in the range of the Lazear and Michael (1988) and OECD scales and are typically found in scales constructed for statistical purposes, which often use fixed increments for additional family members. These scales generally have elasticities in the neighborhood of 0.72. The BLS scale falls into this range overall as well, although for families of three or less its elasticity is about 0.55.

The next largest elasticities are most often found in scales constructed by experts, typically for policy uses such as defining benefits

Table 4.5 RELATIVE POVERTY RATES IN 1980 FOR VARIOUS DEMOGRAPHIC
GROUPS UNDER ALTERNATIVE ADJUSTMENTS FOR FAMILY SIZE

	Expert— statistical	Expert— program	Consumption based	Subjective
Family size elasticity	.72	.55	.36	.25
Poverty rate[a] for:				
All persons	17.2	17.2	17.8	17.9
Single mothers				
With one child	37.5	39.7	42.9	44.6
With two or more children	65.5	62.9	60.5	57.6
Married couples, head under age 60				
No children	4.0	4.2	5.0	5.4
One child	5.3	5.4	5.7	5.7
Two or more children	15.6	13.0	10.1	8.2
Head age 60 or over				
Single men	26.8	34.4	44.3	48.3
Single women	30.5	38.1	48.2	52.2
Married couple	13.5	14.5	16.0	17.4

Source: Derived from Buhmann et al. (1988, Tables 10 and 12). Based on CPS for
1980.
[a]Poverty rates shown are based on poverty thresholds calculated by setting three-
person standard at 50 percent of median income. This threshold is about 160 percent
of the official poverty threshold for 1980.

for social programs. These scales generally have elasticities around
0.55, the general neighborhood of the overall value for the official
U.S. scale, as well as for the Canadian LICOs, the Lampman scale,
and the constant elasticity scale constructed for this study.

Scales that rely on consumption-based measures of relative utility,
like the Van der Gaag and Smolensky scale, typically have lower
family size elasticities. The LIS researchers chose an elasticity of
0.36 as typical of this group.[13]

The final set of scales found by the LIS group are those based on
subjective surveys of well-being, such as the Danziger et al. (1984)
and De Vos and Garner (1989) scales. These scales typically imply
much smaller adjustments for additional family members than do
the expert scales (although they also typically have much higher
thresholds to begin with). The LIS group chose an elasticity of 0.25
as typical of this group of scales as a whole (although both the subjective scales based on U.S. data considered here have elasticities
higher than this).[14]

Poverty Rates under Alternative Scales

Unfortunately, the poverty definition used in the LIS study, and shown in table 4.5, is not strictly comparable with the official definition. Under the LIS poverty definition, the three-person standard is set at 50 percent of the median income, and other thresholds are adjusted accordingly. Of course, because table 4.5 examines four different family size adjustment factors, the actual thresholds implied by different family sizes will differ across the various scales.

Because the poverty threshold levels are higher across all these scales than the levels contained in the official U.S. definition, poverty rates also will be uniformly higher. For 1980, the year examined by the LIS group, this poverty definition gives a basic threshold level of about 160 percent of the official standard, a level somewhat higher than that seen for 1980 under any of the thresholds considered in chapter 3, for example. Despite this difference, the estimates shown in table 4.5 are helpful in illustrating the general effects of alternative equivalence scales. As the second line of the table shows, even very different family size elasticities do not necessarily imply very different overall poverty rates for the population as a whole. Under this poverty definition, the rate for all persons ranged from 17.2 percent to 17.9 percent.[15]

As would be expected, however, poverty rates do vary systematically across the scales within any given family type. In general, families with fewer than three members will have higher poverty rates with the subjective scales and lower poverty rates under the expert scales, whereas the converse will be the case for families with more than three members. For those with exactly three, the four types of scales are almost equivalent (because in fact the median family size is just over three).

OTHER ADJUSTMENTS FOR DIFFERENCES IN FAMILY NEEDS

So far, this study has followed standard Census Bureau practice in focusing on demographic differences between families, and particularly family size, as the major source of differences in their needs. In fact, however, one could argue that family needs vary as much or more by other family characteristics.

Adjusting for Other Demographic Characteristics

Other demographic characteristics in addition to family size could be considered in setting thresholds, as indeed they were in Orshansky's original studies. Both the consumption-based and subjective methods of estimating relative needs, for example, consistently have found the age and gender of family members to have more effect on their "needs" than does family size. These differences are not an appropriate basis for adjustments in need standards that are to be used primarily for program and policy assessment, however. Because such differences in estimated "need" arise primarily out of differences in utility functions that themselves may be at least partially a function of family income, they are not consistent with a "minimum adequacy" approach to estimating need. Few policymakers have any interest in equating utility across family types, and differences in utility that arise from differences in expectations rather than differences in income adequacy, as more broadly defined, are therefore of little policy concern.

An alternative approach taken by Susan Mayer and Christopher Jencks (1989) following in the tradition of the Townsend (1979) study discussed in chapter 2, involves estimating "material hardships" directly, by asking survey respondents about their unmet needs for food, housing, and medical care. Mayer and Jencks find a relatively low correlation between a family's poverty ratio and the number of hardships reported in their surveys, which cover about 1,400 Chicago residents in 1982–83 and another 950 residents in 1984–85. They were able to raise the correlation between the number of hardships reported and estimated "needs" by reestimating the determinants of need, although even with these adjustments only about 35 percent of reported hardships were explained. The determinants of need Mayer and Jencks find particularly important include age and health status, with hardships decreasing with reported age and increasing with increasing health problems. They also find a much higher family size elasticity—0.91—than any of the other approaches considered here.

The Mayer and Jencks approach is interesting, although because degree of hardship is self-reported many of the same biases that occur in subjective studies also may apply here. The finding that the elderly, in particular, suffer less material hardship than other families (particularly holding heath status constant) may relate at least partly to lower expectations rather than to lower needs. Further, the selection of specific hardships from the list of all possible forms of deprivation seems a somewhat daunting task. Economists tend to use income as a proxy for well-being, after all, at least partly because they assume that specific material hardships may take many different forms. More broadly, if high-income families report certain problems—inability to pay the rent, not enough to spend on food—most people are likely to blame poor consumption choices rather than the inability to afford these goods for any material deprivation that has occurred.

In general, then, until there is some better basis for estimating differences in family needs across demographic characteristics other than size, the few family type distinctions that remain in the equivalence scales should be removed, and others should not be added. If programs are to discriminate among households on the basis of these scales, a relatively high standard of proof is needed. To justify different need statements, therefore, it must be shown that these households actually have different levels of needs and not simply different average incomes, expectations, or consumption patterns.

Adjusting for Geographic Differences

Other than differences in family size and type, the major source of possible differences in need that analysts have considered as a basis for adjustment are differences in places of residence. Because some parts of the country have higher prices than other parts, families that live in relatively expensive areas actually may need higher incomes to maintain the same level of consumption as lower income families in less expensive places. A family living in New York City, for example, is likely to pay more rent than one living in rural Alabama, and the New York family probably will have to pay more for most other goods as well. These price differences imply in turn that those in more expensive areas need higher incomes to maintain given minimally adequate levels of consumption, and that possibly our poverty thresholds should be adjusted accordingly.

Table 4.6 confirms that price levels are indeed significantly higher in some parts of the country than in others. The Northeast, for example, has substantially higher price levels overall than do either the Midwest or the South, and prices are continuing to rise at a faster rate in the Northeast as well. In addition, urban areas within each region have higher prices overall than do rural ones.

As might be expected, areas with higher price levels also have higher median incomes. Although the rank ordering of median incomes by region remains the same if they are adjusted for differences

Table 4.6 CONSUMER PRICES, POVERTY RATES, AND MEDIAN INCOME LEVELS BY REGION AND CITY SIZE, OCTOBER 1989

Region and area size	CPI-U in October 1989[a]	Percentage change since October 1988	Poverty rate, 1988	Median family income, 1988
Northeast				
All urban	130.6	5.2	10.2	$30,425
Size A—more than 1.2 million people	131.1	5.0		
Size B—500,000 to 1.2 million people	130.0	6.1		
Size C—50,000 to 500,000 people	128.9	5.9		
Midwest				
All urban	123.0	4.1	11.5	$27,540
Size A—more than 1.2 million people	124.3	4.4		
Size B—360,000 to 1.2 million people	122.5	3.6		
Size C—50,000 to 360,000 people	122.9	4.4		
Size D—nonmetropolitan (less than 50,000)	118.2	3.5		
South				
All urban	123.0	4.1	16.2	$24,670
Size A—more than 1.2 million people	123.9	4.2		
Size B—450,000 to 1.2 million people	124.5	4.2		
Size C—50,000 to 450,000 people	121.7	3.9		
Size D—nonmetropolitan (less than 50,000)	120.7	4.1		
West				
All urban	126.1	4.5	12.7	$28,836
Size A—more than 1.25 million people	127.8	4.6		
Size C—50,000 to 330,000 people	123.7	3.6		
U.S. Average			13.1	$27,225
All urban	125.6	4.5	12.2	$29,346
Nonmetropolitan	121.3	3.9	16.0	$21,385

Source: Columns 1 and 2 from "Consumer Price Index—October 1989," U.S. Department of Labor News, November 21, 1989, Bureau of Labor Statistics, Washington, D.C., Table 3, p. 9. Column 3 from U.S. Bureau of the Census (1989c, Table 21, p. 66). Column 4 from U.S. Bureau of the Census (1989c, Table 1, p.19).
[a] 1982–84 = 100.

in price levels, the gap falls substantially. The median in the Northeast is less than 2 percent higher than in the West after adjustment, for example, compared with almost 6 percent in the unadjusted figures. Similarly, the difference between the Northeast and the Midwest becomes 4 percent rather than 10 percent, and that between the Northeast and the South becomes 16 percent rather than 23 percent.

Just as relative median incomes change if one adjusts for price differentials, so too might poverty rates. Using the official thresholds (which do not adjust for price differences across regions) one finds that areas with high median incomes (and high prices) have low poverty rates compared with areas with lower incomes and lower prices. If thresholds were set higher to account for price differences in high-priced areas, more families in those areas would be found to have incomes below the threshold, raising the relative poverty rates for these areas.[16]

It is difficult to know, of course, how much of the difference in prices across regions is offset by differences in income, and how much represents other differences in the quality of life. Prices may be higher in one place than in another primarily because of differences in the amenities they offer, and these differences in amenities may not all be captured in differences in income. In some broader sense, over the long run the "quality of life"—taking into account both prices and wage levels—should equalize roughly across areas, because presumably otherwise people would continue to migrate to the pleasanter areas, causing prices to rise and wage rates to fall.[17]

However, as discussed with regard to many other topics in this book, for the purpose of measuring poverty broader measures of the "quality of life" are not as relevant as direct measures of minimum needs. Even if the quality of life is higher in some more abstract sense in one place than another, people in the more desirable place surely still should be considered poor if they cannot pay a reasonable rent or buy enough to eat.

Considering the magnitude of the price differentials seen across regions, a strong case can be made for some adjustment of the poverty thresholds to take account of these differences. Additional adjustments for urban versus rural residence within region perhaps could be justified as well. In the past, the Census Bureau has opposed such adjustments because the data base used to compute official poverty statistics (the CPS) is not really representative across detailed geographic categories and because the within-region differences in price levels also can be substantial, so that regionwide adjustments may change thresholds for some areas inappropriately. The CPS is currently due for a redesign, however, and it seems possible that differentials for at least major geographic divisions could be incorporated into the new sample design. And, although this type of adjustment, like any other, does run the risk of introducing new errors in an attempt to fix old ones, the evidence presented in table 4.6 implies that regional price differences persist over a variety of city size categories and therefore probably would not introduce major distortions in measures of relative well-being, at least on average.

This study has implicitly defined poverty, at least for policy purposes, as lack of access to minimally adequate resources. This chapter has argued that if a poverty definition is to be fair as a guide to policy, one's definition of minimal adequacy should be the same for all families unless one has compelling evidence that needs in fact do differ. On these grounds a number of adjustments in the official thresholds have been rejected; although there may be differences in need in some cases, the evidence is simply not strong enough to justify differing policy treatments.

Introducing differences in need standards not justified by the evidence may understate the economic well-being of some families relative to others. At the same time, the opposite error—neglecting adjustments in cases where there clearly are differences in needs— also distorts comparisons between groups. As long as there are some variations in needs within groups as well as between them, any adjustment decision will lead to distortions in some cases. In choosing among possible adjustments, the aim should be to minimize the distortions in estimates of relative well-being as much as possible, within the limits of available data. In other words, the analyst must balance the possibility that a given adjustment will distort needs estimates in some cases against the potential error that may result if no adjustment is done.

Differences in needs across geographic areas represent an example of the potential for this second type of error. The data are simply not available for detailed, city-specific adjustments for price differences for every city in the United States, and even if they were it is doubtful that any resulting improvement in our estimates would be worth the costs involved. On the other hand, many analysts are skeptical of adjustments across very large areas such as regions, arguing that within-region variations in prices are also large. If we adjust poverty standards for the entire Northwest region upward to account for the higher price levels in New York and Boston, they argue, we will overstate needs in Pittsburgh and Syracuse substantially.

In evaluating this argument, it must be remembered that a failure to adjust poverty standards for regional price differences implicitly treats costs (and therefore, income needs) in New York and Boston as if they were the same not only as those in Pittsburgh and Syracuse but also as those in Birmingham and even in rural Mississippi. As table 4.6 demonstrates, this is quite unrealistic, and implicitly allows a higher standard of living to those designated "poor" in low-cost areas. Further, if regional price adjustments are introduced they may indeed overstate costs in Pittsburgh, but costs in the highest price areas such as New York and Boston will still be understated—just not by as much as in the absence of an adjustment.

In general, adjustments are appropriate where the evidence implies that fewer errors would be introduced into the system by the adjustment than would be corrected by it. Although this book opposes most new complications to our system of poverty thresholds, the evidence for real differences in price levels across regions has become too compelling to ignore.

Other Potential Adjustments

Finally, in addition to the differences across families discussed above, a host of other factors may affect family needs. The number of earners in the family may affect work expenses, for example, and the presence of a spouse at home certainly will affect the family's child care costs. Government-provided benefits not counted in the income measure may affect family resources, as may assets or nonmarket income. Although some have advocated equivalence scale adjustments to account for all these, this study instead has considered most of them in chapter 7, which discusses the definition of income and other components of the resource measure. Before turning to those questions, however, the next two chapters discuss topics even more crucial in the measurement of resources—the period over which they are to be measured and the unit whose resources are to be counted.

Notes

1. See Lebergott (1976:33–43) for a presentation of the first view, and Datta and Meerman (1980) for the second, for example.

2. This literature dates back to the works of Engel and Pareto a century ago, and a

great deal has been written on this topic over the years. The more recent literature tends to be primarily concerned with cross-household comparisons of utility and with calculations of the effects of equivalence scales on measures of economic inequality, rather than with the determination of minimal standards of income adequacy by family size. As a result, its relevance to the issues considered here is in many cases rather limited. Nevertheless, useful studies of the past several decades that consider aspects of the equivalence scale problem include Barten (1964), Buhmann et al. (1988), Danziger and Taussig (1979), Danziger et al. (1984), Deaton and Muellbauer (1986), Lazear and Michael (1980; 1988), Mayer and Jencks (1989), Muellbauer (1974b; 1977; 1980), Nicholson (1976), Prais and Houthakker (1955), Pollak and Wales (1979), Van der Gaag and Smolensky (1982), and Watts (1977). Several of these studies are reviewed in more detail later in this chapter.

3. A legal challenge to the practice of setting lower allowances for female-headed households was in fact the event that prompted a reconsideration of these thresholds.

4. The complete set of thresholds by family size for 1987 is given in U.S. Bureau of the Census (1989a, Appendix Table A.2).

5. This measure of elasticity is calculated as the power to which an increase in family size must be raised to generate the proportionate increase in family income specified in the official thresholds. Essentially, this approach creates an index varying between zero and one, with a low value implying very little increase in need for each additional family member, and a high value implying a large increase. At the extremes, a value of zero would imply no adjustment for additional family members, whereas a value of one would give a per capita income adjustment. This method of specifying the effects of increasing family size on need is discussed in detail later in this chapter.

6. The reduction in the number of cells that occurred when distinctions by gender of head were eliminated in 1981 may have added further irregularities to the distribution of equivalencies, because the weighted average thresholds that resulted would have depended at least in part on the mix of male- and female-headed families within each cell. I am grateful to Mark Littman of the Census Bureau for the insights he shared with me on these issues.

7. See, for example, Borzilleri (1978), Bowsher (1982), Bridges and Packard (1981), Hagemann (1982), Kokoski (1988), Michael (1979), and U.S. Bureau of Labor Statistics (1988). Radner (1989) discusses broader comparisons of the well-being of individuals in different age categories.

8. See Van der Gaag and Smolensky (1982) for an example of the first approach, and Danziger et al. (1984) or De Vos and Garner (1989) for examples of the second.

9. Except for the BLS and Lampman scales, which were produced at about the same period as the Orshansky scales and, in some sense, were viable alternatives, this discussion largely focuses on scales produced since 1980, because relative family needs may well change over time. Similarly, except for the Canadian and OECD scales, which represent alternative official approaches, scales based on U.S. data have been selected for examination, because alternative institutional arrangements in other countries may produce legitimate differences in relative family needs. As a result of these choices, however, many classic articles on the estimation of alternative family size adjustments have been neglected. See note 2 above for a more complete list of such studies.

10. This is done by computing the point at which the distribution of "minimum income" responses and the distribution of reported current incomes intersects within each population group being considered. See chapter 2 for more discussion of this methodology.

11. Throughout this discussion comparisons are based on nonelderly values where no average value is given in the study in question, unless the elderly value is cited

specifically. Similarly, where no average value for a single adult was given, the value for a nonelderly male has been used as the numeraire.

12. Detailed examination of the Van der Gaag and Smolensky and Danziger et al. scales illustrates this problem—in at least some categories, both fail the "does it make sense?" test. For example, the first of these scales gives a value of 1.28 equivalent adults for a couple age 35, but 1.27 equivalent adults for a couple age 35 with a child under age 6. A low marginal increase in family needs with the addition of a young child might be explained by assuming that the birth of the child typically causes the mother to leave the labor force, thereby lowering her work-related expenses, but as Van der Gaag and Smolensky note, it is implausible that family needs would be the same or even lower in total in families with three rather than two members. This increase in family size very well may lower family income, however, resulting in lower levels of consumption and of estimated needs. Similarly, the Danziger et al. scale estimates needs for two people over age 65 to be only 80 percent of the amount needed by one man under age 65. This result is also inherently implausible, especially given the consumption data shown in table 4.2, and is probably more related to the actual income levels and expectations of the two groups than to their relative needs.

13. Because the Van der Gaag and Smolensky (1982) study estimated a large number of alternative equivalences based on a variety of family characteristics, it is possible to select values at specific family sizes that lead to somewhat different estimates of elasticities. Indeed, Van der Gaag and Smolensky found that demographic factors other than family size—for example, gender and age—had a larger impact on estimated needs than did family size adjustments. The specific values selected for this study, which were chosen to reflect the actual distribution of characteristics within family size groups in today's poverty population as closely as possible, in fact would result in an estimated elasticity of about 0.32. Buhmann et al. (1988) report an elasticity of 0.38 for this study, implying that they must have chosen a different array of values from those considered in this study in calculating their family size elasticities. (Although Van der Gaag and Smolensky estimate family size elasticities of consumption for specific goods, no overall estimates are given.)

14. The family size elasticity for the Danziger et al. (1984) scale is about 0.31 overall, although the authors found a much lower effect of family size on needs when other family characteristics such as age and gender of head were taken into account. In their more complete regression equation, the family size elasticity of need is estimated at about 0.21. De Vos and Garner (1989) estimate family composition and size effects jointly, noting that the family size elasticity of need is not constant across demographic groups. Overall, however, the elasticity of the De Vos and Garner family size adjustment scale is about 0.42.

15. This estimate is based on Current Population Survey data for 1980.

16. The regional price indexes shown in table 4.6 are adjusted for differences in reported prices across region only. To the extent that the goods consumed also differ across regions, these price indexes may not reflect accurately total differences in the cost of living.

17. The measurement of "quality of life" and its relationship to prices and wage levels has been the subject of much research. See for example Bloomquist et al. (1988), Roback (1982), and Rosen (1979).

Chapter Five

THE ISSUE OF TIME IN MEASURING POVERTY

Methods of setting and adjusting the poverty threshold are clearly fundamental to the design of any poverty measure. Perhaps for this reason, they have been debated at length by economists and statisticians, and alternative measures using different poverty definitions, different indexing methods and different equivalence scales frequently have been proposed and even estimated. The subject of this chapter—the time period over which income and poverty are to be measured—has received much less attention in the literature on poverty measurement, although analysts have long recognized that measures of income distribution are quite sensitive to the accounting period chosen. (See, for example, Steurle and McClung (1977) or Morgan (1984) for a more detailed discussion of this point.)

Part of the reason for this relative lack of attention has perhaps been that most of our data on incomes comes from annual, cross-sectional surveys that collect information only on incomes over the past year. With data of this type, options for alternative accounting periods are very limited. Even the existing longitudinal panel surveys, such as the Panel Study of Income Dynamics (PSID), which collect information on the same individuals over a period of time, typically have collected income information in annual questionnaires. Under these circumstances, the use of an annual accounting period—considering total income over the past year, for example—seems perfectly natural. Indeed, standard institutions such as our tax system also lead people to think of their own incomes in annual terms. People normally compute their income taxes each year by adding up all income over the past calendar year, and often salaries are set and adjusted on an annual basis.

Yet an annual income measure is not really as natural as it might seem when it comes to measuring poverty. Many episodes of poverty are associated with temporary setbacks or with problems of one type or another in one's personal life—for example, a spell of unemployment, death or disability of a wage earner, a divorce or separation, or even the birth of a child out of wedlock.[1] Such problems can crop up at any point during the year, and their appearance can create a sharp break in a person's or family's income stream. Someone whose earnings were more than sufficient to remain above the poverty line for the first six months of the year may have little or nothing to draw on in the second six months if, for example, he or she becomes unemployed. Similarly, someone who is poor for several years probably experiences greater hardships than someone who is poor for only one. Yet as long as annual cross-sectional data are used to measure poverty we cannot tell the difference between those who are poor over the short versus the long run.

Instead, therefore, this chapter considers poverty from the point of view of the poverty *spell*—the amount of time over which a family lacks access to minimally adequate levels of consumption. Clearly, in examining poverty spells the accounting period chosen for measuring income is very important, especially if short-term spells are being considered. The next section of the chapter therefore considers the meaning of poverty in the context of a subannual accounting period and illustrates the effect of alternative accounting periods on simple cross-sectional measures of poverty incidence.

The chapter then presents estimates of the duration of poverty spells, first using a relatively short accounting period and then under a standard annual accounting period. The effects of accounting period issues on the measurement of long-term or persistent poverty also are discussed in detail. The concluding section of the chapter considers methods of integrating alternative approaches to the accounting period into our system of poverty measures.

DEFINING AND MEASURING POVERTY OVER THE SHORT RUN

If someone has inadequate resources for part but not all of a year, is that person "poor"? Those who design the major U.S. assistance programs for the low-income population clearly believe that severe economic hardships may occur if resources are inadequate for periods of much less than one year. Eligibility for these programs is uniformly based on monthly rather than annual income. In many cases emergency assistance is available on even shorter notice. Yet this difference in accounting periods between assistance programs and the official poverty statistics leads to an anomalous finding: even though thresholds for assistance are almost always well below the poverty line, a significant proportion of those receiving assistance do not appear poor when income is measured on an annual basis.

To see how this can happen, consider for example the case of a woman with one child who separates from her husband in January 1987 and who does not receive child support. Suppose she has little in the way of assets and no current income, and so she becomes eligible for assistance from the Aid to Families with Dependent Children (AFDC) program, and receives benefits over a period of several months. Now suppose that in June she realizes that her separation is likely to become permanent, so she goes out and finds a job with an annual salary of $16,000 (which is slightly below the median for a woman working full time).[2] This salary is much too high to allow her to continue to receive assistance, and so she loses her AFDC benefits. Further, even though she is employed for only six months in 1987, the $8,000 she earns in this period is more than enough to put her family of two over the poverty line—particularly once the $1,700 or so in assistance that she received during the first six months of the year is added in.[3] In fact, her total income of $9,700 during 1987 is almost 125 percent of the poverty threshold for her family size and type in that year.

Now consider what happens if data on this woman is included in a national survey used to examine, for example, welfare benefit recipiency. She has quite properly reported receiving six months of AFDC benefits, but her reported income is well above the poverty line. If a policymaker asks, "What proportion of AFDC benefits are received by people who are not poor?", this woman's case will come up, along with others like her. If the role of timing issues is not considered carefully, the policymaker may conclude that these benefits wastefully are being given to people who do not really need them—who, because their incomes are above the poverty line, have enough to get along. This in turn may lead to further initiatives to cut back welfare programs and to eliminate those perennial bogeys of public programs, "waste, fraud, and abuse."

The Meaning of "Poverty" in the Short Run

But was the woman in the example above actually poor? Obviously, the answer depends on what we mean by "poor." If we use a very narrow definition that considers only her income over an entire calendar year, clearly she was not poor. If we use a concept that lines up a bit more closely with people's intuitive notions of poverty, however, she probably was. If, for example, we consider a "spell" of poverty to be a period during which economic resources are so limited that minimally adequate levels of consumption cannot be maintained, then during the first six months of 1987 this woman was poor.

There is a great deal of room for disagreement as to what constitutes "minimally adequate consumption" over any given period. The U.S. system of poverty thresholds purports to say what income is required over the period of a year to support such consumption, although elsewhere in this book it is argued that the system does not always do a good job even in this relatively limited goal. In any case, just dividing the annual threshold by the appropriate number to obtain a prorated threshold for any amount of time of less than one year is probably not the right way to measure minimal adequacy over shorter periods.

Over a long period, such as a year, many expenses come due that cannot be postponed or avoided, but over shorter periods people may be able to find ways to get by on less. One could argue that it is impossible to be poor for one day, for example, because there is no consumption that cannot be postponed for that long. Over a week it would be harder to postpone all consumption—it would become necessary to eat—but with the aid of soup kitchens or meals eaten with friends it might be possible to get by with very limited resources indeed. Over a month the problem would become more desperate—rent and perhaps utility bills would fall due even if certain other expenses, such as the purchase of clothing or other durable goods, could be avoided. Inadequate resources over two months or more will likely cause serious problems. Being more than two months behind on the rent or the mortgage, for example, may well result in eviction. And, by the time a poverty spell has lasted for six months or more a family may begin to need clothing and other consumer goods as well, especially if there are growing children.

Without special consumption studies focusing on subannual periods, it is difficult to know exactly how to adjust existing thresholds to take account of differences in needs over shorter periods. Later in this chapter three alternative poverty spell measures are introduced, illustrating some possible approaches to solving this problem. Here, however, it is sufficient to argue that very low resources over a period even as short as a month can cause significant hardships if no other sources of support are available.

In the case of the woman considered above, for example, her total monthly cash income over the first six months of 1987 would have been $282. In addition, she would have been eligible for a maximum of $115 in food stamps, with the exact amount depending on her housing expenses. Her total income, therefore, would have been at most just under $400 per month. In contrast, one-twelfth of the annual poverty standard for her family size would have been about $650. Although she might be able to postpone some annual consumption needs during her first months in poverty, if she did not have any savings to draw on her ability to pay the rent and put food on the table still would be seriously constrained with an income level this low.

Indeed, her economic problems actually could be worse in the short run than they would be over the year as a whole, because she may have expenses, such as rent, that are fixed in the short run at relatively high levels. Once this woman has adjusted to a permanent separation from her husband she might move out of the house that they shared and find someplace cheaper to live, but if she and her child are not to be evicted in the short run she must pay at least some of the rent.

The Incidence of Short-Run Poverty

If the concept of poverty is meaningful in the short run, then the incidence of short-run poverty is also of interest. Until recently we have not had any nationally representative data that allowed us to look at income in the short run, but with the advent of the Census Bureau's new Survey of Income and Program Participation (SIPP), in which income is reported on a monthly basis, alternative poverty measures have become possible.

One of the clearest findings of the SIPP data on monthly incomes is that many people experience substantial variations in income on a month-to-month basis. Table 5.1 shows four alternative poverty measures for 1984 as calculated from the SIPP for persons and families of several different types. These four measures, all of which are based on cash income only, include an annual poverty rate, based on each individual's family income summed over the year as a whole; an "ever poor" rate, showing the proportion of people who were poor—that is, had an income below one-twelfth of the annual threshold—for at least one month during the year; an "always poor" rate, showing the proportion poor in every month during the year; and finally an average of the monthly poverty rates calculated for each specific month during calendar year 1984.[4] A fifth poverty rate, the

Table 5.1 ALTERNATIVE POVERTY RATES BY FAMILY TYPE, 1984
(in percent)

| Family type | Survey of Income and Program Participation | | | | Current Population Survey 1984 annual rate |
	Annual rate	Poor all 12 months	Poor in any month	Average of monthly rates	
All persons	11.0	5.9	26.2	13.7	14.4
Married couples with children	7.4	2.8	24.3	10.2	10.5
Single parents with children	39.9	25.8	60.8	42.7	44.7
Unrelated individuals	17.7	11.0	35.9	21.9	21.8
Other persons	4.5	2.0	14.3	6.3	5.3
Elderly persons	10.3	6.8	18.5	12.1	12.4

Source: Ruggles and Williams (1986). Tabulations of data from the Survey of Income and Program Participation and the Current Population Survey.

official poverty rate for 1984 as calculated from the Current Population Survey (CPS), has been included in the table for comparison.

Poverty rates under each of these alternative definitions are shown for each of five population subgroups as well as for the population as a whole. The first four categories have been defined as mutually exclusive, and together account for the entire population. A fifth category, consisting of all persons age 65 and over regardless of family situation, is also shown in the table. It should be noted that all those in this category are also included in one of the other four, however.

Perhaps the most striking feature of the poverty rates shown in table 5.1 is the large amount of within-year movement into and out of poverty that they imply for all five population subgroups, as well as for the population as a whole. For all subgroups, the proportion of people poor on average in any given month, based on their monthly income, is always higher than the proportion who are poor when their incomes over the year as a whole are taken into account. The ratio of monthly to annual poverty rates varies somewhat across these population subgroups, however, generally in ways that might be expected. For example, elderly persons and single-parent families, who are most likely to rely on transfer incomes that typically vary relatively little from month to month, have annual poverty rates that are fairly close to their monthly rates, whereas families headed by married couples with children, who may be more likely to depend primarily on employment incomes, have annual and monthly poverty rates that diverge somewhat more.

The effects of within-year movements into and out of poverty can be seen even more clearly by comparing those who are poor in at least one month with those who are poor over the year as a whole. For the full sample, the proportion poor at least one month is more than four times as high as the proportion poor in every month—about 26 percent, compared with about 6 percent. Again, the fluctuations seen differ across the five subgroups considered, with single-parent families having the most stable (and most consistently low) incomes, and with married couples with children experiencing the greatest fluctuations. These estimates imply, for example, that whereas married couples with children are almost as likely to be poor in at least one month as is an average member of the population as a whole, they are less than half as likely to be continuously poor for an entire year. Elderly persons, on the other hand, are substantially less likely than the average to experience at least one month of poverty, but those who are poor are more likely to stay poor over the year as a whole.

Estimating the Duration of Subannual Poverty Spells

As these figures imply, a large number of people who are not poor on the basis of their annual incomes do experience subannual spells of very low income, although these cross-sectional estimates alone cannot tell us much about the total durations of these spells. To examine the duration of a subannual poverty spell, it is necessary to have some concept of poverty that applies to a period of less than a year. As discussed above, it is not easy to adjust annual poverty thresholds to give a meaningful concept of "minimum income adequacy" for specific subannual periods.

To get around this problem without undertaking a major new study of total consumption needs over shorter accounting periods, this study considers three alternative definitions of a poverty spell. The first and simplest definition is just monthly poverty—that is, family income in any month below one-twelfth of the appropriate annual income threshold (using the official poverty thresholds).[5] Measuring poverty by comparing monthly income with a monthly poverty threshold has been widely criticized, however, both for the reasons discussed above and because many people may have little or no income in a given month—for example, when changing jobs — without being

poor in any real sense.[6] Further, even very small changes in income—
for example, an extra pay period falling into some months but not
others—could put some borderline cases on one side of the line or
the other, resulting in apparent short poverty spells with very little
real change in income.

To address these objections, two more stringent poverty definitions
also were used. The first, referred to as *alternative criterion one*,
attempts to eliminate short spells that result from very small fluctuations in income by requiring a fairly large change before an entry
or exit is recorded. Thus, for a spell entry to occur under this criterion, income must decline by at least one-third, and the poverty
line must be crossed. For an exit to be recorded, income must increase
by a similar dollar amount, resulting in a percentage increase of at
least 50 percent, and the poverty line must be crossed again. To
terminate poverty spells for cases that eventually reach fairly high
incomes but do so by small increments, poverty spells were also
considered finished if total income reached 125 percent of the poverty line.

The second criterion, *alternative poverty criterion two*, is designed
to eliminate short spells resulting from very temporary income fluctuations caused, for example, by temporary changes in employment
status such as taking two weeks off between jobs. It uses the same
definition as the first alternative, but in addition the person must
maintain the new status for at least two consecutive months for an
entry or exit to be coded.

Table 5.2 shows survival rates—the proportion of those entering
poverty who are still poor after a given number of months—for poverty spells under these two alternative definitions.[7] Although the
estimated durations of poverty spells do vary across the definitions,
as expected, most entrants leave poverty within a surprisingly short
time under all three.

Table 5.2 includes all cases with a poverty entrance under the
appropriate definition at any time during the 32 months of the SIPP
panel file. Under the least restrictive poverty definition—monthly
income less than monthly poverty threshold—about 23 percent of
the sample experienced an entrance. The addition of restrictions on
the amount of change necessary to record an entrance or exit does
eliminate a substantial number of these entrances. Under alternative
criterion one, 19 percent of the sample had a poverty entrance over
the 32-month period, and under criterion two less than 15 percent
of the sample did so. Nevertheless, cases that do remain still typically

Table 5.2 SPELLS OF MONTHLY POVERTY UNDER THREE POVERTY CRITERIA

	Monthly income less than monthly poverty threshold	Alternative criterion one[a]	Alternative criterion two[b]
Number of cases with a poverty entrance	14,951	12,198	9,383
Percent with a poverty entrance	25.1	20.4	15.7
Percentage of spells surviving after:			
1 month	100	100	100
4 months	42.7	51.6	74.6
8 months	19.8	24.9	41.2
12 months	12.6	15.9	28.7
16 months	9.2	12.0	22.6
20 months	7.7	9.6	18.8
24 months	6.6	8.3	17.3
28 months	5.4	7.0	14.3
Percentage of spells censored[c]	19.7	24.8	38.7

Source: Computed from a 32-month file drawn from the 1984 panel of the Survey of Income and Program Participation. These data cover the period from September 1983 to June 1986.
Notes:
[a]Monthly income below monthly poverty threshold *and* income decline of at least one-third for entry; for exit, increase to above monthly threshold *and* by at least one-half *or* increase to 125 percent of monthly poverty threshold.
[b]As for criterion one, *and* must maintain new state for at least two months for entry or exit to be coded.
[c]Censored spells are those still in progress in the last observed month.

experience relatively short spells. Using the monthly income less than monthly poverty threshold criterion, median spell length is less than 4 months. Use of criterion one increases the median by about 1 month, whereas under criterion two the median is just over 6 months. At 12 months, the probability that an entrant will still be in poverty ranges from less than 13 percent under the least restrictive definition to nearly one-third under criterion two. By 24 months, more than 80 percent of entrants have left poverty under all three definitions.

The figures on spell durations cited above imply that estimates of poverty spell durations are indeed somewhat sensitive to the specific definition used. Even under a definition designed to eliminate very short spells or those arising from trivial income changes, however, very long spells—those lasting two years or more—appear relatively rare.[8]

Comparing across definitions, it also appears that restricting the minimum duration of spells has much more impact both on the number of spells observed and on the durations of spells than does restricting the amount of income change needed. This in turn implies that accounting period issues are quite important in considering the extent and depth of poverty in a comparative context.

Comparing Subannual and Annual Accounting Periods in Measuring Poverty Spells

The importance of the accounting period as a factor in perceptions of poverty is reinforced by examining the duration of poverty spells for those who are and are not in poverty on the basis of their annual incomes, as shown in tables 5.3 and 5.4. In each table, two sets of estimates are supplied. First, spell entries in 1984 are classified by 1984 annual income, and second, spell entries in either 1984 or 1985 are classified by poverty status over the two-year period.[9] Under either definition, only about 20 to 25 percent of all those with spell entries would be counted as poor on the basis of annual income. Although there are some clear differences in spell durations for those who are poor on an annual basis and those who are not, over half of those poor on an annual basis still leave poverty within 12 months of entry under two of the three poverty definitions. For alternative criterion two, spells for those poor on the basis of their 1984 annual incomes are somewhat longer—only about one-third leave poverty in the first 12 months, and the median spell length is just under 18 months.

Nevertheless, even these spells are short compared with the median poverty spell length of two years or more found in studies using annual income data from the Panel Study of Income Dynamics (PSID), discussed below. And of course, spell lengths for poverty entrants who are not in poverty on the basis of their annual incomes are much shorter, as shown in table 5.4. The median is just under three months for the monthly income less than monthly poverty threshold definition, about four months for criterion one, and just under six months for criterion two.

Because entrants who stay in poverty longer are more heavily represented in the cross-sectional statistics than are those with short stays, however, these findings should not be interpreted to mean that

Table 5.3 POVERTY ENTRANCES AND SPELL DURATIONS UNDER ALTERNATIVE POVERTY DEFINITIONS, FOR PERSONS WITH ANNUAL INCOME BELOW THE POVERTY LINE

	Cases with 1984 annual income below poverty threshold and 1984 poverty entry[a]			Cases with average annual income in 1984 and 1985 below average of 1984–1985 thresholds and poverty entry in either 1984 or 1985[a]		
	Monthly income less than monthly poverty threshold	Alternative poverty criterion one[b]	Alternative poverty criterion two[c]	Monthly income less than monthly poverty threshold	Alternative poverty criterion one[b]	Alternative poverty criterion two[c]
Number of cases with poverty spell entrance	2,124	1,469	1,062	2,724	1,977	1,411
Percentage of all entries with annual income below poverty line	26.7	22.3	24.1	23.5	19.9	20.3
Survival rate for poverty spells after:						
1 month	1.00	1.00	1.00	1.00	1.00	1.00
4 months	.682	.809	.951	.715	.830	.956
8 months	.487	.535	.810	.492	.618	.842
12 months	.292	.362	.662	.381	.481	.767
16 months	.207	.240	.545	.299	.406	.680
20 months	.175	.225	.443	.247	.346	.579
24 months	.144	.201	.379	.221	.313	.518
28 months	.127	.175	.273	.195	.276	.389
Percentage of spells censored[d]	31.7	39.1	57.7	41.3	51.3	71.2

Source: Computed from a 32-month file drawn from the 1984 panel of the Survey of Income and Program Participation. These data cover the period from September 1983 to June 1986.

Notes:

[a] "1984" income includes months 5-16 of the panel; "1985" includes months 17-28. These months correspond to slightly different sets of calendar months for interviewees in different rotation groups. See Coder et al. (1987) for further discussion.

[b] Monthly income below monthly poverty threshold and income decline of at least one-third for entry; for exit, increase to above monthly threshold and by at least one half or increase to 125 percent of monthly poverty threshold.

[c] As for criterion one, and must maintain new state for at least two months for entry or exit to be coded.

[d] Censored spells are those still in progress in the last observed month.

Table 5.4 POVERTY ENTRANCES AND SPELL DURATIONS UNDER ALTERNATIVE POVERTY DEFINITIONS, FOR PERSONS WITH ANNUAL INCOME BELOW THE POVERTY LINE

	Cases with 1984 annual income above poverty threshold and 1984 poverty entry[a]			Cases with average annual income in 1984 and 1985 below average of 1984–1985 thresholds and poverty entry in either 1984 or 1985[a]		
	Monthly income less than monthly poverty threshold	Alternative poverty criterion one[b]	Alternative poverty criterion two[c]	Monthly income less than monthly poverty threshold	Alternative poverty criterion one[b]	Alternative poverty criterion two[c]
Number of cases with poverty spell entrance	5,833	5,127	3,352	8,874	7,951	5,538
Percentage of all entries with annual income above poverty line	73.3	77.7	75.9	76.5	80.1	79.7
Survival rate for poverty spells after:						
1 month	1.00	1.00	1.00	1.00	1.00	1.00
4 months	.329	.408	.671	.301	.428	.681
8 months	.083	.120	.287	.092	.137	.315
12 months	.053	.078	.203	.050	.080	.220
16 months	.033	.053	.150	.027	.047	.151
20 months	.027	.043	.119	.017	.036	.113
24 months	.026	.038	.112	.016	.031	.098
28 months	.026	.035	.107	.016	.027	.088
Percentage of spells censored [d]	10.7	13.5	23.5	11.5	15.3	27.8

Source: Computed from a 32-month file drawn from the 1984 panel of the Survey of Income and Program Participation. These data cover the period from September 1983 to June 1986.

Notes:

[a]"1984" income includes months 5-16 of the panel; "1985" includes months 17-28. These months correspond to slightly different sets of calendar months for interviewees in different rotation groups. See Coder et al. (1987) for further discussion.

[b]Monthly income below monthly poverty threshold and income decline of at least one-third for entry; for exit, increase to above monthly threshold and by at least one half or increase to 125 percent of monthly poverty threshold.

[c]As for criterion one, and must maintain new state for at least two months for entry or exit to be coded.

[d]Censored spells are those still in progress in the last observed month.

most of those seen in annual poverty at a given point in time are actually in short spells. Again, the statistics presented here refer to expected spell durations for a sample of entrants, not for a representative sample of those in poverty at a given point in time. Less than 40 percent of those in poverty on an annual basis over the 1984 calendar year also have an observed entry during the sample period, and of course those without an observed entry—that is, those already in poverty at the start of the survey—are likely to include a higher proportion of longer-spell cases.

Nevertheless, the results shown in tables 5.3 and 5.4 have important implications for thinking about poverty. Specifically, they imply that a very large proportion of those who spend some time in poverty are not poor on the basis of their annual incomes and are consequently not picked up in the official poverty statistics. This finding is particularly important in considering issues such as the estimated size of the population eligible for means-tested programs. Because typically only one or two months of low income are needed to qualify for benefits, the population eligible for AFDC or the Food Stamp Program, for example, may be much larger than would be estimated using annual income data alone.

To some extent, the importance one attaches to short spells of poverty depends on the longer term income levels attained by those who experience such spells. If, as one observer suggested, these people are all "college professors taking the summer off"—that is, people with reasonably substantial resources over the longer period, who experience short spells with low incomes—there may be less call for any policy response to these spells than there might be if those experiencing them also had relatively low annual incomes.

As table 5.5 demonstrates, however, the "college professor" scenario is not typical. The two panels of table 5.5 show the distribution of annual incomes for poverty entrants under each of the two annual income measures examined in tables 5.3 and 5.4. Under all three poverty definitions and both annual income measures, almost 90 percent of poverty entrants have an annual income at or below 300 percent of the poverty line, a level approximately equal to the median income for the population as a whole. Under the annual income definition based on 1984 incomes, over half of all entrants have incomes below 150 percent of poverty, and about three-fourths are below 200 percent. Even when annual incomes are averaged over a two-year period, the distribution of annual incomes edges up only slightly. Most entrants, in other words, still have quite low incomes, even over a fairly long accounting period. Thus, although there are

Table 5.5 PERCENTAGE DISTRIBUTION OF POVERTY ENTRIES BY ANNUAL
INCOME AS A PERCENTAGE OF ANNUAL POVERTY THRESHOLDS

	Monthly income less than monthly poverty threshold	Alternative criterion one[b]	Alternative criterion two[c]
1984 annual income level for cases with 1984 poverty spell entries[a]			
Number of entries:	7,957	6,596	4,414
Percentage with annual income:			
Less than 50 percent of threshold	2.8	3.2	3.1
50–100 percent	23.9	19.1	21.0
100–150 percent	32.6	31.1	35.1
150–200 percent	16.2	18.3	17.4
200–250 percent	9.2	10.1	8.4
250–300 percent	5.2	6.0	4.3
Over 300 percent	10.1	12.0	10.7
Average annual income, 1984–1985, relative to average poverty threshold, for cases with poverty spell entries in 1984 or 1985[c]			
Number of entries:	11,598	9,928	6,949
Percentage with annual income:			
Less than 50 percent of threshold	2.2	2.5	2.1
50–100 percent	21.3	17.4	18.2
100–150 percent	28.5	27.4	30.8
150–200 percent	17.5	18.9	18.8
200–250 percent	12.1	13.0	11.9
250–300 percent	6.5	7.4	6.2
Over 300 percent	11.8	13.4	11.9

Source: Computed from a 32-month file drawn from the 1984 panel of the Survey of
Income and Program Participation. These data cover the period from September 1983
to June 1986.
Notes:
[a] "1984" income includes months 5-16 of the panel; "1985" includes months 17-28.
These months correspond to slightly different sets of calendar months for interviewees
in different rotation groups. See Coder et al. (1987) for further discussion.
[b] Monthly income below monthly poverty threshold *and* income decline of at least
one-third for entry; for exit, increase to above monthly threshold *and* by at least one
half *or* increase to 125 percent of monthly poverty threshold.
[c] As for criterion one, and must maintain new state for at least two months for entry
or exit to be coded.

a few cases of relatively high income individuals who experience
short spells of low income, the typical case is someone with a low
annual income who probably does not have enormous resources to
call on in withstanding even a short poverty spell.

Poverty Spell Durations by Demographic Characteristics

The data shown in table 5.1 on poverty rates by family type under
alternative measures implied very different poverty spell durations,

as measured in months, for those in different demographic groups. About 37 percent of the elderly who were poor in any month were poor in all twelve months of 1984, for example. For married couples with children, the comparable figure was less than 12 percent. These findings imply that although the elderly may be much less likely to enter poverty than those who are younger, once they enter they are also much more likely to remain poor.

Table 5.6, which shows poverty spell durations for those in different age categories, confirms this implication.[10] Comparing the figures in table 5.6 with those in table 5.2 (which shows poverty spells for the entire population) makes it clear that the elderly are only about half as likely to enter poverty. The proportion of the elderly in poverty who are still poor at any given month, however, is much higher under any poverty definition than are comparable figures either for children or for the population as a whole.

So far this chapter has considered the issue of accounting period as it affects relatively short spells of poverty. In that context, it is clear that our picture of the effects of poverty may be very different when spell durations rather than simply cross-sectional statistics based on annual data are considered. The study of durations of time spent in poverty—as opposed simply to the incidence of poverty— also can change one's view of poverty over the long run, as the next section discusses.

MEASURING LONG-TERM POVERTY: HOW MANY ARE PERSISTENTLY POOR?

Data on the duration of long spells of poverty have been almost as hard to find as data on short spells. The major longitudinal data base used to study such long spells, the Panel Study of Income Dynamics (PSID), started tracing its panel of 5,000 families in 1968 (collecting information in that year on 1967 incomes). The first longitudinal studies using these data did not appear until the early 1970s (see Morgan et al. 1974), and the first study to address the issue of long-term poverty explicitly by analyzing the probability of remaining poor over a specified period appeared in 1977 (Levy 1977). Since then, other studies have examined the persistently poor and have considered the extent to which they differ significantly from the poverty population as a whole.

Table 5.6 POVERTY ENTRIES AND SPELL DURATIONS BY AGE UNDER THREE
POVERTY CRITERIA

	Monthly income less than monthly poverty threshold	Alternative criterion one	Alternative criterion two
I. Age 18 and under			
Number of entries	4,547	3,726	2,857
Percentage with entry	32.5	26.6	20.4
Percent surviving after:			
month 1	100.0	100.0	100.0
month 4	42.6	53.0	76.1
month 8	19.9	25.3	42.9
month 12	12.5	16.3	30.7
month 16	9.4	12.7	25.2
month 20	8.0	10.0	21.7
month 24	6.5	8.4	20.3
month 28	5.1	6.9	17.1
Percentage censored	16.1	21.4	36.9
II. Age 65 and over			
Number of entries	744	483	415
Percentage with entry	12.9	8.4	7.2
Percentage surviving after:			
month 1	100.0	100.0	100.0
month 4	65.9	71.5	86.8
month 8	39.5	45.3	54.3
month 12	29.6	36.6	44.3
month 16	23.7	29.2	36.6
month 20	18.9	25.4	32.1
month 24	16.7	24.6	31.1
month 28	15.1	20.9	26.7
Percentage censored	29.2	36.9	46.0

Source: Computed from the 1984 panel of the Survey of Income and Program Participation. Sample includes only those cases present in fourth wave of survey, although
data shown are drawn from all 32 months.
Note: Poverty criteria defined as for table 5.2. Censored spells are those still in progress
in the last observed month.

Measuring Long-Term Poverty

Annual cross-sectional statistics on the poverty population as a whole—
like the official poverty statistics—help track changes in the low-
income population over time. But one cannot tell from these cross-
sectional data whether this population contains the same particular
individuals from year to year or whether it consists of many more

individuals, each of whom spends only a relatively short period of time living in poverty (although the data on within-year turnover in the poverty population seen above would appear to be generally more consistent with the second hypothesis). Clearly, these two possibilities have quite different implications for the policies that might be designed to alleviate the problems of poverty.

As Frank Levy pointed out in his 1977 paper on the size of the persistently poor "underclass," most writers of the 1960s implicitly assumed that the bulk of those in poverty were poor over the long run. (Levy 1977:5–6). It seems to have been widely assumed that most of those in poverty typically remained poor from year to year, with minor fluctuations at the margins of the poverty population resulting from changing economic conditions. If the poverty population was basically static over time, then cross- sectional statistics of the type cited earlier could be used to form a fairly accurate picture of its long-run characteristics.

To the extent that significant numbers of individuals move in and out of the poverty population over the fairly short run, however, the characteristics of the long-term poor may diverge from those of the poverty population as a whole. Both Morgan et al. (1974) and Levy (1977), using data from the PSID, found that in fact significant numbers of people leave and enter the poverty population each year. Levy went on to estimate the probability of remaining poor for a cohort of persons who were poor in 1967 and concluded that fewer than half could be considered "permanently poor." These findings raised the possibility that the long-run poor might be significantly different from the poverty population as a whole, as it was known from cross-sectional data.

Estimates of the Incidence of Long-Term Poverty

Since Levy's study, several writers have explored the numbers and characteristics of the persistently poor in the United States.[11] Almost all of those who have attempted to produce estimates of the total numbers of such permanently or persistently poor persons have relied on the PSID, which has a number of advantages for such studies. For example, it is the only nationally representative survey that follows a panel of the same individuals on a year-by-year basis over a long period of years. In some sense, the PSID tracks income and poverty status over a period of years in much the same way that the SIPP data presented earlier do over a period of months. Clearly, for studying the persistence of poverty, a sample that follows specific individuals through a long period is necessary.[12]

As table 5.7 demonstrates, even using a common data base it has been possible for researchers in this area to produce a wide range of estimates of the number of persistently poor. To some extent, of course, the estimated number of long-term poor depends on the year being considered. Presumably, as both the U.S. population as a whole and the poverty population have expanded, the number of persistently poor also has gone up. Even if all estimates are standardized to a single year, however, the range is still large. For example, if all the estimates in table 5.7 were standardized to 1978 (the last year of PSID data typically available for use in these studies) the range still would be from about 3 million to about 20 million persons, or from about 12 percent to about 80 percent of the number appearing poor in 1978 on a cross-sectional basis.

Even a cursory inspection of table 5.7 makes it clear that most of these differences in the estimated incidence of long-term poverty can be accounted for by differences in the definitions of poverty used and in the specific populations being measured by the various authors under consideration. Most of the writers included in the table have used Census Bureau poverty thresholds to determine who is or is not in poverty at any given time, although one writer, Lee Rainwater (1981) uses a relative poverty measure—50 percent of the median income.[13] In addition, another pair of authors, Mary Jo Bane and David Ellwood (1986), use 125 percent of the Census Bureau threshold as their poverty threshold, in an attempt to compensate for the fact that a larger proportion of total income is reported on the PSID than on the Bureau of the Census' Current Population Survey (CPS).[14]

The number of years over which one must be poor to qualify as "permanently" or "persistently" poor varies even more across authors. At one extreme, Richard Coe (1978) required members of his "permanently poor" group to be poor in every year over a 9-year period. Not surprisingly, this results in a relatively small estimate of the permanently poor population—about 12 percent of the poverty population as a whole, or about 3 million people in 1976. Most of the other authors considered those with some short intervals out of poverty poor if they were poor most of the time. Levy (1977), for example, required poverty in 5 of 7 years, whereas Hill (1981) and Duncan et al. (1984) considered those who were poor in at least 8 of 10 years among the long-term poor. Bane and Ellwood considered

Table 5.7 ESTIMATED SIZE OF THE "PERSISTENTLY POOR" POPULATION: REVIEW OF SEVERAL STUDIES

Author(s)	Data	Definition of "persistently poor"	Estimate of size
Levy (1977)	PSID 1967–73	In poverty (Census poverty thresholds) at least 5 years between 1967 and 1973.	10 million to 11 million persons; 40 to 45 percent of poor on an annual basis (base is 1967 poverty population).
Coe (1978)	PSID 1967–75	In poverty (Census poverty thresholds) every year from 1967 through 1975.	3 million persons; 12 percent of the annual poverty population (1.1 percent of the U.S. population). (Base is 1976 poverty population.)
Rainwater (1981)	PSID 1967–76	Always in poverty (relative income definition) over various income averaging periods, 1967–76.	1) Annual income below poverty threshold: 11 million persons—5.2 percent of U.S. population (45 percent of CPS-based poverty population, 1976 base). 2) Three-year average income below poverty threshold: 20 million persons—9.4 percent of U.S. population.
Hill (1981)	PSID 1969–78	In poverty (Census poverty thresholds) at least 8 out of 10 years, 1969–1978; also in poverty (same definition) every year from 1969 through 1978.	1) Eight of 10 years: approximately 6 million persons—2.6 percent of U.S. population (20 to 25 percent of annual poverty population—1978 base). 2) Every year for 10 years: approximately 1.6 million persons—0.7 percent of the U.S. population (about 6 percent of annual poverty population, 1978 base).

continued

Table 5.7 ESTIMATED SIZE OF THE "PERSISTENTLY POOR" POPULATION: REVIEW OF SEVERAL STUDIES

Author(s)	Data	Definition of "persistently poor"	Estimate of size
Duncan et al. (1984)	PSID 1969–78	In poverty (Census poverty thresholds) 8 or more years.	5 million to 6 million persons; 2.2 percent or 2.6 percent of total U.S. population (depending on whether person or household weights are used); 20 percent to 25 percent of annual poverty population (1978 base).
Bane and Ellwood (1986)	PSID 1970–82	Spell of poverty lasting more than 9 years; Census poverty thresholds times 1.25. Nonelderly only.	1) 12 percent of nonelderly beginning spells of poverty will experience spells lasting more than 9 years. (13.1 percent are beginning spells of more than 8 years). 2) 51.5 percent of nonelderly poverty population are in the midst of a spell of poverty lasting more than 9 years (53.8 percent are in spells lasting more than 8 years).

those poor for more than 8 years "permanently poor," but unlike the other authors they examined only the nonelderly poor.

Rainwater (1981) examined a variety of different definitions of the long-term poor, including several based on income averaging periods of different lengths. In each case, people were considered long-term poor only if their incomes were below Rainwater's poverty thresholds in every averaging period examined, however. His estimates for the one-year averaging period correspond to estimates of the long-term poverty population based on annual income measures, therefore. Rainwater's estimates for the three-year period, which compare total income over three years to a poverty standard equal to three times his one-year standard, allow some fluctuations in income as long as the average remains low.

A comparison of Rainwater's results for the one-year accounting period to Coe's "poor in every year" statistics, which refer to almost the same set of years, indicates how generous Rainwater's relative poverty standard is compared with the CPS poverty thresholds. Aside from the poverty threshold used, these two measures are almost identical, yet according to Rainwater's definition, about 11 million persons in 1976 would have been always poor over the preceding 10 years, compared with Coe's estimate of about 3 million.

Methodological Problems in Measuring Long-Term Poverty

Finally, in addition to definitional differences, methodological differences also account for some substantial variations in the estimates. Generally, three different measures of the base population are used as a basis of comparison in these examinations of the long-term poor. The most common approach, used by Hill (1981), by Duncan et al. (1984), and implicitly by those who use an "always poor" definition, is also in some ways the simplest. Under this approach, the base population consists of all those those present throughout the observation period, and the "persistently poor" are those who are poor for some specified proportion of those years, whenever such years may fall.

Although this approach has some intuitive appeal, particularly for studying the characteristics of those who are among the long-term poor, it does not provide a very good estimate of the size of the persistently poor population (and in fact may result in some distortions of reported distributions of characteristics as well). The major problem is that some of those who are not poor for some specified number of years during the observation period—for example, 8, to use the number chosen by Duncan et al.—are in fact in the midst of spells of poverty that have been going on or will go on for a total 8 or more years, although unfortunately some of these years happen to fall outside the period for which data were collected. Thus, the true number of individuals in the sample who were actually poor for at least 8 of 10 years (at least some of which fell during the sample period) cannot be estimated using these data, because the years of poverty falling outside the sample period are not observed.[15]

An alternative approach was taken by Levy (1977), for example, who used what is essentially a cohort approach. He estimated the probability that those who were poor in 1967 would remain poor in at least five of the next seven years. Although he was not able to take into account the number of years those in poverty already were poor, Levy's estimate does have the advantage of being usable to predict what proportion of those who are poor at a given point in time will remain poor for a specified number of years into the future.

In other words, although Levy did not entirely solve the problems of censoring that affect the estimates produced by Hill (1981) and Duncan et al. (1984), his estimates at least can be readily interpreted in policy terms. Using Levy's technique it is possible, for example, to generalize that of those found poor on a cross-sectional basis in a given year, a certain percentage (according to Levy, 40 to 45 percent) will remain "permanently poor." Because policy options can only affect the future poor, this group within the poverty population as a whole is likely to be of particular interest. It represents those who, without intervention, are likely to remain poor, and therefore those for whom intervention of some type is most likely to be necessary. Levy's estimate still may be an underestimate of the persistently poor as a proportion of all who are poor in a given year, however, in that presumably some longer-term poor will be ending long spells of poverty during the early years of his cohort analysis, and so will not be picked up as members of his "permanently poor" population.[16]

A third approach to measuring the proportion of those in annual poverty who are "persistently poor" is taken by Bane and Ellwood (1986). Unlike the other analysts discussed here, Bane and Ellwood have made an explicit effort to adjust their estimates of this population for biases related to sample censoring. That is, they have adjusted for bias resulting from the fact that some individuals who are in the midst of long spells of poverty during the observation period may not be picked up among the "persistently poor," because some of their poverty years fall outside the years being observed. As discussed above, biases of this type lower most other estimates of the proportion of the poverty population that is persistently poor.

Bane and Ellwood adjust for this problem by examining the distribution of completed spells of poverty (that is, spells of poverty for which both a beginning point and an end point are known) that can be observed over the years of PSID data that they had available, and then essentially computing a survival distribution like that computed for short spells using the SIPP data in the section above. (A brief survey of the methodology for estimating such survival rates is given in appendix B). Bane and Ellwood estimate that about 52 percent of all persons in poverty are in spells of more than 9 years, and about 54 percent in spells of 8 or more years.

Use of this methodology, although a substantial improvement over techniques that ignore the problem of censoring, does require somewhat more heroic assumptions in considering very long spells than for short ones. For example, Bane and Ellwood's estimates pool data across all the available years of the PSID, assuming that there are no important systematic variations in the average numbers or duration of poverty spells over time. This "steady state" assumption is necessary, in that unless data from different years somehow can be combined, sample sizes for completed spells will be too small to be analyzed. Nevertheless, such pooling may obscure important changes that do take place over time. For example, both poverty rates and unemployment rates were much higher in the last two or three years of the 1970 through 1982 period than they had been in most of the rest of the period, and the relatively large numbers of new entrants into the poverty population seen in those years could have substantially increased the incidence of relatively short observed spells.

Pros and Cons of Alternative Approaches to Measuring Long-Term Poverty

In summary, the major differences seen in the estimates presented in table 5.7 for the most part can be attributed to methodological differences in their preparation. Any of the approaches used are potentially appropriate for specific policy or analytic purposes. Estimates such as Hill's (1981) or Duncan et al.'s (1984), however, which count only those appearing poor over a given number of years without correction for biases resulting from sample censoring, generally are less helpful in considering the proportion of those poor at a point in time who might qualify as "persistently poor," because, as discussed above, they will tend to underestimate the relative size of the persistently poor population.

Cohort-based estimates such as Levy's, on the other hand, are potentially useful for policy purposes even though they do not fully adjust for sample censoring, because they can be used to consider what proportion of the currently poor population will remain poor over some specified period. In practical terms, because the cross-sectional data typically do not contain any information on the amount of time the poor already have been poor, information on total spell lengths is less useful for prediction purposes than are estimates applying to specific poverty cohorts. For many policy purposes, as well, the most relevant question is how many people are likely to remain poor rather than how many eventually will experience total spells (including time already poor) of some specified length.

In terms of an analysis of the "persistently poor," however, estimates such as Bane and Ellwood's, which take into account the total amount of time that those who are poor at a given time will eventually spend in poverty, are probably the most useful. For this purpose, the aim generally is to consider how many people, and with what characteristics, spend a relatively large part of their lives being poor. Although it is clear from these analyses that the details of the definitions and the methodologies used can significantly affect the answers to this question, in very broad terms the answer seems to be that about half of the nonelderly who appear poor at a given time are in fact members of this "persistently poor" population.

Who Are the Persistently Poor?

As seen in the last section, a "best guess" based on the evidence of the PSID is that about 40 percent of those poor at a point in time will remain poor for some years to come (using Levy's estimates) and, according to Bane and Ellwood, perhaps half or a bit more of the nonelderly poor are in the midst of longer term spells of poverty, including the years that they have already been poor. Table 5.8, which presents a variety of estimates relating to the composition of the persistently poor population, illustrates the range of characteristics associated with this group.[17]

There are some significant differences between the persistently poor, however measured, and the population that is poor on an annual basis. First, it is clear that the persistently poor are considerably more likely to be elderly than are those in the annual poverty population as a whole. To some extent, this may result from the fact

Table 5.8 ESTIMATES OF THE DEMOGRAPHIC COMPOSITION OF THE PERSISTENTLY POOR POPULATION, FROM VARIOUS STUDIES[a]

Percentage in household with head who is:	Levy (1977)	Coe (1978)	Rainwater[b] (1981)	Hill (1981) (Poor 8 of 10 years)	Hill (1981) (Poor in every year)	Duncan et al. (1984)
Elderly: age 65 or over	22.6%	22.1%	36.1%	32.4%	26.4%	33%
Disabled						
All		35.9		38.5	32.3	39
Nonelderly	14.2					
Female						
All		73.9		60.9	81.1	61
Nonelderly	26.4[c]			43.4	58.9	44
Unmarried with children		56.2		37.2	48.6	
Black		77.0	32.8[d]	61.8	60.8	62
Employed at least 1,500 hours		13.6[e]		16.0	9.2	

Notes:

[a] For definitions of "persistently poor" population used, see text and table 5.6.

[b] Percentages refer to all adults, not household heads as for other studies.

[c] Nondisabled non-elderly only.

[d] Minority—includes both blacks and Hispanics.

[e] In 1975 (final year of panel examined by Coe).

that the persistently poor population, at least as measured by these studies, is biased toward those present in the poverty population in relatively early years, because they have more chances to have relatively long observed spells. As pointed out earlier, poverty rates for the elderly have fallen dramatically over this period. Levy's study, which examined the 1967 poverty cohort, found a percentage of elderly persons fairly comparable to the annual statistics for that year, for example—22.6 percent versus 19.4 percent. Nevertheless, all of these studies found higher percentages of elderly among the persistently poor than among the poverty population as a whole.

It is further worth noting that the less stringent the poverty definition used, in terms of either continuousness of poverty or the level of the poverty threshold used, the higher the proportion of the persistently poor population that is likely to be over 65. For example, Hill's "poor in every year" measure resulted in a persistently poor population of about 26 percent elderly, whereas her "poor 8 out of 10 years" measure found more than 32 percent elderly. Rainwater's (1981) definition, which is the least stringent of those considered in terms of the dollar value of the poverty thresholds used, also found the highest percentage of elderly—about 36 percent. This generally supports the view, also supported in the cross-sectional data, that although the elderly are no longer typically among the poorest of the poor, they are relatively likely to be in the "near poor" category.

The disabled are a second group that is heavily represented among the persistently poor. These studies fairly consistently find 35 to 40 percent of the persistently poor in households headed by disabled persons, compared with 10 to 14 percent of the annual poverty population. Some of this difference may result from overlaps between the disabled and elderly populations in the Coe (1978), Hill (1981), and Duncan et al. (1984) studies. Nevertheless, it seems clear that the persistently poor are significantly more likely to be disabled than are the temporarily poor. Even Levy, who excluded the elderly disabled, found more than 40 percent more disabled among the persistently poor in the 1967 cohort than in the 1967 poverty population as a whole. Levy's estimates are still much lower than those of the other authors, but some of this difference is probably accounted for by differences in the span of years examined as well. Because disabled persons now account for a larger proportion of those poor on a cross-sectional basis than they did in 1967, it seems likely that they also account for a larger proportion of the persistently poor.

Those in female-headed households and nonwhites are also relatively likely to be among the persistently poor. For example, estimates of the persistently poor who are in female-headed households range from the 61 percent found by Duncan et al. to the 81 percent found using Hill's "poor in every year" definition. Either measure is substantially higher than the 25 to 35 percent found for the poverty population as a whole. Blacks are also considerably overrepresented among the persistently poor. Some 60 percent or more of this group are black, compared with 30 percent or less of the annual poverty population. And some 40 to 50 percent of the persistently poor are in households headed by an unmarried person with children. Further, the situation for these groups is just the opposite of that for the elderly. In these cases, the more stringent the definition of persistent poverty, the higher the proportion that have these characteristics. This supports the view that the poorest of the poor are also the most likely to be black and in female-headed families.

Finally, the view that the persistently poor are likely to have a relatively low level of labor force attachment is also supported by these data. According to these estimates, some 10 to 15 percent of the persistently poor were in families whose heads were employed for at least 1,500 hours in the first (or in Coe's case, last) year of their observed poverty spell. In contrast, in 1976, for example, about 20 percent of family heads poor on an annual basis worked full-time for 40 or more weeks, and another 4 percent worked part-time for at least 40 weeks. As might be expected, for the employed, like the elderly, tighter definitions of "persistently poor" tend to lead to smaller estimates of their share of this population.

CONCLUSION: ALTERNATIVE TIME CONCEPTS IN MEASURING POVERTY

This chapter has argued that the period over which poverty is measured has important effects on perceptions of poverty, influencing both our measures of poverty incidence and also our views on the composition of the poverty population. The chapter has shown, for example, that the number of people who are poor for some significant period within a year is much larger than the number who are poor on the basis of their annual incomes alone. Similarly, very long spells of poverty, lasting eight years or more, are relatively rare overall, with substantial turnover occurring in the poverty population from year to year.

The timing of consumption matters a great deal to the individual—

one cannot eat all one's meals for the year in one day—and individuals with incomes that fluctuate widely over relatively short periods may have limited ability to adjust their consumption. To deal with this issue, more effort should be made to incorporate information on the timing of income recipiency relative to needs in the official statistics. This problem is particularly relevant to the measurement of shorter spells of poverty, but it could be helpful in considering longer periods of deprivation as well.

Until recently, the data that would have been needed to consider the timing of income recipiency within an annual period simply were unavailable. With the advent of the SIPP, however, it is now possible to consider the incidence of poverty over shorter periods. This chapter neither has exhausted the ways in which this could be done nor has explored every possible problem with such measures. Indeed, the chapter suggests that additional research on consumption needs over short periods would be very useful in assessing the effects of shorter periods of very low income. And, in any case, the use of a shorter accounting period clearly makes the incorporation of data on resources as broadly defined—including assets and perhaps access to borrowed funds, for example—even more desirable than under an annual accounting period. Nevertheless, the findings presented here strongly imply that most of those with below-poverty incomes even over a few months also have fairly low resources over the longer run. This implication is explored in more detail in chapter 7, which considers the asset holdings of the low-income population.

More broadly, this chapter also suggests that for many analytic and policy-related purposes the spell is a more natural measure of poverty incidence than is a measure based on income over some arbitrarily defined annual period. This is seen very clearly with regard to measures of long-term poverty—the size and even the composition of the persistently poor population look very different depending on the approach used to estimate "persistence," and only spell-based measures offer a reasonably unbiased estimate of the proportion of the population that is poor over the long run. Even for subannual poverty measures, however, there are clearly major differences in the expected duration of poverty spells among families of different types.

These differences, which we have only started to explore, can have important implications for antipoverty policies. For example, with spell-based measures of this type it becomes possible to see which types of poverty are largely transitory in nature anyway, and therefore call primarily for limited forms of emergency assistance, and which are likely to develop into long-term spells that may require other types of aid.

For these reasons, perhaps the Census Bureau could consider adding some spell-related poverty measures to those it calculates on a regular basis. As more panels of the SIPP become available, for example, it would be possible to combine data across panels to estimate rates of poverty entrance in each year and the distribution of spell durations for those entering poverty in each year. In this way, patterns in spell duration could be traced across time, and, as sample sizes permitted, across demographic groups. Measures of this type have the potential to expand significantly our understanding of changes in poverty and in the composition and needs of the poverty population over time.

Notes

1. See, for example, Ruggles and Williams (1986) for a discussion of the association of such events with poverty entries and exits.

2. Median earnings for female year-round full-time workers in 1987 were $16,909. See U.S. Bureau of the Census (1989d, Table 688, p. 408).

3. AFDC benefits for a woman with one child were $282 per month in the median state in 1987, or $1,692 over six months.

4. Although the concept of monthly poverty defined simply as income below one-twelfth of the poverty threshold is somewhat suspect, as discussed above, the major purpose of this section is to illustrate monthly fluctuations in income and their effects on alternative measures. For that purpose the specifics of the threshold chosen—at least within fairly broad ranges—are not enormously important. See Williams (1986) or Ruggles and Williams (1986) for more discussion of these measures and their derivation.

5. See U.S. Bureau of the Census (1986b) for a table of these thresholds for 1984. SIPP monthly poverty thresholds are also adjusted on a monthly basis for changes in price levels (that is, the annual adjustment to the thresholds is allocated evenly across the months).

6. The larger issue here is that for very short accounting periods income may be an even poorer measure of total resources than it is over the annual period. Instead of adjusting the threshold or the poverty measure to account for this problem, an alternative approach would be to include assets directly in the resource measure. This approach is explored in chapter 7.

7. Appendix B discusses the data and methods used to estimate poverty spell durations in more detail.

8. The spells shown here include only first poverty spells within the observation period—if multiple spells were included, total durations of course would be longer. The incidence of multiple spells varies across definitions, with about 40 percent of

those with entries having more than one under the least stringent definition. Most of these multiple entries represent minor income fluctuations that are smoothed out under the most stringent definition, under which only 14 percent have more than one entry over the 32 months. See Ruggles and Williams (1989) for more discussion.

9. An individual has been defined to have been in poverty on the basis of 1984 annual income if his or her family income, summed over all months of 1984, was less than the monthly poverty thresholds for his or her family in each month, summed over the same months. For individuals not in the sample for all months of 1984, this calculation was made including all months in which they were present. Poverty status based on average annual income over the 1984–85 period was computed similarly, by summing family income over all 24 months and comparing it with the sum of family poverty thresholds over the same months. For the purposes of this analysis, months 5 through 16 of the panel have been considered 1984, and months 17 through 28 have been considered 1985. These periods include slightly different sets of calendar months for different sets of respondents, although in all cases at least 9 of the 12 months included will fall in the designated calendar year. See Coder et al. (1987) for more detail.

10. Distributions of poverty spell durations by other demographic characteristics may be found in the appendix tables in Ruggles and Williams (1989).

11. This discussion focuses almost exclusively on long-term poverty defined in terms of lack of economic resources. There is a much larger literature, however, that discusses topics such as the intergenerational transmission of poverty and the size and growth of the "underclass" as more broadly defined. See for example Corcoran et al. (1985), Ricketts and Sawhill (1988), and the discussion of this literature in Sawhill (1988) and Ruggles (1989b).

12. The major drawback of the PSID is its relatively small sample size—the panel as a whole consisted of 5,000 families first interviewed in 1968, and there has been some attrition since then. This sample is divided into a subsample of 2,000 that focuses particularly on the low-income population, and one of 3,000 that is nationally representative. For most analytic purposes, these samples must be combined to achieve a sufficiently large number of cases for analysis.

13. Further, because the PSID collects only annual income data, all of these poverty measures are based on annual income only, and thus they overstate the average duration of poverty relative to a measure based on monthly income, such as the SIPP estimates discussed above.

14. Because of the income reporting differences mentioned above (and, possibly, because of sampling differences as well), without some correction poverty rates computed from the PSID will be significantly lower than those computed from the CPS (in fact, generally comparable to the SIPP poverty rates reported above). (See Minarik, 1975, for details on poverty measurement in the PSID.) Bane and Ellwood (1986) state that the use of the 125 percent threshold causes rates computed from the PSID to align more closely with the CPS. Use of this threshold also increases the size of the sample of poor households, making more detailed analyses possible.

15. This type of problem, in which complete observations on some sample items (in this case, spells of poverty) cannot be obtained because the sample is incomplete at one or both ends, is generally known as sample censoring. Statistics derived from such a censored sample cannot be used either to predict the proportion of any given year's poverty population that will be persistently poor in the future or to estimate the proportion of those poor at a given point in time that are in the midst of long spells of poverty, because the information on the individual spells observed in the sample is not complete, leading to an underestimate of the average length of the observed spells. This issue is discussed in more detail in appendix B.

16. In addition, Levy's estimate pertains to the 1967 cohort, and, given the changes

both in economic circumstances and in transfer programs serving the poor that have occurred since then, it may no longer be an appropriate basis for generalizing about the long-term poor. Levy's technique is not difficult to apply, however, and this estimate is one that could be updated usefully with relatively little effort.

17. Unfortunately, the sample size of the PSID is not large enough to allow spell durations to be disaggregated by demographic characteristics, because not enough poverty entries are observed. As a result, all the estimates shown in table 5.8 are based on the population observed in poverty over some relatively long period. As discussed elsewhere in this chapter, this population is not comparable with the population entering poverty at a point in time.

Chapter Six

CHOOSING THE UNIT OF ANALYSIS:
WHOSE INCOME SHOULD BE COUNTED?

Any income measure, including those used to assess poverty status, will depend not only on the specific income types included and the period over which they are measured but also on the units—persons, families, households, and so on—over which the measure is aggregated. Household income is not necessarily the same as family income, and family income is certainly different from personal earnings. Further, poverty measures that count the number of families or households that are poor will get different results from those that count poor people, even when the income measures used are the same.

This chapter briefly considers some criteria that might be used to help choose an appropriate unit of analysis for poverty measurement. It first considers this issue in a cross-sectional context and then discusses its application to longitudinal poverty measures. The final section of the chapter considers the unit of analysis in making comparisons across time.

THE UNIT OF ANALYSIS IN POVERTY MEASUREMENT

Decisions about the unit of analysis actually must be made twice in constructing a poverty measure. First, one must decide at what level to measure income—should one consider all people who live in a given household as an economic unit, or only those who are related? And second, one must decide how to aggregate across those found poor—should one count them as families or as the individuals who live in those families? Although these questions may sound arcane, their answers can have surprisingly large implications for the resulting measures of poverty.

Choice of an appropriate unit of analysis for measuring income depends primarily on what one believes about how income is shared among family and household members. If for example people who are related and living together—husband-wife couples, parents and children—typically pool their incomes and make joint consumption decisions, then it is appropriate to measure income at the family level. ("Family" is the term used by the Census Bureau to refer to all related persons living at the same address; the broader category "household" may include unrelated persons as well.) In considering income adequacy one should presumably count all income actually available so that if people can call on incomes received by other family members to meet their consumption needs, they should all be considered part of the same income unit.[1]

If one believes that parents typically do not pool income with adult children living at home, on the other hand, one may wish to measure income at the "subfamily level" instead, treating such adult children, at least if they have dependents, as separate economic units. This type of decision matters in measuring poverty because some households whose total incomes are above the poverty threshold for the family as a whole contain smaller units with little or no income. An AFDC recipient living with her own small child and her mother, for example, may be poor if only her own income is counted (as would happen in setting her AFDC benefits) but not poor if her mother's earnings also are taken into account.

Ultimately, of course, it is very difficult to know how people do or do not pool incomes within households and families. Indeed, the answer undoubtedly varies from family to family, and in some cases perhaps from month to month. It is probable that in some families whose total income is above the poverty line the actual access to consumption of specific family members is completely inadequate. Children whose parents are addicted to drugs or alcohol, for example, may have below-poverty levels of personal consumption even if the family's total income is above the poverty level. Given the lack of data on the within-family allocation of resources, however, most researchers—and the official poverty measures—assume that incomes are pooled at the family level.

Even if income is measured at the family level, however, it does not necessarily mean that the numbers of units below the poverty line also must be counted at the family level. Indeed, because different types of people typically live in families of different sizes, poverty counts based on families can be misleading in making comparisons across groups. In addition, if poor people typically live in smaller or larger families than the average, even the overall poverty rate can be different if measured across all people or across all families.

Table 6.1, which shows both the percentage of people and the percentage of families in poverty, demonstrates this point. According to the Current Population Survey (CPS), 13.5 percent of people, but only 13.2 percent of families, were poor in 1987.[2] Much more striking, however, are the differences in poverty rates seen for the elderly and the nonelderly, depending on whether one is considering persons or families. The poverty rate for elderly persons in 1987 was 12.2 percent; for the nonelderly—those age 64 or less—it was 13.9 percent. The poverty rate for families with elderly heads, however, was more than two percentage points higher, at 14.7 percent, whereas the poverty rate for families with nonelderly heads was lower, at 12.7 percent. In other words, the view that the elderly are less likely to be poor than the nonelderly depends entirely on whether poverty is measured at the person or family level.

Why this dramatic difference in relative poverty rates depending on the unit chosen for aggregation? The main reason is that poor elderly persons typically live in smaller family units than elderly who are not poor, whereas the reverse is true for the nonelderly. Thus, for example, almost three-fourths of poor elderly persons live in one-person units, but over half of the nonpoor elderly live in units with two or more members. The elderly poor therefore form a larger proportion of all elderly-containing units in poverty than they do of all elderly in poverty. Among families with nonelderly heads, however, family sizes are larger for the poor than for the nonpoor. As a result, the poor appear as a larger proportion of the nonelderly population when measured by people than when measured by families.[3]

The appropriate unit for analysis depends, of course, on the purposes of the analysis being undertaken. In analyzing welfare policy, for example, it may be very appropriate to examine the incomes and

Table 6.1 POVERTY RATES FOR ALL PERSONS, ELDERLY, AND NONELDERLY, AGGREGATED OVER PERSONS AND OVER FAMILIES

Category	Percentage of persons in poverty	Percentage of families in poverty
All	13.5	13.2
Elderly/elderly head	12.2	14.7
Nonelderly/nonelderly head	13.9	12.7

Source: Calculated from the 1987 CPS (unrevised).
Note: "Family" is defined as all related individuals living together. Unrelated individuals are considered one-person families for this analysis.

poverty status of units eligible for welfare. For general comparisons of income adequacy and economic need, however, it is probably least misleading to consider poverty status over all persons rather than over economic units as such. Any other aggregation basis effectively weights poverty rates by average family size across the various demographic and economic groups.

For social policy purposes, one presumably is equally concerned about additional people in poverty whether they live in large families or by themselves, and so an aggregation method that attaches equal weights to each individual in poverty seems most appropriate. In other words, the economic unit is useful in determining the poverty status of its members, but once that status has been determined, each family member probably should be counted separately to arrive at an estimate of the poverty rate for the population as a whole.[4]

LONGITUDINAL UNITS OF ANALYSIS

Choosing the unit of analysis for longitudinal research poses some problems that do not generally arise in cross-sectional analysis. Unfortunately, even relatively straightforward terms such as *household* or *family* lose a great deal of their precision when they are considered longitudinally. Although one may think of the family income reported in the CPS as applying to essentially the same "family" over the period of a year, for example, in fact families may change substantially in that time. This problem is addressed in the data set used for the official poverty estimates, as in many cross-sectional surveys, by fixing the family composition at the point of the interview and by collecting retrospective data on incomes over the previous year from each family member regardless of whether that person was a member of that family for the entire year.

This approach can be duplicated in a panel survey such as the SIPP, but it seems somewhat cumbersome (and potentially misleading) when actual monthly data on both family composition and income are available. Indeed, because many of the policy and research issues that are of interest in a longitudinal context involve the relationship between changes in family composition and income, using a fixed family composition to measure income could undermine the advantages associated with longitudinal analysis as a whole.

Table 6.2, which is taken from a paper by Citro and Watts (1986), illustrates this point. Citro and Watts used data from the Income

Table 6.2 HOUSEHOLD SIZE AND POVERTY STATUS BY LONGITUDINAL
FAMILY STATUS, 1979

Original family type	Stable: Unchanged Composition	Changed in family type and size	Changed in size only	Total changed
	Average size			
Husband-wife family	3.3	3.1	4.1	3.9
Female-headed family	3.0	2.4	4.5	3.4
Singe male nonfamily	1.2	1.4	2.2	1.9
Single female nonfamily	1.0	1.0	1.6	1.2
Total	2.5	2.3	3.9	3.4
	Percentage in poverty over life of household			
Husband-wife family	11.1	23.5	14.4	15.9
Female-headed family	35.9	33.3	54.5	43.5
Single male nonfamily	29.4	0.0	22.2	14.3
Single female nonfamily	56.9	44.4	0.0	33.3
Total	26.5	29.5	20.0	22.6

Source: Citro and Watts (1986). Unweighted tabulations of ISDP 18 percent sample extract.
Note: By definition, stable households were unchanged for a full year. Each household in the "changed in size only" category had the same size each month of its duration until it was terminated by a size change. Two households in the "changed in family type and size" category differed in size from month to month, because, in the assignment to categories, family type change took precedence over household size change in terminating the household's existence. Poverty status is measured over the time period of each original household's existence—that is, until a change in type or size—by dividing the sum of monthly household income by the sum of monthly poverty thresholds for the months of the household's duration.

Survey Development Program (ISDP), the pilot survey for the SIPP, to examine poverty rates for households based on their original composition and on changes in their composition over time. As that table shows, households that change family composition have higher poverty rates within most family types than do those that remain stable over time (although the opposite is true for individuals who join families over the course of the survey.) Overall, however, because certain types of households, especially female-headed households, are both relatively less likely to experience any change (if size change is considered) and relatively more likely to be poor, total poverty rates actually are a bit lower for all changers than for all stable households. Households that change type as well as size, however, have higher poverty rates overall than do stable families.

Differences in poverty rates across stable and changing households illustrate some of the problems associated with the use of a fixed family composition over time. Citro and Watts (1986) found that overall a retrospective, fixed family definition such as the definition used in the CPS misrepresents about 7.5 percent of households in the ISDP as stable over the course of a year. Analysis of the SIPP data indicates that the proportion misrepresented under a fixed definition would be even higher. Further, the biases resulting from such a definition would have differential effects across family types (see, for example, Citro et al. 1986 or Williams 1986 for further discussion).

Unless family or household composition is fixed arbitrarily at some point in time, however, longitudinal analysis at the family or household level requires a set of new longitudinal definitions of what it means to be a family or a household. In other words, one must decide how much change is acceptable within the limits of the term "family." If a couple has a baby, is that a new family, or a continuation of the old one? If they get divorced, is one of the new units a continuation of the old family, or are they both new? What if an elderly parent of one member moves in? Is the resulting family the continuation of both previous families, of one of them, or of neither? Should the answer to this question depend on who is designated as the head of household in this new arrangement? And, perhaps most crucially of all, how does one include statistics on these households that exist for only part of the year in the overall measures of household income and poverty? According to Citro and Watts (1986), for example, the average observed duration of households that experience change over the year is only about six months, whereas estimates done by Citro and colleagues (Citro et al. 1982, Table 2) using SIPP data found an average duration for part-year households of just five months.

Considerable analysis of the implications of alternative family definitions in a longitudinal context has been carried out by Citro and others at the Census Bureau (Citro et al. 1986, Citro and Watts 1986, Ernst 1985, and McMillen and Herriot 1984). This research has compared a number of different longitudinal household definitions, basing the continuation of the household on the presence of the same reference person, on the continuation of family type, on the continuation of family size, and on a more complicated definition developed at the bureau to track the majority of family members who continue to live together over time.

Summarized broadly, their major finding was that the specifics of a longitudinal family definition are relatively unimportant in considering issues such as changes in poverty status but that the use of some longitudinal definition produces results that are significantly different from those seen when family composition is treated as fixed. In addition, because part-year households are different in both income and composition from those present for the full year, the means chosen to incorporate these households can have important implications for the aggregate statistics that result.

Given the need to define an economic unit such as the family as the basis for measuring income, it can be tempting to try to construct such a unit on a longitudinal basis as well. The work done by Citro et al. (1986) demonstrates, however, that the use of a longitudinal family concept can be problematic, because families experience so much change even within a one-year period. Over a longer period, such as the 32 months of the full SIPP panel, an even larger proportion of the sample presumably would change composition. Part-period families cannot simply be excluded in measuring income and poverty, because, among other factors, they have much higher poverty rates than do families that exist for the entire period.

Citro et al. (1986) suggest time-weighting these families—that is, including them at a weight set in ratio to their observed time in existence. This approach at least has the advantage of producing estimates that are reasonably stable over time and across family types. Nevertheless, definitions of the family that emphasize continuity still will produce higher proportions of families with observed poverty spells than will definitions that emphasize change. And, as in the cross-sectional case, family-based poverty estimates essentially count large families at lower weights than smaller ones, at least compared with person-based estimates.

In general, for a measurement concept to be useful, minor variations in its specification should not result in major differences in the quantities being measured. When measures are not robust in this way, it is difficult to tell whether specific outcomes are related to actual differences in behavior, or to some other factor across groups, or whether they are simply artifacts of the measurement method. Longitudinal concepts of the family typically fail this test.

In addition, use of such a concept actually can impede longitudinal analysis, because the very factors that are of interest for much policy research—the effects of divorce, out-of-wedlock births, deaths, and so on—also tend to change family composition, and under many definitions result in new families. Linking these new families with their predecessors in a way that facilitates an understanding of the effects of these transitions can become very difficult, because families can combine and recombine in many different ways over a 32-month observation period.

As a result, therefore, longitudinal linkages at the person level generally are preferable, because the person is the only unit of observation that truly can be considered reasonably constant over time. Although people do move in and out of the sample over a period of time, the identification of a specific individual during his or her time in the sample can be made unambiguously. Further, as in the cross-sectional case, counts of the number of people with a given characteristic or behavior pattern are generally at least as useful for policy purposes as are counts of families or other aggregate units. If one is able to estimate that 50,000 people will experience poverty spells as the result of a given legislative proposal, for example, one may not much care whether those 50,000 people are in 15,000 families or in 25,000. Indeed, if two proposals could be shown to affect the same number of people but different numbers of families (if one particularly targeted large families, for example) most analysts would consider it misleading to cite only the numbers of families involved.

Nevertheless, person-level linkages have the disadvantage that they do not correspond directly to the economic unit whose resources are being measured. Specifically, personal income (without family income information) does not provide a very good estimate of the resources actually available to each person. The solution to this problem in the longitudinal context is similar to the approach taken in the cross-sectional case. Even though one links records—and measures poverty—at the person level, one can compute income at the family level. For each person, family income in each month can be compared with a threshold for the appropriate family size to determine whether or not the person is in poverty that month.[5] Poverty spells for each person then can be calculated by aggregating poverty status information across the months. In other words, economic status still is measured at the family level, but measures are aggregated both across time and across units using person-level data.

To facilitate the analysis of income change over time, therefore, substantial modifications must be made in the simple person-level linked longitudinal file. For the most part, these modifications involve moving additional information on the family and household in which each person resided in each month onto the person record— in essence, creating a personal longitudinal family history for each person in the longitudinal file. In particular, it is necessary to record information on family income and family size for each person in each month to construct meaningful longitudinal estimates of poverty status.

THE UNIT OF ANALYSIS IN MAKING POVERTY COMPARISONS ACROSS TIME

So far, this chapter has focused on poverty comparisons carried out over a fairly narrow span of time—at most, 32 months. Perhaps the single most common use of poverty data, however, is to make comparisons across a span of years. The choice of a unit of analysis also may affect such choices—sometimes in unexpected ways.

Many of the longer run effects of specific choices in units of analysis arise from shifts in the demographic structure of the population over time. As family size and composition change, the relations between poverty measures based on different units of analysis also change. An example of such a shift is the decline in median family size since the mid-1960s. As families have become smaller on average, and poor families have come to resemble the nonpoor more closely—at least in terms of family size—the differences between family-based and person-based poverty measures also have declined somewhat.

Long-term changes in demographic patterns can even change aggregate measures of poverty for the population as a whole. For example, one long-term trend has been an increase in the tendency of the elderly to live alone rather than with their children or other family members. To some extent, this shift has been fueled by rising Social Security benefits, which have provided the income many older people needed to maintain their own homes. In some cases, however, elderly persons who would not have been counted as poor if they had been part of a larger household—where some of the living expenses were paid by other family members—appear poor when they are considered on their own. Ironically, then, this is a case in which rising incomes in fact may have contributed to a higher poverty rate, largely as a result of changes in income units over time.

Finally, demographic change can interact with the peculiarities of the system of equivalence scales to produce odd changes in income units and poverty rates over time. The most blatant example has to do, again, with the reduced need standard used for the elderly. As the population ages over time, and more people become age 65 or over, this differential in equivalence scales for the elderly will cause a decline in poverty rates even if no one experiences any change in real income. Other changes, such as the decline in the number of very large families, also may affect poverty rates and other measures even if the distribution of family incomes remains unchanged.

Thus, particularly in making comparisons across groups and across time, a measure aggregated over persons rather than over families or other groups will provide the most consistent estimates. Because income is not very meaningful at the person level, however, the use of a family unit, or something like it, is inescapable in measuring economic resources. As a result, even person-based poverty measures will have some implicit family characteristics built in, because each individual's poverty status will still be determined on the basis of his or her family income and family size. In considering trends in poverty status over time, therefore, the effects of changes in family size and living arrangements also should be considered, even when the poverty rates being considered are based on the number of people rather than the number of families counted as poor.

Notes

1. Other bases for determining the income unit might include legal factors—parents are typically required to support their minor children, for example—and observed within-family or within-household transfer patterns, to the extent that data on such transfers can be obtained. See Piachaud (1982) for more discussion. Lazear and Michael (1988) also discuss and estimate the allocation of income within the household, focusing particularly on the share going to children. Their work is discussed in more detail in chapter 4.

2. The Census Bureau defines a family as two or more related persons living together, and all one-person units are considered "unrelated individuals." This is not particularly helpful for most analytic purposes, because it makes it difficult for the analyst to use published census data to aggregate income over economic units, which include one-person families. It would be extremely helpful to users interested in income issues if the Census Bureau would publish at least some estimates that are based on economic family units—including one-person units. All "family" estimates shown here include one-person units (and are therefore not consistent with those published by the Census Bureau).

3. Theoretically, some of the difference also could result from the fact that units with elderly heads may have some nonelderly members, and some elderly persons may live in units with nonelderly heads. As a result, the population age 65 and over and the population living in units headed by someone age 65 or over are not exactly identical. In fact, however, minor changes in the measurement basis—examining all people in families with elderly heads, for example, or examining all families with elderly members—do not change the basic finding that poverty rates for the elderly are much higher when one measures over families than when one measures over people.

4. This point applies not just to poverty measures, of course, but also more generally to measures of income distribution as a whole. Danziger and Taussig (1979) discuss its application in this broader context and conclude that measures that weight each individual equally are preferable for distributional analyses.

5. More complex definitions of a poverty spell also can be implemented using a similar methodology. See appendix B for more discussion.

Chapter Seven

MEASURING ECONOMIC RESOURCES: WHAT SHOULD WE COUNT?

To determine whether or not someone is poor, it is necessary to have not only an appropriate poverty threshold but also a measure of the individual's own economic resources to compare with that threshold. Probably the most frequently challenged characteristic of the official poverty measure, at least in the recent past, has been its reliance on before-tax cash income as its basic measure of resources. Ideally, the resource measure used to determine whether or not a family is poor should be as complete as possible, taking into account all the resources that actually are available to the family.[1] The importance of a comprehensive resource measure for policy analysis has been nicely summarized by Marilyn Moon and Eugene Smolensky who stated: "More comprehensive measures of economic status, which better distinguish poor from non-poor families, increase the likelihood of policy improvements that will treat those who society views as equals equally." (Moon and Smolensky 1977: p.2).

Most of the recent literature on the resource measure has focused on the inclusion or exclusion of noncash benefits such as food stamps, housing subsidies, or Medicare, but other economic resources also could be considered for inclusion. For example, assets above some threshold level could be counted, as they are for most means-tested benefit programs. Similarly, one conceivably could take into account the amount of nonmarket income households receive. At the same time, it makes sense to subtract out any sources of income that in fact are not available for consumption purposes, including for example tax payments.

The income measure used in compiling official poverty statistics includes only income received in cash and does not subtract out tax payments. In this regard it may be misleading, overstating incomes for those who pay taxes but receive little noncash income, and understating incomes for those who have substantial noncash resources but who pay little in taxes.

This chapter considers alternatives in the measurement economic resources and their effects on poverty estimates. Economic resources have been defined broadly here, to include not only cash and non-cash incomes but also nonmarket income and even assets. This topic has been quite controversial over the past several years, and a great deal has been written not only on the pros and cons of different approaches but also on their empirical effects. In fact, following up on the work of Timothy Smeeding (1977, 1984), the Census Bureau now produces an annual volume giving estimates of the poverty population under a variety of alternative income definitions, although even their most inclusive measures do not consider either assets or nonmarket, nongovernment resources.[2] The Census Bureau's publications, however, give relatively little guidance to the analyst in considering which income measure is appropriate for what purpose, a central aim of this book. Before turning to that discussion, a review of both the existing official methodology and the alternatives now being estimated by the Census Bureau is in order.

THE RESOURCE MEASURE IN OFFICIAL POVERTY ESTIMATES

When Mollie Orshansky set out to measure poverty in the early 1960s, comprehensive income data from a regularly updated, nationally representative survey was only just becoming available for use by policy analysts interested in topics such as poverty. As seen in chapter 3, Orshansky's choices in setting the poverty threshold were constrained by the consumption data available to her, and within those constraints her choices were generally reasonable. Nevertheless, it is not so clear that all of those choices should be maintained now that much more data (and a much greater capacity for rapid data analysis) has become available. This argument applies even more forcefully when it comes to measuring income.

The official poverty statistics, like the measures Orshansky constructed 25 years ago, depend on a very basic concept of family income. Under this concept, all cash income received by the family is included, and no adjustments are made either for noncash transfers received or for taxes paid out. The adoption of such a measure in the early 1960s is understandable, on conceptual grounds as well as practical ones. For example, although most analysts would now agree that after-tax disposable income is a better basis for judging income adequacy than is before-tax income, in the early 1960s income tax thresholds were high enough so that the poor were much less likely to owe tax anyway, and payroll tax rates also were considerably lower than they are now.

According to Joseph Pechman's (1985) estimates of the distribution of tax burdens, for example, the individual income tax rate for the bottom 10 percent of the population was about 1 percent in 1966, compared with about 4 percent in 1985. Similarly, payroll taxes rates varied between 2.6 percent and 4.5 percent for the bottom tenth in 1966, depending upon the tax incidence assumptions used, compared with a range of 9.4 percent to 10.8 percent in 1985 (see Pechman 1985, Table A-1, p. 77 and A-4, p. 80). Consequently, the choice of after- rather than before-tax income for use in measuring poverty would have had less effect, although the adjustments to the data that this would have entailed would have been costly and time-consuming, given the technology then available. Considering the relatively crude nature of the measure as a whole, such an adjustment hardly would have been justified.

Similarly, it is not surprising that the addition of noncash income sources to the basic income measure was not considered in the 1960s. Noncash transfers—both public and private—have expanded dramatically over the past 20 years. Programs such as the Food Stamp Program (FSP), Medicare, and Medicaid add considerably to the resources available to low-income families. The FSP did not even exist at the national level in 1970, however, whereas spending in the two programs providing medical benefits is now more than 12 times as high as in 1970. Although some of this increase reflects rising prices for health care services, there has also been a major expansion in the receipt of health benefits. Privately provided fringe benefits, such as health insurance coverage and employer-provided pensions, also have become much more common and now represent a much higher share of total compensation than they did two decades ago.

In the face of these changes in the structure of family incomes, different choices might well be made if an official poverty measure were being designed now. It is likely that if an analyst were setting out today to define an income concept for measuring poverty, at a minimum he or she would consider adjusting both for taxes paid and for noncash income received. The next section of this chapter therefore considers these two potential adjustments to income in turn.

POTENTIAL CHANGES IN THE MEASUREMENT
OF INCOME

The basic measure of economic resources on which most poverty research is founded is income. Although the latter part of this chapter considers additional sources of support, it is unlikely that official measures will ever be revised to take account of resources that cannot be included in the income measure—and indeed, for most purposes one would not argue in favor of such a revision. This section therefore focuses on the pros and cons of specific possible changes in the Census Bureau's basic concept of income.

The Treatment of Taxes in Measuring Income and Poverty

Probably the least conceptually controversial change in the computation of income for measuring poverty that could be suggested would be the move to an after-tax income concept. As discussed above, taxes for the low-income population were a substantially higher proportion of income, at least for earners, in the mid-1980s than they were in the mid-1960s—although recent tax changes have reduced income taxes for the poor and have increased offsetting tax credits. Nevertheless, if the major goal of poverty measurement is the assessment of income adequacy, it is appropriate to focus on disposable rather than pretax income in making that assessment. This is particularly important in comparing income adequacy across time and across groups. Assessments based on pretax income may give a misleading picture of relative needs if the taxes paid by the groups being compared—and consequently, their relative after-tax incomes—are very different.

Although most analysts would agree that disposable income would be preferable to the current concept for assessing adequacy, then, there remains some question about exactly which taxes should be subtracted from income to arrive at a disposable income concept. Some taxes are relatively noncontroversial—for example, the payroll tax paid by employees almost certainly should be deducted from their earnings in computing net resources. Income taxes also should be deducted, but they are a bit harder to compute, because tax filing units do not always line up perfectly with the households observed in our surveys, and most household surveys do not collect income tax information directly. Further, most of the states impose some income tax of their own on top of the federal income tax system, but the variations in these state systems make them difficult to model.[3]

Table 7.1 IMPACTS OF EXCLUDING FEDERAL INCOME AND PAYROLL TAXES
FROM INCOME IN MEASURING POVERTY, 1986

	Number of persons added to poverty (in thousands)	Percentage increase in poverty rate	Percentage increase in poverty gap
All persons	2,261	7.4	4.0
All persons in families with children	1,627	8.2	3.5
Persons in single-parent families with children	338	3.0	0.8
Persons in units with all members aged 65 or over	10	0	0.3

Source: Computed from Tables 16–20, pp. 962–71 in Committee on Ways and Means, *Background Material and Data on Programs within the Jurisdiction of the Committee on Ways and Means,* 1989 edition. Based on Current Population Survey data.
Note: Tax impacts computed on an income base that includes inputed food and housing benefits.

Both of these are problems that can be solved, however, and this effort would improve our estimates of the income available to families and individuals for consumption purposes. The Census Bureau has argued that it cannot use income net of taxes as its basic income concept for measuring poverty because the effort needed to compute net income precludes a timely release of the data. The bureau has produced estimates of disposable income net of both federal income and employees' payroll taxes on a less timely basis, however. If incomes including in-kind benefits can be computed routinely, surely the process of estimating net income also could be automated enough to allow the use of an after-tax income measure as the basis for computing poverty statistics.

The move to an income concept that excludes direct taxes would be both conceptually preferable and computationally feasible, therefore. Even with today's higher tax rates for the poor the actual amounts of tax—at least, of federal direct taxes—paid by the low-income population remains relatively low, however. Table 7.1 shows the effects of excluding direct federal taxes from income on a variety of poverty measures for the year 1986, as computed by the Congressional Budget Office (CBO) for the Ways and Means Committee.[4] For all persons, the exclusion of direct taxes from income would increase the observed poverty rate by just under one percentage point (or in this case, from about 12.2 percent to about 13.1 percent). This represents an increase in the poverty rate of just over 7 percent. The poverty gap, on the other hand, would increase by only about 4 percent.

The increase in the poverty rate for all persons in families with children would be slightly larger, but the effect on the poverty gap for this group would be even smaller, because most of those affected have incomes near the poverty line under the official measure. Most of the effect seen comes from the inclusion of payroll taxes, so those groups with relatively low labor-force participation rates—poor single parents and the elderly, for example—would be relatively unaffected.

The relatively small poverty gap effects seen imply that even for those poor and near-poor who do pay taxes, the taxes paid are a relatively small proportion of income. Because those with near-poverty incomes are much more likely than the very poor to pay taxes, the move to a disposable income concept may move a relatively large number of people across the poverty line, but the magnitude of their income deficit will not be very large.

Further, it should be noted that these estimates do not take into account the effects of recent tax reforms that have further reduced income taxes owed by low-income workers. In addition, under current law most of the federal taxes that low income families pay will be offset through the Earned Income Tax Credit (EITC), a refundable tax credit for low-income earners with children.

The treatment of indirect taxes is somewhat more problematic than the treatment of direct taxes in computing disposable income. Sales and excise taxes, for example, are certainly paid by the poor, as they are by all consumers. In general, however, they are not included in adjustments to income. Instead these taxes are treated as a cost of consumption, and as such they presumably ought to be taken into account in setting need standards rather than in computing economic resources. Similarly, property taxes may be treated as a component of shelter costs rather than as a deduction from income.

Because, with minor exceptions, sales taxes are approximately proportional to expenditures for all consumers, failure to account for these taxes may overstate purchasing power but does not necessarily distort comparisons across groups.[5] On the other hand, if the share of total government revenues coming from this type of tax (as opposed to direct taxes) changes over time, including one type but not the other in an income measure may distort comparisons of income adequacy across time. This problem is even more likely to arise in comparing poverty rates across countries, because different national governments have very different mixes of revenue sources.[6]

Noncash Income and the Income Measure

The problem of incorporating noncash incomes into the resource measure differs from the calculation of after-tax incomes in at least two important ways: there is little consensus as to how—or even whether—it ought to be done, and the potential effects of such an adjustment could be very large. These factors, plus the inherent measurement problems involved in estimating noncash income, have generated a lively debate on this issue. (See for example U.S. Bureau of the Census (1986a) for several different views.)

Noncash income has become a particularly important part of total resources for the poor over the past 10 or 15 years, as more and more spending on programs for the low-income population has been concentrated on benefits that are provided in kind rather than in cash. Indeed, some of the original impetus for including these benefits in the resource measure for estimating poverty came from the belief that excluding them in effect failed to give our society credit for some of the progress against poverty that had been made over this period. As mentioned above, both food programs (especially the FSP) and medical programs have increased their spending dramatically over the last two decades, and a large share of these benefits go to those with below-poverty cash incomes.

One approach to measuring the value of these noncash income sources has been simply to add them into the income measure at their market value—the amount that it would cost to obtain similar goods in the private market. Noncash benefits, unlike cash, however, cannot be used at will by the recipient to meet any need or perceived need that arises. As a result, they may be worth less than their general market value to the recipient, who may be forced to overconsume one good at the expense of others. In the simplest terms, recipients cannot eat medical benefits, and a very large supply of such benefits will do little for those who are hungry.

A great deal of work has been undertaken over the past seven or eight years in attempting to reconcile the need to include noncash benefits in income for at least some purposes and the need to maintain a poverty definition that is a realistic measure of actual needs. Timothy Smeeding's work as a research fellow at the Bureau of the Census pioneered the use of a variety of measurement techniques and income definitions in examining these issues. The Census Bureau has followed up on Smeeding's work in this area, sponsoring a conference to discuss the conceptual and measurement issues involved.[7] The Census Bureau currently publishes poverty estimates under five different combinations of income definition and valuation techniques. Although the provision of a variety of estimates is useful (and is a marked departure from the Census Bureau's practice in other areas of poverty measurement), the analyst must still decide just which measure is appropriate for a particular application.

In general, the appropriate method of valuing noncash benefits depends on the purpose of the measure being constructed. If the purpose is to gauge whether specific households or types of households meet some standard of minimal income adequacy, it is appropriate to count only those income sources that can be used to meet an individual's most pressing needs.[8] If a person cannot afford adequate amounts of food or a place to sleep at night, the availability of other noncash benefits such as health care does nothing to change the fundamental inadequacy of that person's basic resources.

In measuring income adequacy, then, the fungibility of a resource—the extent to which its benefits can be applied to different consumption needs, depending on which is most pressing—is very important. Cash, of course, is totally fungible, in that it can be spent for food, housing, heat, or whatever else is most needed. In practice, food stamps are also fairly fungible. Very few recipients get more in food stamps than they would have to spend on food anyway, and so the stamps effectively free up cash for other purposes. For many U.S. families, housing benefits may also replace spending that would have occurred anyway. Health care entitlements such as Medicare or Medicaid, however, are not very fungible, in that they do not substitute for other needs and they normally exceed the amounts recipients would have spent otherwise.[9]

To get around this problem, the Census Bureau has calculated a second measure for noncash benefits, which it calls the *recipient value*. The recipient value is adjusted to take account of the possibility that recipients might not have chosen to spend as much on the good or service in question as its private market cost. Such an adjustment is problematic, however. Although in many cases the recipient might have spent little or nothing on the good in question if it had not been provided for free, that does not mean that it has no value to the recipient if it is provided free. Even in cases in which consumption of the good would have occurred without the subsidy, for a good such as emergency health care the subsidy may only replace charity care or reduce the debt incurred by the individual, without increasing the individual's ability to consume other goods.

Indeed, for a good such as medical care, true recipient value is likely to be related to how sick the person is—someone who is not sick at all during the measurement period may care very little that medical care would have been provided, particularly if other necessities have not been available. If recipient value really could be measured, therefore, those who were most likely to be sick would presumably value health care more.[10] This in turn would lead to higher measures of economic well-being for those groups most likely to be sick, even if all their other resources were identical to those of groups with which they were being compared. Indeed, even under our current measures, which probably do not represent true recipient values, the very old must be substantially worse off than the middle-aged in terms of all other goods in order to be considered poor when the value of medical care is included in income.

Adjustments to the income measure, then, no matter how estimated, are probably not the best way to take the value of nonfungible benefits into account in assessing income adequacy. Instead, a number of analysts have proposed the development of two separate poverty standards to be used in measuring the adequacy of resources—one for cash and "cashlike" benefits such as food stamps, and one for those needs, principally medical care, that are often met out of nonfungible resources.[11] Under this system a person would have to meet both standards to be considered nonpoor. Any fungible resources left over after meeting a basic need standard in that area could be applied to the health care standard, but excess health benefits would not be applied to other needs, because they cannot actually be used to meet those needs.[12]

Impacts of Including Noncash Benefits in Measuring Poverty

The last section argued that although it was appropriate to include some noncash benefits such as food stamps in income for the purpose of measuring poverty, nonfungible benefits such as medical care should not be included unless a separate poverty standard is developed for them, because to do so would be to give a misleading picture of income adequacy for groups that receive such benefits.[13] The estimates presented in table 7.2 illustrate this point. For the population as a whole the inclusion of medical benefits in income, for example, does reduce the poverty rate significantly, particularly if a market valuation method is used. Overall, the poverty rate for 1987 based on CPS data goes from 13.5 percent under the official definition down to 8.5 percent if all noncash benefits are included and are valued at market rates. For those age 65 and over, however, the impact of including all noncash benefits is even more dramatic. Poverty rates

Table 7.2 POVERTY RATES FOR 1987 UNDER CURRENT INCOME DEFINITIONS
AND ALTERNATIVE METHODS OF VALUING NONCASH BENEFITS

Group	Cash income only (official poverty standard)	Cash income only, food and housing benefits		Cash income plus food, housing and medical benefits	
		Market value	Recipient value	Market value	Recipient value
All persons	13.5	12.0	12.4	8.5	11.0
Persons in female-headed families	38.3	32.8	34.2	21.6	30.9
Persons aged 65 and over	12.2	10.2	10.7	2.1	6.4

Source: U.S. Bureau of the Census (1988a, Table 1). Based on Current Population Survey Data. Meaning of the terms *market value* and *recipient value* are discussed in text; for method of computation see source.

for this group fall from 12.2 percent under the official definition to 2.1 percent if all noncash benefits are included at market valuation. In contrast, the inclusion of food and housing benefits valued at a recipient value (an approximation of "cashlike" income) results in poverty rates of 12.4 percent for the total population and 10.7 percent for the elderly—a much more realistic comparison of the relative shortfall in income adequacy.

Noncash Benefits and Trends in Poverty Over Time

The major argument in favor of incorporating noncash benefits into income for the purpose of measuring poverty is that failing to do so neglects a major source of increases in the well-being of the poor. Because so much of the budget for programs assisting the poor now goes to noncash benefits, especially food and medical benefits, and because the rate of growth in these programs has been so high, failure to include them may understate real improvements in the well-being of these groups. Indeed, many people wonder how the nation can spend so much on antipoverty programs and have so little impact on measured poverty. At least part of the answer may be that much of the spending goes for programs whose benefits, although real, are not captured in our official poverty measures.

There is no question that incorporating the cost of providing noncash benefits into the income measure would substantially lower measured poverty rates in any given year, as table 7.2 has demonstrated. It is less clear, however, that this approach would have a

Figure 7.1 TRENDS IN POVERTY UNDER ALTERNATIVE INCOME CONCEPTS

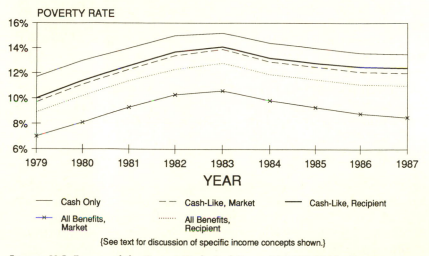

{See text for discussion of specific income concepts shown.}

Source: U.S. Bureau of the Census Technical Paper 58 (1988, Table 1).

major impact on trends in measured poverty over time. Figure 7.1 illustrates the trend in poverty since 1979 under each of the five income definitions that were shown in table 7.2. Although the level of the poverty measure varies according to the definition chosen, the trend in these measures is remarkably similar, at least over this time period. In fact, the official cash-only measure has actually risen less, in percentage terms, since 1979 than have any of the other measures.[14]

The period since 1979 was chosen for this figure only because the Census Bureau's estimates of poverty rates under various income definitions are unavailable before this date. Much of the expansion in noncash benefits took place before 1979, and it is possible that if estimates for earlier years were available the effects of their inclusion would be larger. However, virtually all the rise in measured poverty rates has occurred since 1979. If noncash benefits did make any significant difference to poverty trends in the 1970s, they would only have lowered relative rates for this decade still more.

Even if noncash benefits are included in income, in other words, it is clear that overall poverty rates have risen significantly since the late 1970s. If such a measure could be extended back even further, to the early 1970s or late 1960s, it might cause poverty trends over the decade of the 1970s to look a bit more favorable. Given the relative magnitude of spending on noncash benefits over this decade, however, it is unlikely that incorporating them would more than slightly increase the mild downward trend in poverty rates over the decade as a whole.[15]

In summary, noncash benefits are an important source of support for the low-income population, and their inclusion in the income measure clearly will lower measured rates at a given time. Over the long term, however, U.S. spending on these benefits has not been high enough, and has not changed dramatically enough, to cause major alterations in long-term trends in measured poverty rates.

Other Issues Concerning Noncash Incomes

So far, most of the discussion of noncash incomes has focused on the inclusion of publicly provided noncash benefits in income and their effects on measured poverty rates. This focus mirrors the debate on this issue, which has concerned these benefits almost exclusively. Publicly provided benefits are by no means the only possible source of noncash income, however. There are two other specific issues with regard to noncash income that are much less widely discussed but that also have potential effects on poverty measures. These are, first, the treatment of employer-provided fringe benefits, and, second, the treatment of imputed income streams from durable goods, especially from owner-occupied housing.

Employer-provided fringe benefits have been growing as a component of income almost as rapidly as publicly provided noncash benefits have grown as a component of total government spending for the low-income population. The two major components of such benefit plans are health insurance programs and pension entitlements. Given the shift in employee compensation plans that the growth of these benefits represents, it may well be appropriate to take them into account, at some valuation, in considering total income growth and changes in the distribution of income over time. In addition, if a separate health need standard is ever developed, employer-provided health insurance certainly should be taken into account as an offset against that need standard. For the purpose of assessing income adequacy, however, the arguments for excluding publicly provided health benefits from income apply equally to health benefits that are privately provided.

The issue of pension entitlements may be slightly more complex, because in some cases employees can borrow against these entitlements, making them at least partially fungible. Because pensions are counted as income when paid out—as is surely appropriate in assessing income adequacy—counting them as income when they were accrued as well would lead to some double counting. Instead, it probably makes more sense to consider fungible pension accruals as an addition to total assets rather than as an addition to income. In practice, this issue is of only minor relevance for the low-income population in any case, because very few have significant pension accruals.

A much more important issue, at least in terms of its potential impact on incomes, is the treatment of durable goods and especially of owner-occupied housing. One issue that comes up repeatedly in comparing, for example, elderly and nonelderly persons in poverty, is that the low-income elderly are much more likely to own their own homes than are the nonelderly. Because in many cases they own the home outright, or at least owe only a relatively small amount on their mortgages, housing costs for these elderly may be much lower than for people who are not homeowners. Because housing costs in turn are a major component of total consumption needs, the "correct" need standard for such households actually could be much lower than for households that rent their housing at current market rates.[16]

Developing separate poverty thresholds for home owners and renters would be a relatively cumbersome process, and separate poverty thresholds would be difficult to implement with existing survey data in any case. Further, these separate thresholds would be only a partial approximation of the actual differences, because the extent to which needs differ depends not just on the type of tenure but, for home owners, on the carrying charges for the house—which in turn depend on the amounts still owed.[17] An alternative approach, consistent with the methodology used in computing national income, for example, would be to impute housing "income" to home owners. This income would represent the implicit income stream derived from home ownership, which could be calculated by comparing actual housing costs with the rental value of the house.

In some ways this methodology is an attractive solution to the problems of comparing total needs and resources across a population that includes both home owners and renters, and again it may be appropriate if one's aim is to make generalized comparisons of relative economic well-being. As a means of assessing income adequacy, however, especially in the short run, it has some drawbacks. Specifically, imputed income from owner-occupied housing fails the fungibility test. Many of the elderly who own their own homes are overinvested in housing, in the sense that the rental-equivalent value of their housing is more than they would need to spend in the open market to obtain "adequate" housing. Including imputed income from that housing in their total income measure therefore may over-state the resources they have available for other types of consumption. Although to some extent their failure to sell their houses and move in order to increase the income available for other needs is an issue of tastes, rather than of adequacy, in practical terms many do not see such a move as a real option.

An alternative approach that seems more promising, therefore, is to treat housing equity not as a source of imputed income, but, more realistically, as an asset. Under current measurement techniques, assets are not considered in assessing the adequacy of resources, but as long as one is careful not to double count the asset and its income stream as potential sources of support, there is no reason why assets should not be included in an expanded measure of total resources. Indeed, one might anticipate that in some cases individuals might entirely offset the effects on consumption of short spells of low income by drawing down their asset holdings. This issue is discussed in detail later in this chapter. Before turning to that discussion, however, the next section considers another potential source of resources not counted in the official measure—income from nonmarket and nongovernment sources.

NONMARKET INCOME IN MEASURING POVERTY

People who have major doubts about the validity of our poverty measures as a whole often point to the exclusion of nonmarket (or in some cases, black market) incomes as an important source of error in estimating total resources. Specifically, many believe that the poor— or at least, those who appear poor in the survey data—receive a great deal of income either from unreported "moonlighting" or from criminal activities ranging from shoplifting to burglaries and large-scale drug transactions.

The "Underground Economy" and the Reporting of Income

It is extremely difficult to estimate either the magnitude or the distribution of income received from illegal sources. For obvious reasons the recipients do not tend to report such income to Census Bureau survey takers, and the criminal justice system does not keep its statistics in a form that makes it easy to estimate the proceeds even from reported crimes. Similarly, income from unreported employment is difficult either to estimate or to allocate across income classes.

It is clear that the poor are relatively more likely to be arrested for property crimes than are the well-to-do, although white-collar crimes may produce more average revenue for the criminal. Crime, however, particularly violent crime, is probably not a very good source of income over the longer run. Apart from the fact that at least some stolen goods are found and returned to their original owners, people who make crime a career are likely to spend a significant part of their lives in jail, and probably also have lower-than-average life expectancies.

Clearly, if we could measure income from such sources, it would be important to consider both the accounting period problem and the unit of analysis. In practice, because prisons and cemeteries are outside our sample universe—the population base over which poverty is estimated—a large proportion of those who benefit from criminal activities over a given year will not be included in the poverty population in any case. In fact, to the extent that such people are relatively likely to lack a fixed address, they are also likely to be excluded from our surveys even if they are not in jail.

In summary, although unreported income from moonlighting and from criminal activities may provide some support for the poverty population observed in our surveys, it is likely that a large proportion of the recipients of such income are—like the income itself—excluded from our sample frame. Although family members and friends may receive some support indirectly from such activities, such transfers are probably relatively small and irregular, making it difficult to estimate their effects on poverty even if they were better reported.[18]

Income from Home Production

A second—and probably far more widespread—source of nonmarket income is income derived from home production. Home production can take many different forms. Farmers who grow their own food, seamstresses who make clothes for their families, carpenters who fix up their own houses are all engaging in "home production." Traditionally, the U.S. statistical system has tried to take account of the major sources of such home-produced goods by adjusting measures of need. For example, until 1981 there were separate farm and nonfarm poverty standards, because it was assumed that farmers would be producing at least some of their own food and would thus need less market income. As farm work became more specialized and as the number of family-run farms declined, however, this assumption became more questionable.

In practice, the largest source of home-produced consumption goods today is almost certainly the work that housewives—and especially mothers—do in the home.[19] Although women at home always have contributed in substantial ways to the resources of the household, until recently this source of household support could be implicitly built into poverty thresholds with relatively little difficulty. Most married couples with children included a family member—ordinarily the mother—whose role it was to provide child care and other support services in the home, and so need standards for such households could be set assuming these services were being provided. No additional market income needed to be set aside to purchase them. Single parents were more likely to need to purchase such services, and their poverty thresholds probably should have been adjusted accordingly, although even this group was more likely 20 years ago than they are today to have either a mother at home or children old enough to be in school at least part of the time.

As more and more women have joined the labor force, however, and particularly as mothers of very young children have gone to work, real differences have arisen in the levels of home-produced support services available to otherwise similar families. A family with a father who earns $20,000 a year and a mother who stays home with their two children is in fact better off economically than is a similar family with two earners making $10,000 each and paying $2,500 a year for someone else to provide child care.[20]

The mother at home is providing a valuable service that otherwise comparable families must purchase. Imputing income to the family to cover the value of this service is problematic—after all, the service is clearly in the category of nonfungible goods. As argued above, fungibility is extremely important in considering income adequacy. More and better child care services will not compensate for a lack of food, and children whose mother is at home with them should still be considered poor if the family cannot buy enough to eat or cannot find shelter they can afford. On the other hand, it may be appropriate to adjust poverty thresholds upward for families where there is no parent at home, to take into account the higher incomes they need to cover child-care expenses.

There are of course a myriad of other goods and services produced by both mothers and fathers in the home and by other family members as well. So far, however, child care services are the major home-produced good that also constitutes a major budget item for many families. Although mothers who work outside the home also may produce fewer in-home services of other types—for example, time spent cleaning or cooking—they are less likely to purchase these services in the marketplace, and so their minimum income needs are less likely to be affected. In other words, their families may have lower standards of living in some broader sense than families with a comparable market income where the mother stays home, but it would be harder to argue that these differences materially affect their access to basic consumption needs.

INCLUDING ASSETS IN THE RESOURCE MEASURE

In addition to nonmarket sources of income, many people who appear poor, especially in the short run, may have access to savings or other assets that they can use to tide themselves over a period of low income. Designers of income-support programs are quite sensitive to this point. All income-tested support programs have some sort of asset test as well, and potential recipients do not become eligible unless their resources are below the thresholds for both income and assets.

The official poverty measures, however, have never attempted to include a measure of asset holdings in considering access to resources. The major reason for this has been strictly practical—we simply have not had adequate data on the asset holdings of the low-income population. The Survey of Income and Program Participation (SIPP) is the first survey to combine reasonably good asset data with a large, reasonably representative sample of the low-income population. Second, analysts have tended to think of poverty as an aspect of income distribution rather than as a measure of minimal access to resources. As a result, they have often assumed that assets could be adequately taken into account by incorporating their associated income streams into the income measure.

Despite the absence of good data on the asset holdings of the low-income population, economists traditionally have been relatively unconcerned about short spells of poverty because they have believed that individuals are likely to have some ability to "smooth" their consumption over time, even if income streams vary considerably. Thus, people with short spells of poverty may not be forced to reduce their total consumption if they have other resources they can use in the short run. Typically, these other resources would be expected to come either from the individual's accumulated asset holdings or from borrowed funds. As demonstrated in chapter 5, however, most of those with poverty spells also have relatively low incomes over an annual or even two-year period, which, given the realities of credit markets, means that they are unlikely to be able to borrow much unless they have something to offer as collateral (or have rich relatives—another unlikely event).[21]

Financial Assets in the Low-Income Population

As a practical matter, therefore, most of those with short spells of poverty will be forced to rely on their own asset holdings if they are to maintain their consumption levels during their poverty spells. Table 7.3, which shows the distribution of financial assets across income categories, indicates that most poor individuals have very little access to such assets, however, making the neglect of asset data in our standard poverty measures appear less important, overall, than otherwise might have been expected.[22] More than half of those with below-poverty incomes report no financial assets at all, and more than half of the remainder report less than $1,000 in assets. About 7 percent of those below the poverty level report assets between $1,000 and $3,000, whereas about 13 percent have assets in excess of $3,000.

Although asset holdings are low for the low-income population as a whole, they are important in assessing relative resource levels for subgroups within that population. As the bottom panel of table 7.3 illustrates, the elderly are particularly likely to have higher asset levels, even when incomes are very low. About 60 percent of the elderly in poverty hold more than $3,000 in assets. In contrast, about 92 percent of poor children are in families with less than $3,000 in total financial assets. Even at slightly higher levels of monthly income—up to 200 percent of the poverty line—more than half of all respondents report less than $1,000 in financial assets.

Accounting for Assets in Measuring Poverty

A number of different methods of taking assets into account in measuring poverty have been suggested by economists and other researchers. The simplest approach is to choose some cutoff level of assets, above which people are no longer considered poor. Under a cutoff of $3,000 in assets, for example, about 12.9 percent of those with at least a month in poverty over the 1984–86 period would no longer have been counted as poor (based on the SIPP data shown in table 7.3). Those who are in poverty on the basis of their annual rather than monthly incomes have even lower asset holdings, on average—of those whose annual incomes in 1984–85 were below the official poverty thresholds, only 7.4 percent had financial assets above $3,000, and in fact slightly fewer than 12 percent had assets over $1,000.[23]

The simple cutoff approach is used by means-tested support programs such as Aid to Families with Dependent Children (AFDC) and the Supplemental Security Income (SSI) program for the aged, blind, and disabled. It has some drawbacks as a measure of economic resources over any very long period, however, in that presumably many of those with some assets at the point of entering poverty will be forced to spend those assets long before they are able to leave poverty.

An alternative approach, derived from the work of Weisbrod and Hansen (1968) and applied, for example, in Moon (1977) to estimate the effects of the asset holdings of the elderly, is to convert assets into an annuity and then to add the value of this annuity back into income. (Of course, to avoid double counting, any reported income from these assets first must be subtracted from the income measure.) This approach is appealing in dealing with poverty among the elderly, many if not most of whom may be expected to remain poor for the rest of their lives once they enter poverty. In dealing with the nonelderly population, however, an annuity approach may understate the potential contribution of assets to economic resources, because it will spread the spending of those assets over an unrealistically long period.

A more direct approach is to assume that people draw down their assets on a dollar-for-dollar basis whenever they enter a poverty spell. This approach may overstate the possible contribution of assets to reducing poverty, because it is assumed that no one spends a dollar more in any month than it would take to put them over the poverty line, thereby making their assets last as long as possible. Nevertheless, asset holdings at the levels reported for the poverty population imply that with the exception of the elderly, most people with low incomes will be unable to offset the consumption effects of even fairly short poverty spells by spending down their assets.

Table 7.3 PERCENTAGE DISTRIBUTION OF FINANCIAL ASSET HOLDINGS BY INCOME CATEGORY

Monthly income as a percentage of poverty	No assets	$1 to $1,000	$1,000 to $3,000	$3,000 to $10,000	$10,000 to $100,000	Over $100,000	Total cases	Percentage of cases in this category
I. All people								
Under 100%	55.3	25.1	6.7	5.9	6.6	0.4	7,340	14.3
100% to 150%	33.2	34.4	11.9	10.6	9.5	0.5	5,105	10.0
150% to 200%	22.2	36.2	14.0	12.5	14.8	0.4	5,406	10.5
200% to 300%	13.7	33.4	17.3	15.8	19.0	0.9	11,246	21.9
300% or over	7.0	16.7	15.6	22.1	33.6	5.0	22,194	43.3
Total cases	10,044	13,006	7,267	8,329	11,360	1,285	51,291	100.0
Percentage of cases in this category	19.6	25.4	14.2	16.2	22.1	2.5	100.0	
II. People age 18 or under								
Under 100%	61.9	24.8	5.0	4.1	4.1	0.2	3,157	21.0
100% to 150%	34.7	40.8	10.6	8.6	5.3	0.0	1,740	21.0
150% to 200%	21.7	41.3	15.8	12.6	8.5	0.2	1,804	12.0

200% to 300%	12.5	37.5	20.1	16.7	12.7	0.5	3,548	23.6
300% or over	6.3	18.2	18.1	25.0	28.9	3.4	4,793	31.9
Total cases	3,695	4,441	2,210	2,300	2,209	187	15,042	100.0
Percentage of cases in this category	24.6	29.5	14.7	15.3	14.7	1.2	100.0	

III. People age 65 or over

Under 100%	22.8	11.6	5.8	10.3	42.9	6.7	718	12.3
100% to 150%	13.3	7.7	6.3	9.4	53.4	9.9	948	16.3
150% to 200%	7.4	6.0	3.0	6.3	57.4	19.8	823	14.1
200% to 300%	4.7	1.1	1.5	3.1	60.5	29.1	1,368	23.5
300% or Over	4.2	0.3	0.5	1.6	34.0	59.5	1,971	33.8
Total cases	497	225	156	290	2,785	1,875	5,828	100.0
Percentage of cases in this category	8.5	3.9	2.7	5.0	47.8	32.2	100.0	

Source: Computed from the 1984 panel of the Survey of Income and Program Participation.
Note: Total financial assets includes cash, securities and other fungible assets held by the individual or by other co-resident members of the individual's family, gross of any liabilities. Income levels shown refer to monthly family income in the month when the asset information was collected.

Effects of Asset Spend-Downs on the Number and Duration of Poverty Spells

Table 7.4 examines simulated poverty entries and spell durations if assets are used to bring the consumption levels of those with below-poverty incomes to the poverty line for as long as possible. For example, if an individual is in a family whose total income falls $500 short of the poverty line for each of two months, that individual would need $1,000 in family assets to eliminate his or her recorded poverty spell. If the individual was in a family with only $500 in assets, the recorded spell length would be reduced by one month, but an entry into poverty still would be recorded.[24]

Using this approach, measures of poverty entries and spell durations with and without asset "spend-downs" have been constructed under each of the three poverty criteria defined in chapter 5. As table 7.4 demonstrates, almost two-thirds of observed poverty entries remain even when asset holdings are taken into account.[25] In other words, about two-thirds of those entering poverty do not have enough assets to eliminate their entire "poverty gap" over the duration of their poverty spell.

In addition, although the percentage distribution of durations is similar for any given poverty criterion whether or not assets are considered, the definitions that include the asset spend-down uniformly result in slightly longer average spell durations. This occurs because very short spells are, not surprisingly, those most likely to be eliminated as the result of counting assets, and this impact more than offsets the small reductions in spell length that occur for some remaining poverty entrants when their assets are taken into account.

The impacts of asset spend-downs are also shown separately for two major demographic groups, children and the elderly, in table 7.4. Overall, trends in poverty entries and durations are quite similar for children and for the population in general. Children are slightly more likely to experience an entry under any given definition, and their spells last slightly longer on average, but the effects are not large. Similarly, counting assets is slightly less likely to eliminate a spell for those age 18 or under, but again the effect is not large.

Poverty entries and spells for the elderly, on the other hand, are quite different from those for the population as a whole, and counting assets has a substantial effect on their incidence. Overall, as discussed in detail in chapter 5, the elderly are much less likely to enter poverty under any given definition, even if asset holdings are not taken into account.

Including assets in the resource measure makes this contrast even more dramatic for the elderly. As noted in table 7.3, the low-income elderly are far more likely than other low-income people to have significant amounts of assets. As a result, including assets in resources eliminates more than half of observed poverty spell entries for elderly persons, no matter which poverty definition is used. Those who do remain in poverty even when their assets are counted, however, are much more likely to have very long spells. The median spell duration for elderly persons who are in poverty even when assets are included ranges from about nine months under the least stringent criterion to more than a year under criterion two.

In summary, few of those experiencing spells of poverty have any large amount of assets. Using assets to bring incomes up to the poverty line for as long as possible would eliminate about one-third of observed poverty entries for the population as a whole, but it would slightly lengthen the average duration of poverty for those who remained poor. Further, even under the most stringent poverty criterion, more than 10 percent of the population would still experience a poverty entry during the observation period, and almost 16 percent of the population would experience at least one month in which their incomes fell below a monthly poverty threshold and insufficient assets were available to compensate for the drop. These figures would not be significantly different for children in the sample, but for the elderly including assets in calculating resources would have a much larger impact on both poverty entries and estimated spell durations.

Nonfinancial Assets in Measuring Poverty

So far this chapter has considered assets primarily in terms of their potential effects on consumption opportunities over the short run. Because the study has been concerned about the fungibility of these resources, it has concentrated on financial assets, which are fairly readily turned into cash. Over the longer run, however, various other assets, from home equity to human capital, also may be argued to affect resources and consumption needs.

The problem of home equity was considered briefly in the earlier part of this chapter, which argued against including imputed income from home ownership in the resource measure. This argument was based on the fact that such income is often inaccessible to the individual—at least in cash—in the short run. As a result, it could not be considered fully fungible. Nevertheless, in many cases this equity does increase the real resources available to households and families,

Table 7.4 EFFECTS OF ASSET SPEND-DOWN ON POVERTY ENTRIES AND SPELL DURATIONS UNDER THREE POVERTY CRITERIA

	Monthly income less than monthly threshold		Alternative criterion one		Alternative criterion two	
	Income only	With assets	Income only	With assets	Income only	With assets
I. All Cases						
Total poverty entries	13,566	8,425	11,224	6,628	8,662	5,378
Percentage with entry	25.5	15.8	21.1	12.4	16.3	10.1
Percentage of spells lasting:						
1 month	100	100	100	100	100	100
4 months	42.1	48.2	50.8	57.0	74.2	78.6
8 months	19.4	25.1	23.7	29.5	40.7	47.4
12 months	12.4	16.7	15.0	19.9	28.4	34.9
16 months	9.0	12.9	11.3	15.9	22.4	28.8
20 months	7.5	10.8	9.0	12.8	18.6	24.6
24 months	6.5	9.5	7.8	10.6	17.1	22.5
28 months	5.3	7.9	6.5	9.4	14.1	19.3
Percentage of spells censored	16.7	21.9	21.3	27.2	35.3	42.4
Entries under asset spend-down as a percentage of all entries		62.1		59.1		62.1
II. Age 18 and under						
Total poverty entries	4,950	3,399	4,018	2,592	3,113	2,105
Percentage with entry	26.4	18.1	21.4	13.8	16.6	11.2
Percentage of spells lasting:						
1 month	100	100	100	100	100	100
4 months	42.4	49.2	52.7	59.4	55.3	80.7

8 months	19.7	25.5	24.6	30.6	43.1	49.1
12 months	12.4	17.0	15.4	21.0	30.6	36.7
16 months	9.2	12.9	12.1	17.1	25.0	31.0
20 months	7.3	10.8	9.3	13.2	21.1	26.9
24 months	6.4	8.9	7.8	10.4	19.9	24.7
28 months	5.0	7.2	6.4	8.9	16.7	21.5
Percentage of spells censored	16.7	21.3	21.4	28.0	37.2	44.2
Entries under asset spend-down as a percentage of all entries		68.7		64.5		67.6

III. Age 65 and over

Total poverty entries	758	349	487	202	422	180
Percentage with entry	12.7	5.8	8.2	3.4	7.1	3.0
Percentage of spells lasting:						
1 month	100	100	100	100	100	100
4 months	65.8	68.9	71.7	76.1	86.6	87.8
8 months	39.4	44.4	44.7	51.8	54.0	60.6
12 months	29.5	35.4	35.8	41.9	44.1	51.3
16 months	23.6	30.4	28.4	35.8	36.4	44.1
20 months	18.9	24.0	24.6	31.0	31.9	38.2
24 months	16.7	23.0	23.9	29.0	31.0	35.8
28 months	15.1	21.3	20.3	29.0	26.6	35.8
Percentage of spells censored	29.4	37.3	37.2	43.6	46.2	52.8
Entries under asset spend-down as a percentage of all entries	29.4	46.0		41.5		42.7

Source: Computed from the 1984 panel of the Survey of Income and Program Participation.
Note: Asset definitions as on table 7.1. Poverty criteria defined as for table 5.2. Poverty entries and durations computed only for those present in the month when asset data were collected, so totals are slightly lower than those shown in chapter 5.

and even low-income families may have substantial amounts of equity in their homes. Elderly homeowners, in particular, are likely to have some equity even when they have very low incomes.

There are two possible methods of adjusting for home equity in assessing the adequacy of resources (other than the imputed rent method discussed briefly above). One approach would be to follow the same course with imputed income from home ownership already proposed for other large, nonfungible sources of income—that is, adjust the poverty thresholds to take it into account. Yet having separate poverty standards for cash income and health needs is already a bit cumbersome. Adding additional subcategories based on housing costs and resources (as well as possibly for those with different child care needs) would make the system of thresholds considerably more complex. Nevertheless, the computer technology is now available to calculate separate poverty thresholds for every family in our data bases, if an appropriate formula could be agreed upon. This approach therefore cannot be ruled out.

In the case of housing, a second approach is possible: there is now a well-developed market for home equity loans, which makes at least some of the equity held in housing reasonably accessible in the medium term. It therefore may be defensible to add at least that proportion of home equity that would be available for borrowing to financial assets, and then to use this total figure in estimating the resources available to low-income households.[26] Indeed, to the extent that other assets are realizable in the short run, they too could be incorporated into the fungible assets measure.

Intangible Assets and the Measurement of Economic Resources

Finally, in addition to these tangible assets, low-income households also differ with respect to their intangible assets—including the human capital, or skills, of their members. Some analysts would argue, for example, that graduate students living on meager fellowships are not really as "poor" as are unemployed workers living on the same amount in unemployment benefits, because the students are acquiring skills that will raise their lifetime incomes far above those of the workmen. Knowing that the current period represents a mere dip in lifetime income, the students may adjust their consumption upward accordingly—whereas the workmen may feel more constrained by their current low incomes.

The view that consumption is determined by lifetime rather than current income is widely held by economists, and many would also argue that poverty therefore also should be assessed on the basis of longer run income potential, not just current income. It is possible to see the contrast between a student's and a workman's situations in another light, however. Students' higher level of consumption is in fact made possible not by their higher level of human capital as such, but rather by their greater ability to borrow against future income. In the face of illiquid credit markets, a student would be just as constrained by current income as a workman.

In practice, most students are in fact able to maintain relatively high levels of consumption for two reasons, neither of them directly related to their acquisition of human capital. First, much of their consumption is subsidized—by living in dormitories and eating in cafeterias, for example, they are able to capture certain economies of scale not available to a worker living alone. Second, most students come from relatively high-income families, and these families are willing to subsidize their consumption still further while they are in school. Students from very low income families that are not able to help with their expenses may in fact be just as poor, in terms of access to short-run consumption, as are workers with comparable incomes—even if the students' lifetime incomes will be very high.

In summary, then, if one wishes to include human capital in the resource measure, it is probably most appropriate to treat it in the same way as tangible assets and to include it only to the extent that the individual is able to borrow against it to subsidize consumption in the short run. In practice, most such borrowing probably will take the form of transfers from relatives, which (if reported) probably should be included in income in any case. Although the distribution of income over the longer run is an interesting topic for study, for policy purposes, poverty is best understood as a lack of access to necessary consumption on an everyday (as opposed to lifetime) basis. To the extent that assets are available to provide that access, they should be included in the resource measure.

Notes

1. For a summary of the various arguments on this point and a list of references see U.S. Bureau of the Census 1986a or Danziger et al. 1986.

2. See, for example, U.S. Bureau of the Census (1988a), which gives these estimates for 1987.

3. Some large-scale microsimulation models, such as the Urban Institute's TRIM model, do include state tax modules that model the effects of each specific state system. Unfortunately, no recent figures on the effects of excluding state income taxes on poverty measures are currently available. In general, state income taxes are substantially lower than federal income taxes, however, and because even federal income tax payments for the poor and near poor are small, the additional impact of these state taxes presumably also would be small.

4. Unfortunately, the pretax income concept used by CBO in computing these estimates included federal food and housing benefits as well as cash income, so that estimated changes in the resulting poverty measures are not strictly comparable with those that would occur in the official estimates. Food and housing benefits are relatively small compared with total income and have only a small impact on measures of poverty status, however, so the order of magnitude of the results for this measure should be similar to those that would be seen using the official measure.

5. Pechman and others estimated the total incidence of consumption taxes to be fairly regressive, with the bottom tenth of the population facing effective tax rates about three percentage points higher than those for the median consumer in 1985 (see Pechman 1985, Table A-4, p. 80). These differentials arise because some goods, including tobacco, alcohol, and gasoline, for example, are subject to special excise taxes, and to the extent that the poor consume these goods disproportionately to other consumers, the poor bear a higher share of total consumption taxes.

6. Other taxes such as the employers' share of payroll taxes or even the corporate income tax could also be considered for exclusion in computing net income. Pechman's estimates of total tax incidence by income category, for example, include both of these. In both of these cases, however, it would be necessary to make some explicit set of assumptions concerning the incidence of these taxes. The distributional effects of the corporate income tax, in particular, vary enormously depending on the incidence assumptions chosen. To the extent that either of these taxes are assumed to increase prices or to reduce the wages or dividends companies pay out, however, they again will be accounted for already either in the need standard or in reported income, and no additional adjustment is needed. For more discussion of tax incidence and its implications for income measurement see Pechman (1985), Ruggles (1989a), or Kasten and Sammartino (1987).

7. See U.S. Bureau of the Census (1986a). Smeeding's original work for Census appeared in U.S. Bureau of the Census Technical Paper 50 (1982), and some earlier estimates produced by Smeeding are cited in Danziger et al. (1986). Several follow-up studies have been issued by the Census Bureau, with the most recent estimates (for 1987) appearing in Technical Paper 58 (1988a).

8. If the purpose of the measure is a more general assessment of changes in economic well-being over time, a broader income measure may be appropriate. However, as chapter 2 argues, for that goal a poverty measure may not be the appropriate summary statistic in any case.

9. Some small share of medical benefits may be fungible, in that there may be some irreducible minimum amount that recipients would have spent on health care even under very severe budget constraints. The Census Bureau currently estimates the fungible value of medical benefits by assuming that all income above minimal allowances for food and housing is available to pay for medical care, however, which almost certainly overstates the amount recipients actually would allocate to this purpose. (For example, it assumes that recipients would spend nothing on clothing, transportation, utilities, or child care.) Despite this considerable overestimate, including medical benefits so valued in income would reduce the poverty rate by only about one percentage point overall. See U.S. Bureau of the Census (1988b), Appendix B, pp. 223–26 and Table 4, p. 102 for more details.

10. Because medical benefits are valued at their insurance value to the individual, rather than at the cost of the services actually provided to that individual, it is not literally the case that the sicker you are the more you appear to receive. Because insurance values are higher for those who are statistically more likely to be ill, however—the old and the disabled, for example—both the recipient and market values of medical benefits are higher for those who are more likely to be sick.

11. This type of two-tiered measurement was proposed, for example, by Henry Aaron at the Census Bureau's conference on noncash benefits. See Aaron's comments in U.S. Bureau of the Census (1986a). Burtless (in press) has expanded on this idea.

12. The Census Bureau's current approach to estimating "fungible" medical benefits goes partway toward such a standard by counting only the part of medical benefits that could be paid for out of income after minimal food and housing expenditures. See discussion of this point in note 9 above.

13. Public or publicly subsidized housing benefits also may be nonfungible, and thus at least in theory they should be excluded from the category of "cashlike" goods. In the United States, however, such subsidies are relatively small relative to medical benefits, and at least at recipient values are unlikely to exceed the amounts recipients would have had to spend anyway to obtain any housing. Thus, the Census Bureau's estimates of total income including the recipient value of food and housing benefits represent a reasonable approximation of "cashlike" income for the purpose of assessing income adequacy.

14. The estimates underlying figure 7.1 can be found in U.S. Bureau of the Census (1988a, Table 1).

15. Smeeding has produced some estimates of the combined effects on poverty rates of taxes and benefits at recipient values for the 1960s and 1970s, and these are cited in Danziger et al. (1986, Table 3.1, p. 54). These estimates show a larger proportionate decline in poverty during the 1960s than do the official numbers, but the overall poverty rate estimated by Smeeding remains almost flat between 1972 and 1979. These numbers are not strictly comparable with the estimates shown in figure 7.1, but they do indicate that at least since 1972 in-kind benefits have had little effect on the *trend*, as opposed to the *level*, of measured poverty.

16. Offsetting this, as seen in chapter 4, shelter costs as a share of income are just as high for the elderly as for other groups less likely to own homes. In fact, on median, poor home owners pay about 47 percent of their incomes for shelter, compared with about 65 percent for poor renters. (See Leonard et al. 1989, pp. 1–4.) Although renters pay even more, in other words, costs for home owners are still remarkably high, partly because these home owners tend to own fairly large, older houses that are not in particularly good condition. Utilities, maintenance, and property taxes therefore account for most of these costs.

17. In addition, differences in costs among the renter population are potentially large, with those in rent-controlled or subsidized units, for example, often paying much less than standard market rates.

18. There is a fairly large literature that attempts to estimate the size of the "hidden economy" relative to measured national income for various countries. Although both methodologies and total estimates vary considerably across such studies, few authors believe that the total magnitude of this economy is typically much more than 5 percent of national income (although a few estimates range much higher, and some authors argue that this sector of the economy is growing). It is unclear what proportion of this unreported income is received by otherwise low-income households, but clearly some of it goes to self-employed skilled laborers who underreport their incomes to avoid taxes. Similarly, relatively wealthy households are likely to underreport interest payments, and may legally underestimate income from capital gains. See Barthelemy (1988), Blades (1982), Carson (1984), Feige (1979), Franz (1985), Frey and Pommerehne

(1984), Gaertner and Wenig (1985), Tanzi (1982), and Van Eck and Kazemier (1988) for more discussion of measurement issues and estimates relating to unreported economic activity (including crime).

19. This is yet another topic with its own substantial literature. See, for example, Hawrylshyn's survey of estimates of the value of household services (1976). Substantial work on aspects of this topic has also been done by several others. See, for example, Cain (1984), Ferber and Birnbaum (1980), Gronau (1973), Morgan et al. (1966), Stafford (1980), Walker and Gauger (1973), and Walker and Woods (1976). The relationship of nonmarket production to estimates of total national product is discussed in T. P. Hill (1979) and in Chadeau and Roy (1986).

20. The two-earner family would pay substantially more in taxes—another reason such comparisons should be based on after-tax incomes.

21. In addition, the SIPP actually collects information on accumulated liabilities, and, as would be expected, the liabilities of those with low incomes also tend to be small.

22. Financial assets are defined here to include cash, securities, and other fungible assets held by the individual or by other coresident members of the individual's family, gross of any liabilities. Only financial asset holdings are discussed in detail in this chapter, because they are more likely than other assets to be available to offset immediate consumption needs. Distributions of total wealth and of total net worth—wealth minus liabilities—are given in Ruggles and Williams (1989), however.

23. These estimates are computed from the 1984 panel of the SIPP, and poverty status is based on average annual income over the 1984–85 period. More details and additional estimates for variations on the specific income and asset definitions are given in Ruggles and Williams (1989).

24. This method of examining the impacts of asset holdings was originally suggested by Harold Watts. Because the data contain only one observation of asset holdings, and the poverty entry we are observing may in fact start on a different date when true assets could be different, the simulation is less than perfect. However, the asset data are collected in month 12 of the 32-month panel, so the majority of observed entries will occur after the asset information has been collected.

25. As indicated in the notes for table 7.4, the numbers of entries recorded under the "income only" definitions differ slightly from those shown in earlier tables because only those cases present at the time asset data were collected were included in this table. In addition, it is necessary, of course, to subtract any asset-generated income from total income when using those assets to offset an individual's poverty gap.

26. It would be necessary to add the carrying costs of the loan to estimated housing costs. Estimates of asset holdings and poverty entries and durations after spend-down based on alternative asset definitions that include housing are given in the appendix tables to Ruggles and Williams (1989).

Chapter Eight

SUMMARY AND CONCLUSIONS

For the policymaker and the policy analyst, poverty measurement matters for two major reasons. First, the production of some sort of official poverty measure is important because it allows us to assess our general progress in alleviating the most severe forms of need. And second, the methods used to measure poverty matters because alternative measures can lead to different perceptions of the population in poverty and, ultimately, to different policy priorities.

Most of this book has focused on alternative concepts of poverty and methods of measuring the various components of a poverty definition. It has considered alternative means of setting and adjusting a set of poverty thresholds, and alternative concepts of income and resources. Throughout, the major emphasis has been on the conceptual problems that arise in each area, and on the empirical implications of possible solutions to these problems. Although the book has argued that different measures can lead to differing perceptions of poverty, it has made no systematic attempt to explore these perceptions in detail. Instead, it has focused primarily on measurement issues, offering specific alternative measures as illustrations of particular approaches rather than as the basis for alternative choices in antipoverty policies.

Even though the primary purpose of this book has been to discuss measurement issues rather than perceptions of poverty, it is perhaps useful to summarize here the ways in which these measurement issues may influence beliefs about poverty in the United States. After all, if there is any validity to the argument that alternative measures can lead to differing perceptions, it should be possible to explore those differing perceptions even with the limited set of poverty estimates produced under the various measures discussed here. Accordingly, the next sections consider measurement effects both on the overall estimated size of the poverty population and on the relative poverty rates of two important groups—children and the elderly.[1]

POLICY IMPLICATIONS OF ALTERNATIVE POVERTY MEASURES

Probably the single most important aspect of a poverty measure, in terms of its impact on public policy, is the proportion of the population that it suggests to have inadequate levels of consumption. Certainly this basic poverty rate for the population as a whole is the poverty statistic most widely reported in the press, and it is frequently cited by politicians and program analysts. People who know very little else about the poor in the United States often can give this statistic, and they may even know something about its recent trend. Accordingly, before turning to a discussion of the implications of alternative measures for different population groups, this section considers the implications of alternative approaches to the measurement of poverty for the population as a whole.

This book, and especially the discussion in chapters 2 and 3, suggests that in many ways the overall poverty rate estimate is a fairly arbitrary number. Even with very careful studies of consumption and needs one at best can estimate an "adequate" level of consumption for families of different types and sizes. The current official thresholds, however, cannot be characterized as the result of "very careful study." Although they represented a reasonable approach, given existing data, when they were established in the 1960s, the rather minimal consumption data on which they were based became outdated long ago. In addition, the methods used both to update these thresholds over time and to adjust for differences in family size and type are questionable.

But if our current estimates of the total population in poverty are based on a flawed measure, can it be said, at least, whether they are too high or too low, and by approximately how much? Given the large number of criticisms of the measure made throughout this book, which problems are the most important, from an empirical point of view? How do they all balance out?

Several answers to these questions are possible. At the most basic level, even though it may not be possible to design a market basket of basic consumption goods that perfectly defines minimum consumption needs for different types of households, one certainly could come much closer than does the present. If poverty measures are to reflect minimum needs with reasonable accuracy, the consumption studies on which they are based must be updated from time to time, and needs must be reexamined in the light of new information on relative prices and consumption patterns.

As discussed in chapter 3, people's perceived needs change over time, and the mix of goods available for consumption also changes. At a minimum, therefore, the measures should be updated periodically to reflect these changes, even if this is done in a fairly mechanical way—for example, by incorporating new information on budget shares devoted to basic goods. This approach has been used by Statistics Canada, which periodically estimates a new set of Low Income Cut-Offs based on new data on the consumption share of food and other necessities.

More broadly, there is no good reason to continue to rely on a simple multiplier approach to determining needs for goods other than food. Instead, if at all possible, we should examine those needs directly, updating our estimates of minimally adequate budgets at reasonable intervals, such as a decade. A poverty measure based on food consumption data collected in the late 1950s, along with a multiplier roughly estimated from even earlier consumption data, is surely outdated in 1990.

Basing U.S. poverty measures on an expert-determined market basket representing "minimum needs" has a great deal of appeal from a political standpoint, because it ties the determination of poverty to some concrete standard of minimum adequacy. It is easier to defend the view that those labeled poor do indeed have less-than-sufficient levels of resources if we have expert studies to back this up. Although these studies are bound to be imperfect in important ways, one message of this book is that any other method of defining and measuring poverty necessarily will be imperfect as well.

Economists and other policy analysts continue to search for some method of defining concepts such as poverty that will make them more "scientific," removing them from the realm of judgment and giving them an appearance of objectivity, or at a minimum, neutrality. Setting poverty lines by estimating relative individual utilities at given income or consumption levels—whether done through studies of the actual distribution of consumption expenditures or through the use of "subjective" poverty measures—is attractive, for example, because the "equal utility" standard seems neutral, without value judgments imposed by the researcher or policymaker. Relative poverty measures have something of the same appeal. They depend only on a fixed relationship to income, and so one can avoid the awkward and obviously value-laden process of defining "need," except in some very global sense.

Ultimately, however, this approach is not a realistic way to set poverty standards—particularly relative poverty standards for different population groups—for policy purposes. Its basic flaw is that the concept of poverty that most people normally use in fact does imply some fairly specific value judgments, and these judgments are not consistent with the view that only people's relative levels of utility, rather than their actual consumption, matters in assessing poverty. Not all "needs" or desires are generally considered equal in judging whether or not someone should be counted as poor. The need to eat regularly and to have someplace warm and dry to sleep is widely recognized. But the need to own a particular brand of sneakers or jeans, although deeply felt by many teenagers, is rarely considered of equal importance by policymakers.

More generally, social and political concerns about poverty arise for many different reasons, but almost all of them have to do either with basic notions of fairness and justice or with concerns about the effects of very low levels of consumption on future needs, abilities, and behavior. In either case, these concerns are likely to be much stronger with regard to some types of consumption than for others, and therefore it is appropriate, in a policy context, to weight some types of consumption more heavily in determining "need."

As chapter 3 demonstrated, it is possible to argue that today's poverty thresholds are either too high or too low, and to cite some plausible alternatives in either case. Overall, however, price-indexing alone ultimately will cause poverty thresholds to fall behind a realistic measure of needs, as both relative prices and general standards of consumption change. This clearly has happened to our official thresholds, which are now much lower relative to normal family consumption expenditures than they were in the 1960s. Although most other developed countries do not have official poverty lines, the U.S. line is also low in proportion to the relative income levels at which most other countries phase out eligibility for programs serving the low-income population—a kind of unofficial "need" standard.

Most writers on poverty, from Adam Smith to the present, have recognized that ultimately poverty is a relative concept. It is unrealistic to think that we can identify a minimally necessary basket of goods today, and that that same basket, adjusted only for changes in price levels, will represent minimum consumption needs in 50 or 100 years. As people's incomes rise over time, and as the available selection of goods changes, people's concept of a "minimum" is bound to change also. Although comparisons of "absolute" poverty levels, based on thresholds adjusted only for price change, may be meaningful over a decade or so, without some method of updating these thresholds over time, poverty standards will lose their validity as a measure of minimum adequacy.

But how should we readjust our standards over time? One solution would be to build in periodic recalibrations based on new consumption studies—perhaps every decade or so. This proposal would lead to some discontinuities in data series over time, but it would maintain a standard that was firmly grounded in a concept of minimal adequacy, and it would keep the thresholds relatively current as a measure of needs. This standard presumably would rise faster than one adjusted for price changes alone, but over the very long run it might rise less than a standard tied directly to incomes, particularly over periods of sustained growth. Further, unlike an income-based standard, it would not be sensitive to year-to-year fluctuations based on the state of the economy. After all, family needs, unlike real median incomes, probably do not decline even in periods of recession.

If the market basket were updated for changes in consumption patterns at reasonably frequent intervals, the discontinuities that would result would be fairly minor. In practice, we regularly reapportion and rebenchmark most other statistics that matter for policy purposes, from local population estimates to the national income accounts. It is not very realistic to think that, unlike all these other estimates, an estimate of minimum consumption needs can be done once and then updated mechanically for price changes alone forever after.

Although this book does not pretend to offer a comprehensive assessment of all changes in consumption needs since 1967, it does estimate current minimum consumption standards under two alternative market-basket-based approaches, discussed in detail in chapter 3. It must be emphasized that these approaches are at best approximations, and a broader-based examination of minimum needs would be far preferable. Both of these approaches, however, imply that poverty standards today, to be comparable in terms of their consumption implications to the original Orshansky thresholds, would have to be at least 50 percent higher than the official thresholds. In addition, both imply that today's poverty rates are very high by historic standards and that they show little or no downward trend despite improvements in the economy as a whole since 1982.

Of course, as demonstrated in other chapters of this book, thresholds are not the only aspect of poverty measurement that could be reexamined. But they are probably the most important, at least in terms of changing perceptions of trends in poverty over time. For example, although changes in the income measure—including food stamps and other cashlike transfers, for example—might lower poverty rates marginally, they would neither come close to offsetting increases in the thresholds of this magnitude nor change recent trends in poverty.

EFFECTS ON POVERTY RATES FOR THE ELDERLY AND FOR CHILDREN

Probably the most widely known fact about changes within the poverty population is that there has been a dramatic improvement over the last two decades in the poverty status of the elderly. Indeed, this improvement is often cited by those who argue that it is time to reallocate some of our resources and to make the elderly pay for a larger share of the total benefits they receive. Some politicians have even referred to the elderly as "greedy geezers" who continue to lobby for higher benefits and lower tax burdens, even though they now appear to be one of the better-off segments of society.

It should be stated at the outset that there is no measurement change that could entirely eclipse this apparent improvement in the lot of the lower-income elderly. Particularly through the mid-1970s, the relative proportion of elderly who were poor—under any measurement method—clearly did decline. Because poverty rates for this population were over 20 percent in 1970—and were still well above those for the general population in 1979—this improvement, which largely resulted from increasing Social Security benefits, can only be hailed as a major policy success.

Some of the decline in the proportion of the elderly who are poor—especially, the change since 1979—is probably more apparent than real, however. First, the elderly are still more likely than the average to have low incomes, and, as seen in chapter 3, their poverty rates are as high or higher than those of the rest of the population under any threshold that is even a bit higher than the official ones. Second, current official poverty thresholds for the elderly are about 10 percent lower than those for the rest of the population, and, as chapter 4 argues, the evidence in support of this differential need standard is not strong.

Evidence on the potential effects of accounting period changes on poverty rates for the elderly is more mixed. Although there is no question that fewer elderly than others enter poverty within a given year, elderly persons who become poor are likely to remain poor for much longer periods than are the nonelderly. Including assets in poverty measures would disproportionately reduce poverty entries for the elderly, but again would lengthen the average spells of those who remain. In summary, although the elderly as a group are likely to be less poor, especially relative to the rest of the population, than they were in the 1960s, a substantial minority are still poor, and those who are poor have relatively less ability to escape poverty than do the nonelderly poor.

In addition to poverty rates for the elderly, this book also has considered the effects of alternative measurement methods on poverty rates for children and their families. Unlike poverty rates for the elderly, rates for children have declined little in this decade and are still over 20 percent even under the official thresholds. Under the two consumption-based standards almost one American child in three would be counted as poor.

Under any measurement method, today's poverty rates for children are very high by historic standards. Although poverty rates for children always have been a bit higher than those for the general population, in the first half of the 1970s the official rates for children averaged around 15 percent, and even in the late 1970s they remained around 16 percent. Further, even under current measurement methods there is little apparent downward trend in this figure over the past few years.

Even under the official measure we are now approaching the poverty rates for children seen in the mid-1960s, and under a relative income or consumption-based measure today's rates would equal or exceed those of 30 years ago for this group. A policy program that has reversed the improvements in these poverty rates seen in the 1960s and early 1970s, bringing us back to sustained levels of poverty last seen 25 or 30 years ago, cannot be considered a success.

Assessments of the relative importance of poverty among the very old and the very young depend on many factors besides their relative poverty rates, of course. If we care about poverty at least partly because of its implications for future behavior or needs, for example, poverty among children may be of greater concern, because a failure to invest reasonable amounts in children while they are young may contribute to more severe and sustained social problems in the future. If we are concerned about more abstract concepts of fairness, however, we may weight poverty among the elderly, who have already been productive contributors to the economy, relatively more heavily.[2] Nevertheless, under either motivation for concern, today's poverty rates for both of these groups merit a reexamination of our policies.

PRIORITIES IN POVERTY MEASUREMENT

This book has considered a large number of possible revisions in the methods of measuring poverty, and it has discussed their potential effects on our view of poverty and the poverty population. The last sections have attempted to suggest, in general, how some of these factors would offset or reinforce each other, and, among the many choices available, which are most consistent with the measurement needs of policymakers and analysts. This section goes on to summarize the major measurement changes recommended in the book and to discuss their relative importance in improving poverty estimates.

Revision of our system of poverty thresholds is clearly the most pressing priorty in poverty measurement. At a minimum, we should update the consumption standards on which our thresholds are based, ideally by constructing detailed budgets for minimum needs across a variety of consumption categories. Even the much more limited consumption-based standards examined in chapter 3 are an improvement over standards based on consumption data that is now 35 years old, however. Whatever basis for estimating consumption needs is eventually chosen, it is important to build in some mechanism for regular updates. No standard can reasonably be expected to reflect minimum consumption needs accurately forever.

A second major priority is the reexamination of the system used to adjust thresholds for differences in family needs. Unless we can find some firm basis in realistic estimates of minimum family consumption needs for the current irregular system of family size adjustments—a very unlikely prospect—they should be replaced with a more realistic set. Although the overall trend in thresholds by family size is reasonable, and is in the range used by most other "expert"-determined systems of adjustments, the specific adjustments for additional people across family sizes and types appear to be without foundation. Reestimating these needs by family size directly certainly would be the preferred approach, but failing that, the curve could be smoothed out to provide similar adjustments for each additional person regardless of family size.

In addition, we should reconsider our use of lower poverty thresholds for the elderly. It is not clear that there was ever any very good justification for this differential. At this point, unless evidence on differences in consumption needs can be obtained to back it up, the differential probably should be abolished. On the other hand, we already have strong evidence for differences in price levels by region and, to a lesser extent, by urban versus rural residence. Given the size and persistence of these differentials, the time has come to consider incorporating adjustments for them into our poverty thresholds.

Minor changes in the U.S. income concept also have been proposed in this book. *Most notably, we should move to an after-tax basis for measuring income* and *should incorporate "cashlike" in-kind benefits such as food stamps into the measure of disposable income* as recommended in chapter 7. In practice these two changes would largely offset each other for the measured poverty rate as a whole, although, of course, specific individuals would not necessarily be affected by both to an equal degree. Less fungible forms of in-kind benefits should not be included in income for the purpose of measuring poverty, however, because it is not clear how these benefits contribute to minimally adequate levels of consumption for other goods.

The proposed changes in our thresholds—and especially the adjustments to the overall level of the poverty line—are both the most pressing and probably the most controversial changes recommended in this book. *Accounting period changes also have the capacity to change views of poverty over the long run, however, and therefore we should develop spell-based measures of poverty in addition to the current measures based on annual income.* As chapter 5 argues, from the individual's point of view poverty spells are experienced when resources dip below needs, and they continue until resources increase or needs decline. Only coincidentally and occasionally will these spells line up with the period over which annual income is measured. Indeed, some people may be poor for 12 consecutive months or even more without ever appearing in the statistics on annual poverty. If someone's 12 or more months in poverty happen to fall into different income years, and the person has higher resources during the remainder of those years, he or she will not appear poor.

This accounting period problem can be very misleading for many types of analysis. Means-tested income support programs, in particular, typically use a very short accounting period, because one of their major goals is to help people who are in emergency situations. The designers of these programs realize that if one had to wait to see if the family's income was low over the annual period as a whole, many of their potential clients would starve or die of exposure. In consequence, the annual poverty statistics misclassify many of the recipients of means-tested benefits as "nonpoor." This book does not recommend dropping annual statistics in favor of a set with shorter accounting periods. But it would be helpful to analysts if the Census Bureau would start to publish some statistics reporting on poverty spell entries and durations as well. Over the longer term, a program of research on relative consumption needs over differing accounting periods would add to our understanding of many issues of income adequacy.

Finally, *we should consider ways to account for assets and other resources in measuring poverty.* Particularly if we do start to produce some statistics that consider shorter accounting periods, it would be useful to consider methods of including asset data in the assessment of poverty status on a routine basis. Again, this book does not advocate a move to a measure that includes assets as the most basic poverty standard, at least without considerable study. Regular publication of data on the asset holdings of the low-income population, however, would help in assessing the severity of the remaining unmet needs of the poor.

It has now been more than 25 years since Mollie Orshansky's original work on measuring poverty in the United States. The standard she devised was reasonable, given the data and tools she had at hand, and the regular publication of poverty statistics based on that standard in the years since then has proven invaluable to policymakers and analysts alike. Nevertheless, many changes in both our society and our data resources have occurred since the early 1960s. It is past time to overhaul our poverty standards to bring them into alignment with today's world.

Notes

1. Ideally, all of the various types of revisions considered in the different chapters of this book should be combined, so that their total effects (rather than just their marginal effects) could be examined. Unfortunately, the data and processing requirements of such an approach are probably beyond the resources of an individual analyst (or at least, of this individual analyst). As a result, the discussion that follows focuses primarily on the marginal impacts of each proposed type of revision.

2. See Preston (1984) or Smeeding et al. (1988) for more discussion of these tradeoffs.

APPENDICES

CALCULATION OF ALTERNATIVE POVERTY THRESHOLDS

Five alternative methods of setting poverty thresholds, in addition to the official threshold, are considered in chapter 3. These alternatives consist of one additional price-indexed threshold, two sets of thresholds based on median incomes, and two consumption-based thresholds. Details of the calculation of each of these are given in this appendix.

ALTERNATIVE METHOD OF PRICE INDEXING

As discussed in the text of chapter 3, the official threshold was adopted in 1969 (for the 1967 income year) and has been adjusted for changes in prices as measured by the CPI-U in each year since then. Until 1983 the CPI-U based its estimates of housing cost increases primarily on increases in the sales prices of new homes, which many analysts believe overstated price increases in the late 1970s and early 1980s.

An alternative to the CPI-U, the Bureau of Labor Statistics' experimental index known as the CPI-U-X1, has been developed to correct for this problem, relying on changes in the "rental- equivalent" value of housing instead. (The two indexes use the same methodology in 1983 and later years.) The CPI-U and CPI-X1 are shown in table A.1. Adjusted poverty thresholds for years after 1967 have been calculated by multiplying the official threshold for any given individual in the Current Population Survey by the ratio of the CPI-X1 to the CPI-U for the year in question.[1]

Table A.1 ALTERNATIVE PRICE INDEXES, 1967–1987

Year	CPI-U	CPI-XI	Ratio of CPI-X to CPI-U
1967	100.0	100.0	1.00
1968	104.2	103.7	1.00
1969	109.8	108.3	0.99
1970	116.3	113.6	0.98
1971	121.3	118.5	0.98
1972	125.3	122.2	0.98
1973	133.1	129.8	0.98
1974	147.7	142.9	0.97
1975	161.2	154.7	0.96
1976	170.5	163.5	0.96
1977	181.5	173.9	0.96
1978	195.4	185.8	0.95
1979	217.4	203.6	0.94
1980	246.8	226.4	0.92
1981	272.4	248.0	0.91
1982	289.1	263.2	0.91
1983	298.4	274.1	0.92
1984	311.1	285.8	0.92
1985	322.2	296.0	0.92
1986	328.4	301.1	0.92
1987	340.4	312.7	0.92

Source: Williams 1988, Table B-2, p. 103 as corrected; 1987 Estimate computed from Economic Report of the President, January 1989 (U.S. Government Printing Office, Washington, D.C.), Table B-58, p. 373.

"RELATIVE INCOME" THRESHOLDS

A second method of calculating a poverty threshold is to relate it to median income. Two such sets of thresholds are considered in chapter 3: one indexed by the growth in median income, and one that set the threshold for a four-person family at one-half the median income in a given year and used the standard Census Bureau equivalence scales to adjust all other thresholds accordingly.

Table A.2 gives median family income in current dollars in the years 1967–87. Setting the 1967 value equal to 100, an index has been calculated showing the growth in the median over this period. The first relative-income-based threshold has been calculated from this index, by multiplying the official poverty threshold for each individual in the CPS by the ratio of this index to the CPI-U in the relevant year.

The second relative-income-based threshold has been calculated

Table A.2 MEDIAN FAMILY INCOME, 1967–1987

Year	Median family income in annual dollars	Growth in median (1967 = 100)
1967	7,933	100.0
1968	8,632	108.8
1969	9,433	118.9
1970	9,867	124.4
1971	10,285	129.6
1972	11,116	140.1
1973	12,051	151.9
1974	12,902	162.6
1975	13,719	172.9
1976	14,958	188.6
1977	16,009	201.8
1978	17,640	222.4
1979	19,587	246.9
1980	21,023	265.0
1981	22,388	282.2
1982	23,433	295.4
1983	24,674	311.0
1984	27,735	349.7
1985	29,458	371.3
1986	30,853	388.9
1987		

Source: Williams, 1988, Table B-1, p. 102; 1987 Estimate computed from U.S. Bureau of the Census 1989b. Index calculated by author.

by dividing 50 percent of the median income in the relevant year by the official weighted average four-person poverty threshold. The ratio thus derived has then been multiplied by the official poverty threshold given for each individual in the CPS files.

CONSUMPTION-BASED THRESHOLDS

Finally, two sets of thresholds based on housing and food consumption standards, respectively, also have been included in this study. In both cases, the basis for the threshold is a normative judgment by government "experts" about minimum consumption levels for these basic goods.

In the case of housing, the norm in question is the "fair market rent" (FMR) developed by the U.S. Department of Housing and Urban Development (HUD), and shown in table A.3. The FMR series rep-

Table A.3 U.S. AVERAGE MONTHLY FAIR MARKET RENT FOR A
TWO-BEDROOM UNIT, 1980–1988

Fiscal year	As of date	FMR	Basis
1980	Oct. 1979	$261	50th percentile, all recent rentals
1981	Oct. 1980	$285	50th percentile, all recent rentals
1982	Oct. 1981	$316	50th percentile, all recent rentals
1983	—	—	—
1984	April 1984	$379	45th percentile of all recent rentals except new construction and public housing units
1985	April 1985	$398	45th percentile of all recent rentals except new construction and public housing units
1986	April 1986	$426	45th percentile of all recent rentals except new construction and public housing units
1987	April 1987	$448	45th percentile of all recent rentals except new construction and public housing units
1988	April 1988	$467	45th percentile of all recent rentals except new construction and public housing units

Source: Michael Allard, U.S. Department of Housing and Urban Development.

resents a "norm" in the sense that it gives the amount of rent that
HUD will subsidize for low-income families. Higher cost units are
implicitly considered luxuries, not necessities. As discussed in the
notes to chapter 3, the FMR is not the lowest possible rent for a unit
of a given size, but rather a reasonable market rent. Use of this rent
level in conjunction with the equivalence scales implicit in the official thresholds, however, which almost certainly overstate the economics of scale (particularly in rents) available to smaller households,
results in a fairly conservative estimate of the costs of meeting housing needs. (See chapter 3, note 25, for more discussion of this point.)

Unfortunately, the FMR series is not available on a national average basis before October 1979.

Some changes have occurred in the method of calculating the FMR over the past decade. Before 1983, the FMR was set equal to the median rental price among all units rented in a given area in the past two years. More recently, the FMR has been set at the 45th percentile of the distribution of recent rentals, excluding both public housing and newly constructed housing. The net impact of this re-definition has probably been to lower FMRs somewhat compared with the earlier method of calculation.

Because lower standards of provision for the poor were set in almost all assistance programs at about this time, this study has chosen to treat these changes as evidence of a change in our beliefs about how much the poor "need," and has lowered thresholds accordingly. This is a relatively conservative approach, however. Both sets of consumption-based standards would be higher if norms consistent with earlier levels of provision had been used throughout the period.

The basis for the food consumption standard, referred to in the text as the "updated multiplier" approach, is the U.S. Department of Agriculture's Thrifty Food Plan (TFP).[2] The average monthly value of the TFP and its predecessors is shown in table A.4.

As with the housing programs, changes in basic consumption norms for food also occurred in the early 1980s. In the 1975–83 period the TFP was based on the actual food consumption patterns of low-income families, adjusted to meet minimum nutritional standards. When data from the Nationwide Food Consumption Survey of 1977–78 were analyzed in preparation for TFP revisions, however, it was found that updating this methodology to account for changes in the consumption patterns of the low-income population would have caused a 24 percent increase in the TFP (see Peterkin et al. 1983: 9).

Because benefit levels in the Food Stamp program are based directly on the TFP, such an increase could have been very costly. A decision was therefore made to develop new, lower cost food consumption norms that were not closely tied to actual consumption patterns but that could be implemented without changing the overall level of the TFP. Clearly, without this change in methods both the TFP and the poverty standards computed from it in this study would have been substantially higher.

Given a norm for "necessary" consumption of one basic good, it is still necessary to make some judgment about the relationship of

Table A.4 CALENDAR YEAR U.S. AVERAGE MONTHLY COST OF THE
ECONOMY FOOD PLAN (1959–1974)[1] AND THRIFTY FOOD PLAN
(1975–1988)[2] (family of four, two adults and two children)

Year	U.S. average monthly cost	Year	U.S. average monthly cost
1959	$82.96	1974	152.88
1960	82.27	1975	164.08[3]
1961	82.88	1976	165.65
1962	83.31	1977	171.88
1963	84.44	1978	188.34
1964	85.39	1979	207.13
1965	87.50	1980	225.85
1966	91.62	1981	244.45
1967	90.64	1982	252.06
1968	98.00	1983	254.86
1969	103.18	1984	265.73
1970	107.25	1985	268.51
1971	109.68	1986	274.83
1972	114.19	1987	287.36
1973	132.13	1988	300.66

Source: Computed by the Congressional Research Service using data provided by the
U.S. Department of Agriculture, Human Nutrition Information Service.
Notes:
1. Per HNIS instructions, 1959–1964 weekly Low-Cost Plan figures (published quarterly) are multiplied by 4.33 to convert to monthly data, and by 80 percent to
convert to the Economy Food Plan equivalent. From 1965–1968, monthly Low-
Cost Plan data (published quarterly) are multiplied by 80 percent to convert to the
Economy Food Plan equivalent. From 1969–1971, Economy Food Plan data (published quarterly) are used. From 1972–1974, monthly Economy Food Plan data
are used. The 1972 average cost is based on the 9 months of data that have been
published.
2. Monthly data.
3. The 1975 average cost is based on monthly Economy Food Plan data from January
through July, and on monthly Thrifty Food Plan data from August through December.

this good to the rest of the family budget in order to calculate poverty
thresholds. In the case of the housing standard, the Section 8 subsidized housing program (as well as several other HUD programs)
specifies that tenants are not required to spend more than 30 percent
of their income on rent. This amount also was increased in the early
1980s, rising by one percentage point per year for existing tenants
after 1981. To calculate thresholds, therefore, the annualized value
of the FMR for each year has been divided by the specified income
share for that year, to arrive at the minimum income necessary to
pay the FMR without exceeding the allowed budget share.

Table A.5 COMPUTATION OF THE "HOUSING CONSUMPTION STANDARD"
THRESHOLDS FOR A FOUR-PERSON FAMILY, 1977, 1983, 1987

Fiscal Year	U.S. average two bedroom Fair Market Rent		Housing share of income[2]	Implied threshold	Ratio to official threshold
	monthly	annual			
1977	$187[1]	$2,244	.25	$ 8,976	1.45
1982	$316	$3,792	.26	$14,585	1.48
1987	$448	$5,376	.30	$17,920	1.54

Source: Computed using data on FMRs given in table A.3.
Notes:
1. U.S. average not computed by HUD before FY 1980. Figure shown is the FMR for a standard two-bedroom unit in Kansas City, which was close to the median in 1975–1980 period.
2. Based on proportion of income existing tenants in Section 8 subsidized housing would have been required to spend on rent.

Housing programs allow various deductions from income for the purpose of calculating the housing budget share, but this study again has taken a relatively conservative approach, applying the 30 percent standard to a family's gross reported cash income in 1987 and using a similar methodology for earlier years. (See table A.5 for details.) Use of a net income figure would reduce the amount left to pay rent, implying a higher threshold level of income to meet any given rental spending standard.

Choosing a family size to equate to the income standard implied as necessary to rent a standard two-bedroom unit was somewhat more difficult. Such a unit could hold up to four persons without violating HUD standards on overcrowding, and so a four-person family was chosen as the basis for estimation. It should be noted, however, that a three-person family consisting of one adult and two children—the typical nonelderly family in poverty—also would require a two-bedroom unit not to be technically overcrowded. Clearly, this is one instance in which the equivalence scales for three- and four-person families do not allow for a realistic family size adjustment.

In computing actual poverty rates given the four-person threshold the same methodology was used as for the other poverty standards discussed above. The ratio of the four-person housing consumption standard to the average official four-person threshold was calculated for each relevant year, and then the official thresholds reported for each individual in the CPS file were adjusted by multiplying them by this ratio.

Table A.6 COMPUTATION OF THE "UPDATED MULTIPLIER" THRESHOLDS
FOR A FOUR-PERSON FAMILY, 1960–1987

Year	Average monthly value of food plan[1]	Annual cost of food	CPI weight for food[2]	Implied threshold	Ratio to official threshold
1960	$82.27	$987	.335	2,947	.98
1967	90.64	1,088	.252	4,316	1.27
1972	114.19	1,370	.252	5,438	1.27
1977	171.88	2,063	.252	8,185	1.32
1982	252.06	3,025	.204	14,827	1.50
1987	287.36	3,448	.177	19,482	1.68

Source: Food Plan data from table A.4. CPI weights for food supplied by Jesse Thomas,
U.S. Department of Labor (from Report No. 517).
Notes:
1. Average Monthly Value of the Economy and Thrifty Food Plans calculated as noted
in the notes to table A.4.
2. Use of the CPI-U weight for food assumes that the "multiplier" could have been
updated on about the same schedule as the Consumer Price Index. In practice,
updates to the CPI have lagged considerably behind the collection of new consumption data.

Finally, a similar approach was used in calculating the updated
multiplier thresholds shown in table A.6. Annualized values of the
TFP or the Economy Food Plan were calculated for a four-person
family, and these values were multiplied by the weight for food in
the CPI. Although the share of food in the CPI does not always reflect
the most recent available consumption data, it was reasoned that the
government could have been expected to update the poverty thresholds about as fast as they in fact updated the CPI. Because the
objective here was simply to update Orshansky's consumption data
without otherwise changing the basic methodology she used, average
consumption values rather than a value based on the budget share
of food in the low-income population were deemed appropriate.

Given information on both the cost of food consumption and the
budget share to be devoted to food, a new standard could again be
computed for the relevant year by dividing the annualized TFP by
the appropriate budget share. The ratio of this standard to the average
weighted official four-person threshold was then computed, and that
ratio was multiplied by the official poverty threshold given for each
individual in the CPS to produce an adjusted threshold, which in
turn was compared with each person's family income to determine
poverty rates under this standard.

Notes

1. All of the CPS-based poverty rates shown in this study have been computed directly from public-use data tapes for the CPS released by the Census Bureau. Official poverty thresholds and family income amounts are attached directly to each person-record in these files, which allows the researcher to identify persons in poverty fairly easily. In order to allow the poverty rates in this study to be compared to the Census Bureau rates in detail, the myriad of equivalence scales used by the bureau to adjust for family size and type differences has been retained, although chapter 4 of this book argues that many of them should be eliminated in the future.

2. Before 1975 a similar plan, the Economy Food Plan, was used.

DATA AND METHODS USED IN ESTIMATING POVERTY SPELL DURATIONS

Most of the poverty spell estimates shown in chapters 5, 6, and 7 are calculated using data from the Survey of Income and Program Participation (SIPP). The SIPP is a panel survey that interviews participating households every four months. Households are selected for participation in the survey from a universe that includes the civilian noninstitutionalized population of the United States. The sample is stratified geographically to facilitate data collection, and the sample framework is constructed on the basis of randomly chosen household addresses.

Within this framework, information is collected on each individual in the households selected, with a particular focus on sources of income, program participation, and family status and other demographic variables. The 1984 panel of the SIPP, which is the only panel that so far has been released entirely, went into the field in mid-1983, collecting information on an initial sample of about 60,000 people. This sample was divided into four "rotation groups," which were interviewed over a period of four consecutive months. Interviews were then repeated at four-month intervals for each individual in the initial sample, with additional information being collected on those joining the households of the initial sample since the first interview. Each set of interviews over a four-month period is known as a "wave." The 1984 panel of the SIPP includes eight complete waves.[1]

At each interview, three types of information can be collected from SIPP participants. First, certain "control card" information is collected at the initial interview. This information primarily involves questions such as race, sex, age, and so forth that either should not change or should change only in predictable ways over time. Second, "core" information on income, employment status, program partic- ipation, family status, and so forth is collected on a month by month basis. Because each wave of interviews covered four months, re- spondents were asked about each of these areas separately for each of the previous four months, producing a string of four monthly estimates in each wave. Finally, "topical modules" also were ad- ministered at most interviews. These modules, which change from wave to wave, focus on specific topics such as marital history or asset holdings where detailed longitudinal information was not con- sidered necessary.

The accumulation of 32 months of core information, covering more than 200 variables per interview, plus the associated topical modules result in a very large data file. It would have been even larger except for two factors. First, the survey underwent a "reduction in sample" for budget reasons during the fifth wave, in which about 20 percent of the cases, randomly chosen, were dropped. Additionally, another approximately 20 percent dropped out of the survey (either through refusals, exits from the sample universe, or through unfollowed moves) over the 32-month period. As a result, information is available for all 32 months on about 60 percent of the original sample, or about 35,000 people. Because those entering households with original sam- ple members after the start of the panel also were interviewed, how- ever, a total of 64,500 people are present for at least one month in the full panel file. A longitudinally linked research file based on this full-panel sample has been produced by the Census Bureau, and a preliminary edit has been performed on these data to produce income estimates that are reasonably consistent across time. It is this file that has been used to produce the estimates given here.[2]

This file contains up to 32 months of information on all persons ever interviewed during the 1984 SIPP panel. Persons not present for all 32 months of this file do not have panel file weights, however. Because our analysis already adjusts for spell censoring through at- trition, we include part-panel cases. Consequently, we have not used the panel weights—all of the duration analysis results presented here are unweighted. Based on our preliminary analysis of the impacts of alternative weighting schemes that could be used to incorporate these part-panel cases, we believe that these alternatives would make little difference to the overall distributions of spell durations ob- served. Records have been linked at the person level. That is, each person is followed through time as an individual, regardless of changes in his or her family status. Income, however, has been coded as family income in each month, and the individual's poverty status has been derived by comparing that month's income with a needs threshold based on that month's family composition.

The asset information presented in chapter 7 comes from a special "topical module" of the SIPP that collected detailed information on each individual's assets and liabilities. This module was administered during the fourth set of SIPP interviews in the last four months of 1984 and reports total assets by type for all individuals present at that interview. Data from this topical module have been merged with the longitudinal file, so that asset holdings could be examined in conjunction with longitudinal data on income flows.

ESTIMATING SPELL DURATIONS

The estimates of the distribution of spell durations presented in this book have been derived using a simple survival analysis technique. Spells are observed from their beginning either until they end or until the observation is right-censored. For each month, t, the conditional probability of leaving poverty that month given that the case has remained in poverty up to month t is calculated. This probability is equal to

$$h(t , X) = \frac{f(t , X)}{(1 - F(t , X))} ,$$

where f(t,X) is the probability density function for spell exits at t months for an individual with characteristics X, and F(t , X) is the cummulative probability function for exits before time t for such an individual. The survival function, which is essentially the probability that an individual will still be in poverty at time t, is simply the denominator of the expression above: S(t , X) = 1 − F(t , X).

In assessing the distributions of spell durations that result from this analysis, it is helpful to remember that the universe over which spells are examined includes spell entrants only. In other words, left-censored spells are excluded from the analysis. Estimated survival rates thus give the probability that a given entrant into poverty will still be poor t months later. This estimate does not align in a direct fashion with cross-sectional data on poverty, which tell us what proportion of people are poor at a given point in time. Because someone who is poor for a long period has a higher probability of being included in a randomly chosen cross-section of the poverty population than does someone who is poor for only a short period, cross-sectional analyses will include more people with long spell durations than will an analysis based on the population of all people entering poverty over a given period.

Finally, all of the duration estimates derived from the SIPP are subject to "seam bias"—the tendency of respondents to report more transitions in the interview month than in the other months of the wave. As a result, the hazard rate for spell exits is two to three times as great at the wave "seams"—the fourth, eighth, twelfth months, and so on, when interviews are done—than in each of the within-wave months. We believe that this phenomenon results primarily from faulty recall of the dates of income changes, rather than from misreporting of the existence of an income change. In other words, people are more likely to get confused about when a specific change occurred than they are to report a change that did not actually occur.

Consequently, this type of reporting error probably introduces only a small error into our duration estimates, because, given the wave interviewing structure, it would be difficult for respondents to err in their recall by more than four months, and most are probably off by only one or two months. Further, presumably some respondents recall shorter spells than actually occurred, whereas others recall longer spells, causing the errors in duration estimates to offset each other somewhat.[3] On the other hand, this problem may mean that some very short spells—of both poverty and nonpoverty—are missed because they occur entirely within interview waves. This would, however, only strengthen the finding that most spells are short.

Notes

1. Additionally, two of the rotation groups were interviewed a ninth time, but this incomplete set of interviews has been dropped from the longitudinal file.

2. For more information on the SIPP and on the Longitudinal Research File produced by the Census Bureau see Nelson et al. (1984) and Coder et al. (1987). Most of the additional work on the SIPP done at The Urban Institute has focused on increasing the ease with which these files can be used.

3. Further discussion of seam bias and its effects on estimates of various types can be found in Young (1989).

REFERENCES

Atkinson, A. B. 1987. "On the Measurement of Poverty." *Econometrica* 55 (4): 749–764.

Bane, Mary Jo, and David T. Ellwood. 1986. "Slipping Into and Out of Poverty: The Dynamics of Spells." *Journal of Human Resources* 21(1):1–23.

Barten, A. P. 1964. "Family Composition, Prices and Expenditure Patterns." In *Econometric Analysis for National Economic Planning*, ed. P. E. Hart, G. Mills, and J. K. Whitaker, pp. 277–92. London: Butterworth.

Barthelemy, Philippe. 1988. "The Macroeconomic Estimates of the Hidden Economy: A Critical Analysis." *Review of Income and Wealth* 34 (June): 183–208.

Blades, D. 1982. "The Hidden Economy and National Accounts." *OECD Observer*, 15–17.

Bloomquist, Glenn C., Mark C. Berger and John P. Hoehn. 1988. "New Estimates of Quality of Life in Urban Areas." *American Economic Review* 78 (March): 89–107.

Borzilleri, Thomas C. 1978. "The Need for a Separate Consumer Price Index for Older Persons: A Review and New Evidence." *The Gerontologist*. 18 (June): 230–36.

Bowsher, Charles. 1982. "A CPI for Retirees is Not Needed Now But Could Be in the Future." General Accounting Office Study No. GAO-GGD-82-41. Washington, D.C.: GAO.

Bridges, Benjamin and Michael D. Packard. 1981. "Price and Income Changes for the Elderly." *Social Security Bulletin* 44 (January): 3–15.

Buhmann, Brigitte, Lee Rainwater, Guenther Schmaus, and Timothy M. Smeeding. 1988. "Equivalence Scales, Well-Being, Inequality, and Poverty: Sensitivity Estimates Across Ten Countries Using the Luxembourg Income Study (LIS) Database." *Review of Income and Wealth* 34 (June): 115–142.

Burtless, Gary. In press. "In-Kind Transfers and the Trend in Poverty." In *The New Meaning of Poverty*, ed. John Weicher. Washington, D.C.: American Enterprise Institute.

Cain, Glen G. 1984. "Women and Work: Trends in Time Spent in House-work." Institute for Research on Poverty Discussion Paper no. 747–84.

Carson, C. S. 1984. "The Underground Economy: An Introduction." *Survey of Current Business* 64 (5): 21–37.

Chadeau, Ann, and Caroline Roy. 1986. "Relating Households' Final Consumption to Household Activities: Substitutibility or Complementarity Between Market and Non-Market Production." *Review of Income and Wealth* 32 (December): 387–407.

Citro, Constance F., Donald J. Hernandez, and Roger A. Herriot. 1986. "Longitudinal Household Concepts in SIPP: Preliminary Results." SIPP Working Paper Series No. 8611. Washington, D.C.: U.S. Bureau of the Census, U.S. Government Printing Office.

Citro, Constance F. and Harold W. Watts. 1986. "Patterns of Household-Composition and Family Status Change." SIPP Working Paper Series No. 8609. Washington, D.C.: U.S. Bureau of the Census, U.S. Government Printing Office.

Clark, S., R. Hemming, and D. Ueph. 1981. "On Indices for the Measurement of Poverty." *Economic Journal* 91 (June): 515–26.

Coder, John F., Dan Burkhead, Angela Feldman-Harkins, and Jack McNeil. 1987. "Preliminary Data from the SIPP 1983–1984 Longitudinal Research File." SIPP Working Paper Series No. 8702. Washington, D.C.: U.S. Bureau of the Census, U.S. Government Printing Office.

Coe, Richard. 1978. "Dependency and Poverty in the Short and Long Run." In *Five Thousand American Families: Patterns of Economic Progress*, volume 6, ed. by Greg J. Duncan and James N. Morgan, pp. 273–96. Ann Arbor, Mich.: Institute for Social Research.

Colasanto, Diane, Arie Kapteyn, and Jacques van der Gaag. 1984. "Two Subjective Definitions of Poverty: Results from the Wisconsin Basic Needs Study." *Journal of Human Resources* 19 (1): 127–37.

Corcoran, Mary, Greg J. Duncan, Gerald Gurin, and Patricia Gurin. 1985. "Myth and Reality: The Causes and Persistence of Poverty." *Journal of Policy Analysis and Management* 4 (4): 516–36.

Danziger, Sheldon, and Peter Gottschalk. 1983. "The Measurement of Poverty: Implications for Antipoverty Policy." *American Behavioral Scientist* 26 (6): 739–56.

Danziger, Sheldon H., Robert H. Haveman, and Robert D. Plotnick. 1986. "Anti-Poverty Policy: Effects on the Poor and the Nonpoor." In *Fighting Poverty: What Works and What Doesn't*, ed. S. H. Danziger and Daniel H. Weinberg, pp. 50–77. Cambridge: Harvard University Press.

Danziger, Sheldon, and M. K. Taussig. 1979. "The Income Unit and the Anatomy of Income Distribution." *Review of Income and Wealth* 25 (December): 365–75.

Danziger, Sheldon, Jacques van der Gaag, Michael K. Taussig, and Eugene

Smolensky. 1984. "The Direct Measurement of Welfare Levels: How Much Does It Cost to Make Ends Meet?" *Review of Economics and Statistics* 66(3): 500–505.

Datta, G., and J. Meerman. 1980. "Household Income or Household Income Per Capita in Welfare Comparisons." *Review of Income and Wealth* 26 (December): 401–18.

Deaton, A. S. and J. Muellbauer. 1986. "On Measuring Child Costs: With Applications to Poor Countries." *Journal of Political Economy* 94 (4): 720–44.

De Vos, Klaas, and Thesia I. Garner. 1989. "An Evaluation of Subjective Poverty Definitions Comparing Results from the U.S. and the Netherlands." Paper presented at the 21st General Conference of the International Association for Research in Income and Wealth.

Duncan, Greg J., Richard D. Coe, and Martha S. Hill. 1984. "The Dynamics of Poverty." In *Years of Poverty, Years of Plenty*, pp. 33–70. Ann Arbor, Mich: Institute for Social Research.

Economic Report of the President. 1989. Washington, D.C.: U.S. Government Printing Office.

Ernst, Lawrence R. 1985. "SIPP Longitudinal Household Estimation for the Proposed Longitudinal Definition." Washington, D.C.: Bureau of the Census.

Feige, E. L. 1979. "How Big is the Irregular Economy?" *Challenge* 22 (November/December): 5–13.

Ferber, Marianne A., and Bonnie G. Birnbaum. 1980. "Housework: Priceless or Valueless?" *Review of Income and Wealth* 28 (December): 387–400.

Fiegehen, G. C., Lansley, P. S., and Smith, A. D. 1977. *Poverty and Progress in Britain 1953–73.* Cambridge: Cambridge University Press.

Fisher, Gordon M. 1984. "The 1984 Federal Poverty Income Guidelines." *Social Security Bulletin* 47 (July): 24–27.

Foster, J. E. 1984. "On Economic Poverty: A Survey of Aggregate Measures." *Advances in Econometrics* 3: 215–51.

Foster, J. E., J. Greer, and E. Thornbecke. 1984. "A Class of Decomposable Poverty Measures." *Econometrica* 52 (3): 761–76.

Franz, A. 1985. "Estimates of Hidden Economy in Austria on the Basis of Official Statistics." *Review of Income and Wealth* 31(December): 325–36.

Frey, B. S., and W. W. Pommerehne. 1984. "The Hidden Economy: State and Prospects for Measurement." *Review of Income and Wealth* 30 (March): 1–23.

Friedman, Rose D. 1965. *Poverty: Definition and Perspective.* Washington, D.C.: American Enterprise Institute.

Fuchs, Victor. 1967. "Redefining Poverty and Redistributing Income." *The Public Interest* 8 (Summer): 88–95.

Gaertner, Wulf, and Alois Wenig, eds. 1985. *The Economics of the Shadow Economy: Conference Proceedings Bielefeld*. Berlin: Springer.

Goedhart, Theo, Victor Halberstadt, Arie Kapteyn, and Bernard M. S. Van Praag. 1977. "The Poverty Line: Concept and Measurement." *Journal of Human Resources* 12 (4): 503–20.

Gronau, Reuben. 1973. "The Intrafamily Allocation of Time: The Value of the Housewives' Time." *American Economic Review* 63 (4) (September): 634–51.

Haber, Alan. 1966. "Poverty Budgets: How Much is Enough?" In *Poverty and Human Resources Abstracts* 1 (3). Ann Arbor, Michigan.

Hagemann, Robert P. 1982. "The Variability of Inflation Rates Across Household Types." *Journal of Money, Credit, and Banking* 14 (4): 494–10.

Hagenaars, Aldi J. M. 1986. *The Perception of Poverty*. Amsterdam: North Holland Publishing Co.

Hagenaars, Aldi, and Klaas de Vos. 1988. "The Definition and Measurement of Poverty." *Journal of Human Resources* 23 (2): 211–21.

Harrington, Michael. 1962. *The Other America: Poverty in the United States*. New York: Macmillan.

———. 1969. *The Other America: Poverty in the United States*, revised edition. New York: Macmillan.

Harrison, Beth. 1986. "Spending Patterns of Older Persons Revealed in Expenditure Survey." *Monthly Labor Review* 109 (October): 15–17.

Haveman, Robert H. 1987. *Poverty Policy and Poverty Research*. Madison: University of Wisconsin Press.

Hawrylyshyn, Oli. 1976. "The Value of Household Services: A Survey of Empirical Estimates." *Review of Income and Wealth* 22 (June): 101–32.

Her Majesty's Statistical Office. 1942. Social Insurance and Allied Services. (The Beveridge Report), Cmd 6404, London.

Hill, Martha S. 1981 "Some Dynamic Aspects of Poverty." In *Five Thousand American Families: Patterns of Economic Progress*, volume IX, ed. Martha S. Hill, Daniel H. Hill, and James N. Morgan, Ann Arbor, Mich.: Institute for Social Research, pp. 93–120.

Hill, T. P. 1979. "Do It Yourself and G.D.P." *Review of Income and Wealth* 25 (March): 1–17.

Hollister, Robinson G. and John L. Palmer. 1972. "The Impact of Inflation on the Poor." In *Redistribution to the Rich and Poor*, ed. Kenneth Boulding and Martin Pfaff. Belmont, Calif.: Wadsworth.

Jencks, Christopher, and Barbara Boyle Torrey. 1988. "Beyond Income and Poverty: Trends in Social Welfare Among Children and the Elderly Since 1960." In *The Vulnerable*, ed. John L. Palmer, Timothy Smeeding, and Barbara Boyle Torrey, pp. 229–64. Washington, D.C.: Urban Institute Press.

Jenkins, S., and M. O'Higgins. 1987. "Measuring Poverty in the European Community," Mimeo: University of Bath.

Kapteyn, A. 1977. "A Theory of Preference Formation." Ph.D. thesis, Leyden University.

Kasten, Richard, and Frank Sammartino. 1987. *The Changing Distribution of Federal Taxes: 1975–1990.* Washington, D.C.: Congressional Budget Office.

Kokoski, Mary F. 1987. "Consumer Price Indices by Demographic Group." Working Paper 167. Washington, D.C.: Bureau of Labor Statistics, U.S. Department of Labor.

————. 1989. "Experimental Cost-of-Living Indexes: A Summary of Current Research." *Monthly Labor Review* 112 (July): 34–39.

Lampman, Robert J. 1959. "The Low Income Population and Economic Growth." Study Paper no. 12. Washington, D.C.: U.S. Congress, Joint Economic Committee.

————. 1971. *Ends and Means of Reducing Income Poverty.* New York: Academic Press.

Lazear, Edward P., and Robert T. Michael. 1980. "Family Size and the Distribution of Real Per Capita Income." *American Economic Review* 70 (1): 91–107.

————. 1988. *Allocation of Income Within the Household.* Chicago: University of Chicago Press.

Lebergott, S. 1976. *The American Economy, Income, Wealth and Want.* Princeton, N.J.: Princeton University Press.

Leonard, Paul A., Cushing N. Dolbeare, and Edward B. Lazere. 1989. *A Place to Call Home: The Crisis in Housing for the Poor.* Washington, D.C.: Center on Budget and Policy Priorities and Low Income Housing Information Service (April).

Levy, Frank. 1977. *How Big is the American Underclass?* Working Paper 0090-1. Washington, D.C.: Urban Institute.

Levy, Frank, and Richard C. Michel. 1988. *Education and Income: Recent U.S. Trends.* Urban Institute Research Report, Washington, D.C.: Urban Institute.

Lewis, Oscar. 1966. *La Vida.* New York: Random House.

Manser, Marilyn, and Richard McDonald. 1988. "An Analysis of Substitution Bias in Inflation Measurement." *Econometrica* 56 (July): 909–30.

Mayer, Susan E., and Christopher Jencks. 1989. "Poverty and the Distribution of Material Hardship." *Journal of Human Resources* 24 (1): 88–114.

McMillen, David Byron, and Roger Herriot. 1984. *Toward a Longitudinal Definition of Households.* SIPP Working Paper Series no. 8402. Washington, D.C.: U.S. Bureau of the Census.

Michael, Robert T. 1979. "Variation Across Households in the Rate of Inflation." *Journal of Money, Credit, and Banking* 11 (1): 33–46.

Minarik, Joseph J. 1975. "New Evidence on the Poverty Count." In American

Statistical Association, *Proceedings of the Social Statistics Section* pp. 544–59.

Moon, Marilyn. 1977. *The Measurement of Economic Welfare: Its Application to the Aged Poor.* New York: Academic Press.

————, ed. 1984. *Economic Transfers in the United States.* National Bureau of Economic Research. *Studies in Income and Wealth,* vol. 49. Chicago: University of Chicago Press.

Moon, Marilyn, and E. Smolensky, eds. 1977. *Improving Measures of Well-Being.* New York: Academic Press.

Morgan, James N., Ismail Sirageldin, and Nancy Baerwaldt. 1966. *Productive Americans.* University of Michigan Institute for Social Research Survey Research Center Monograph no. 43. Ann Arbor: University of Michigan.

Morgan, James N. 1984. "The Role of Time in the Measurement of Transfers and Well-Being." In *Economic Transfers in the United States,* vol. 49, ed. Marilyn Moon, pp. 199–234. Chicago: University of Chicago Press.

Morgan, James N., David H. Martin, Wilbur J. Cohen, and Harvey E. Brazer. 1962. *Income and Welfare in the United States.* New York: McGraw-Hill.

Morgan, James N., Katherine Dickinson, Jonathan Dickinson, Jacob Benus, and Greg J. Duncan. 1974. *Five Thousand American Families: Patterns of Economic Progress,* volume 1. Ann Arbor, Mich.: Institute for Social Research.

Muellbauer, John. 1974a. "Prices and Inequality: The United Kingdom Experience." *Economic Journal* 84 (March): 32–55.

————. 1974b. "Household Composition, Engel Curves and Welfare Comparisons Between Households." *European Economic Review* 5 (August): 103–22.

————. 1977. "Testing the Model of Household Composition Effects and the Cost of Children." *Economic Journal* 87 (September): 460–87.

————. 1980. "The Estimation of the Prais-Honthakker Model of Equivalence Scales." *Econometrica* 48 (1): 153–76.

Nelson, Dawn, David McMillen, and Daniel Kasprzyk. 1984. *An Overview of the Survey of Income and Program Participation.* SIPP Working Paper Series no. 8401. Washington, D.C.: U.S. Bureau of the Census.

Nicholson, J. L. 1976. "Appraisal of Different Methods of Estimating Equivalence Scales and Their Results." *Review of Income and Wealth* 22 (March): 1–18.

Orshansky, Mollie. 1963. "Children of the Poor." *Social Security Bulletin* 26 (July): 3–13.

Orshansky, Mollie. 1965. "Counting the Poor: Another Look at the Poverty Profile." *Social Security Bulletin* 28 (January): 3–29.

Orshansky, Mollie. 1988. "Commentary: The Poverty Measure." *Social Security Bulletin* 51 (October): 1–4.

Palmer, John L., Timothy Smeeding, and Barbara Boyle Torrey, eds. 1988. *The Vulnerable*. Washington, D.C.: Urban Institute Press.

Pechman, Joseph A. 1985. *Who Paid the Taxes, 1966–1985?* Washington, D.C.: Brookings Institution.

Peterkin, Betty B., Andrea J. Blum, Richard L. Kerr, and Linda E. Cleveland. 1983. "The Thrifty Food Plan, 1983." CND (Adm.) 365, Consumer Nutrition Division, Human Nutrition Information Service. Washington, D.C.: U.S. Department of Agriculture.

Piachaud, David. 1982. "Patterns of Income and Expenditure with Families." *Journal of Social Policy* 2 (December): 469–82.

Plotnick, Robert D., and Felicity Skidmore. 1975. *Progress Against Poverty*. New York: Academic Press.

Podoluk, J. R. 1968. *Income Distribution and Poverty in Canada, 1967*. Ottawa: Dominion Bureau of Statistics.

Pollak, R. A. and T. J. Wales. 1979. "Welfare Comparisons and Equivalence Scales."*American Economic Review* 69 (March): 216–21.

Prais, S. J., and H. S. Houthakker. 1955. *The Analysis of Family Budgets*. Washington, D.C.: Brookings Institution.

Preston, S. 1984. "Children and the Elderly: Divergent Paths for America's Dependents." *Demography* 21 (November): 435–57; also presented as the Presidential Address at the Annual Meeting of the Population Association of America, Minneapolis, Minnesota.

Radner, Daniel B. 1989. "Income-Wealth Measures of Economic Well-Being for Age Groups." Paper presented at the Annual Meetings of the American Statistical Association.

Rainwater, Lee. 1974. *What Money Buys: Inequality and the Social Meanings of Income*. New York: Basic Books.

————. 1981. *Persistent and Transitory Poverty: A New Look*. Joint Center for Urban Studies of the Massachusetts Institute of Technology and Harvard University Working Paper no. 70. Cambridge: MIT:Harvard.

Rein, Martin. 1969. "Problems in the Definition and Measurement of Poverty." In *Poverty in America*, revised edition, ed. Louis A. Ferman, Joyce L. Kornbluh, and Alan Haber. Ann Arbor: University of Michigan Press.

Ricketts, Erol R., and Isabel V. Sawhill. 1988. "Defining and Measuring the Underclass." *Journal of Policy Analysis and Management* 7 (2): 316–25.

Roback, Jennifer. 1982. "Wages, Rents and the Quality of Life." *Journal of Political Economy* 90 (December): 1257–78.

Rosen, Sherwin. 1979. "Wage-Based Indexes of Urban Quality of Life." In *Current Issues in Urban Economics*, ed. Peter Mieszkowski and Mahlon Straszheim. Baltimore: John Hopkins University Press.

Rowntree, B. S. 1901. *Poverty: A Study of Town Life*. London: Macmillan.

Ruggles, Patricia. 1989a. *The Impact of Government Tax and Expenditure*

Policies on the Distribution of Income in the United States. Urban Institute Research Paper. Washington, D.C.: Urban Institute. Also forthcoming in *Readings on Economic Inequality*, ed. Lars Osberg. Armonk, N.Y.: M. E. Sharpe.

————. 1989b. *Short and Long Term Poverty in the United States: Measuring the American "Underclass."* Urban Institute Research Paper. Washington, D.C.: Urban Institute. Also forthcoming in *Readings on Economic Inequality*, ed. Lars Osberg. Armonk, N.Y.: M. E. Sharpe.

Ruggles, Patricia, and Roberton Williams. 1986. *Transitions In and Out of Poverty.* Urban Institute Research Paper, December. Also presented at the Annual Meeting of the American Economics Association, December.

————. 1989. "Longitudinal Measures of Poverty." *Review of Income and Wealth* 35 (September): 225–44.

Sawhill, Isabel V. 1988. "Poverty in the U.S.: Why Is It So Persistent?" *Journal of Economic Literature* 26 (3): 1073–1119.

Sen, A. K. 1976a. "Poverty: An Ordinal Approach to Measurement." *Econometrica* 44 (March): 219–31.

————. 1976b. "Real National Income." *Review of Economic Studies* 43 (February): 19–39.

————. 1979. "Issues in the Measurement of Poverty." *Scandinavian Journal of Economics* 81 (February): 285–307.

Smeeding, Timothy. 1977. "The Anti-Poverty Effectiveness of In-Kind Transfers." *Journal of Human Resources* 127 (March): 360–78.

————. 1984. "Approaches to Measuring and Valuing In-Kind Subsidies and the Distribution of Their Benefits." *Economic Transfers in the United States*, ed. Marilyn Moon, pp. 139–71. National Bureau of Economic Research. *Studies in Income and Wealth*, volume 49. Chicago: University of Chicago Press.

Smeeding, T., B. B. Torrey, and M. Rein. 1988. "Patterns of Income and Poverty: The Economic Status of Children and the Elderly in Eight Countries." In *The Vulnerable*, ed. J. L. Palmer, T. Smeeding, and B. B. Torrey, pp. 89–119. Washington, D.C.: Urban Institute Press.

Smith, Adam. 1776. *Wealth of Nations.* London: Everyman's Library.

Stafford, Frank P. 1980. "Women's Use of Time Converging with Men's." *Monthly Labor Review* 103 (December): 57–59.

Statistics Canada. 1987. *Low-Income Cut-Offs.* Ottawa: Statistics Canada.

Steurle, Eugene, and Nelson McClung. 1977. *Wealth and the Accounting Period in the Measurement of Means.* The Measure of Poverty, Technical Paper VI. Washington, D.C.:U.S. Department of Health, Education and Welfare.

Tanzi, Vito, ed. 1982. *The Underground Economy in the US and Abroad.* Lexington Mass.: Lexington Books.

Thon, D. 1979. "On Measuring Poverty." *Review of Income and Wealth* 25 (December): 429–40.

Tobin, James. 1969. "Raising the Incomes of the Poor." In *Agenda for the Nation*, ed. Kermit Gordon. Washington, D.C.: Brookings Institution.

Townsend, Peter. 1979. *Poverty in the United Kingdom*. Harmondsworth: Penguin Books.

United Kingdom, Parliament. 1942. *Social Insurance and Allied Services* [The Beveridge Report]. Cmd. 6404. London: HMSO.

U.S. Bureau of the Census. 1980. *Characteristics of the Population Below the Poverty Level: 1978*. Current Population Reports, Series P-60, no. 24. Washington, D.C.: U.S. Government Printing Office.

————. 1982. *Alternative Methods for Valuing Selected In-Kind Transfer Benefits and Measuring Their Effects on Poverty*. Technical Paper 50. Washington, D.C.: U.S. Government Printing Office.

————. 1986a. *Conference on the Measurement of Noncash Benefits: Proceedings*. Washington, D.C.: U.S. Government Printing Office.

————. 1986b. *Characteristics of the Population Below the Poverty Level: 1984*. Current Population Reports, Series P-60, no. 152. Washington, D.C.: U.S. Government Printing Office.

————. 1988a. *Estimates of Poverty Including the Value of Noncash Benefits: 1987*. Technical Paper 58. Washington, D.C.: U.S. Government Printing Office.

————. 1988b. *Measuring the Effect of Benefits and Taxes on Income and Poverty: 1986*. Current Population Reports Series P-60, no. 164-RD-1. Washington, DC.: U.S. Government Printing Office.

————. 1989a. *Poverty in the United States: 1987*. Current Population Reports, Series P-60, no. 163, Washington, D.C.: U.S. Government Printing Office.

————. 1989b. *Money Income of Households, Families, and Persons in the United States: 1987*. Current Population Reports, Series P-60, no. 162, Washington, D.C.: U.S. Government Printing Office.

————. 1989c. *Money Income and Poverty Status in the United States: 1988 (Advance Data from the March 1989 Current Population Survey)*. Current Population Reports, Series P-60, no. 166, Washington, D.C.: U.S. Government Printing Office.

————. 1989d. *Statistical Abstract of the United States: 1989*, 109th ed. Washington, D.C. U.S. Government Printing Office.

U.S. Bureau of Labor Statistics. 1982. "Family Budgets—Final Report on Family Budgets: Cost Increases Slowed, Autumn 1981." *Monthly Labor Review* (April): 44—46.

————. 1988. "An Analysis of the Rates of Inflation Affecting Older Americans Based on an Experimental Reweighted Consumer Price Index." Unpublished report.

————. 1989. "The Consumer Price Index." In *Handbook of Methods*. Washington, D.C.: U.S. Government Printing Office.

U.S. Congress. House Committee on Ways and Means. 1985. *Children in Poverty*. Washington, D.C.: U.S. Government Printing Office.

_____. 1989. *Background Material and Data on Programs within the Jurisdiction of the Committee on Ways and Means*. Washington, D.C.: U.S. Government Printing Office.

U.S. Congress. Joint Committee on the Economic Report, Subcommittee on Low Income Families. 1949. *Low Income Families and Economic Stability*. Committee Print, 81st Cong., 1st sess., Washington, D.C.

U.S. Department of Health, Education and Welfare. 1976. *The Measure of Poverty: A Report to Congress as Mandated by the Education Amendments of 1974*. Washington, D.C.: U.S. Government Printing Office.

Van der Gaag, Jacques, and Eugene Smolensky. 1982. "True Household Equivalence Scales and Characteristics of the Poor in the United States." *Review of Income and Wealth* 28 (March): 1728.

Van Eck, R., and B. Kazemier. 1988. "Features of the Hidden Economy in the Netherlands." *Review of Income and Wealth* 34 (September): 251–72.

Van Praag, Bernard M. S., Theo Goedhart, and Arie Kapteyn. 1980. "The Poverty Line. A Pilot Survey in Europe." *Review of Economics and Statistics* 62 (3): 461-65.

Van Praag, Bernard M. S., Jan S. Spit, and Huib Van de Stadt. 1982. "A Comparison Between the Food-Ratio Poverty Line and the Leyden Poverty Line." *Review of Economics and Statistics* 64 (4): 691–94.

Walker, Kathryn E., and William H. Gauger. 1973. "The Dollar Value of Household Workers." Information Bulletin 60, New York State College of Human Ecology, Cornell University. Ithaca N.Y.: Cornell University.

Walker, Kathryn E., and Margaret E. Woods. 1976. *Time Use: A Measure of Household Production of Family Goods and Services*. Washington, D.C.: American Home Economics Association.

Watts, Harold W. 1967. "The Iso-Prop Index: An Approach to the Determination of Differential Poverty Income Thresholds." *Journal of Human Resources* 2 (1): 3–18.

_____. "An Economic Definition of Poverty." In *On Understanding Poverty*, ed. D. P. Moynihan, pp. 316–29. New York: Basic Books.

_____. 1977. "The Iso-Prop Index." In *Improving the Measure of Economic Well-Being*, ed. M. Moon and E. Smolensky. New York: Academic Press.

_____. 1980. "Special Panel Suggests Changes in BLS Family Budget Program." *Monthly Labor Review* 103 (December): 3–10.

_____. 1986. "Have Our Measures of Poverty Become Poorer?" *Focus* 9 (2): 18–23.

Weinberg, Daniel H. 1986. *Filling the "Poverty Gap," 1979–84: Multiple*

Transfer Program Participation. U.S. Department of Health and Human Services, Office of Income Security Policy Technical Analysis Paper no. 32. Washington, D.C.: Department of Health and Human Services.

Weisbrod, Burton A., and Lee W. Hansen. 1988. "An Income-Net Worth Approach to Measuring Economic Welfare." *American Economic Review* 58 (December): 1315–29.

Williams, Roberton. 1986. "Poverty Rates and Program Participation in the SIPP and the CPS." Presented at the Annual Meetings of the American Statistical Association.

———. 1988. *Trends in Family Income: 1970–1986*. Congressional Budget Office Study. Washington D.C.: U.S. Government Printing Office.

Wolfson, Michael C. 1979. "Wealth and the Distribution of Income, Canada 1969–1970." *Review of Income and Wealth* 25 (June): 129–40.

———. 1986. "Stasis Amid Change: Income Inequality in Canada 1965–1983." *Review of Income and Wealth* 32 (December): 337–70.

Wolfson, M. C. and J. M. Evans. 1989. *Statistics Canada's Low Income Cut-Offs: Methodological Concerns and Possibilities*. Statistics Canada discussion paper. Ottawa: Statistics Canada.

Young, Nathan. 1989. "Wave Seam Effects in the SIPP." Presented at the Annual Meetings of the American Statistical Association.

ABOUT THE AUTHOR

Patricia Ruggles is a senior research associate at the Urban Institute. She is currently on leave, and is serving as a senior economist with the Joint Economic Committee. Her primary research interests focus on poverty, public income support programs, and the distribution of income, and she has written extensively on these issues.

In 1987–88, also while on leave from the Urban Institute, Ms. Ruggles was an American Statistical Association/National Science Foundation Fellow at the Bureau of the Census, where she conducted research on the distribution and duration of spells of poverty. In 1980–1984 Ms. Ruggles was a policy analyst at the Congressional Budget Office, where she was responsible for analyses of Social Security and means-tested transfer programs.